ROUTLEDGE LIBRARY EDITIONS:
ENERGY ECONOMICS

Volume 7

ENERGY MANAGEMENT IN INDUSTRIAL FIRMS

ENERGY MANAGEMENT IN INDUSTRIAL FIRMS

LIAM FAHEY

Routledge
Taylor & Francis Group

LONDON AND NEW YORK

First published in 1984 by Garland Publishing, Inc.

This edition first published in 2018
by Routledge
2 Park Square, Milton Park, Abingdon, Oxon OX14 4RN

and by Routledge
711 Third Avenue, New York, NY 10017

Routledge is an imprint of the Taylor & Francis Group, an informa business

British Library Cataloguing in Publication Data
A catalogue record for this book is available from the British Library

ISBN: 978-1-138-10476-1 (Set)
ISBN: 978-1-315-14526-6 (Set) (ebk)
ISBN: 978-1-138-30666-0 (Volume 7) (hbk)
ISBN: 978-1-315-14194-7 (Volume 7) (ebk)

Publisher's Note
The publisher has gone to great lengths to ensure the quality of this reprint but points out that some imperfections in the original copies may be apparent.

Disclaimer
The publisher has made every effort to trace copyright holders and would welcome correspondence from those they have been unable to trace.

Energy Management in Industrial Firms

Liam Fahey

Garland Publishing, Inc.
New York & London, 1984

Library of Congress Cataloging in Publication Data

Fahey, Liam, 1951–
    Energy management in industrial firms.

    (Outstanding dissertations in economics)
    Originally presented as the author's thesis (Ph.D.)—
University of Pittsburgh, 1978) under title: An exploratory
study of the process of energy management in industrial
firms.
    Bibliography: p.
    1. Industry—Energy conservation. I. Title. II. Series.
TJ163.3.F34 1984   658   79-7937
ISBN 0-8240-4187-9

All volumes in this series are printed on acid-free,
250-year-life paper.

Printed in the United States of America

AN EXPLORATORY STUDY OF THE PROCESS OF

ENERGY MANAGEMENT IN INDUSTRIAL FIRMS

By

Liam Fahey

B. Comm., University College Dublin, 1972

M.B.S., University College Dublin, 1973

Submitted to the Faculty of the

Graduate School of Business

in Partial Fulfillment of the Requirements

for the degree of

Doctor of Philosophy

University of Pittsburgh

1978

ACKNOWLEDGEMENTS

A special word of thanks is owed to my dissertation committee chairperson, Samuel I. Doctors, for his continuous support and encouragement throughout this research. His research interests have made this study possible.

I also wish to thank the other members of my dissertation committee, Paul A. Beck, John H. Grant, Paul Y. Hammond and G. Richard Patton for their assistance and cooperation at many phases of this work.

The editorial skills of Bonnie Bloch and Veta Doctors have saved me from many errors of commission and omission.

The secretarial assistance of Robyn Bantile, Karen Guberman, Leethia McFadden and Anne Pyshos were greatly appreciated on many occasions.

Finally, a special expression of gratitude to the person who made it all possible, my wife, Patricia. Her cooperation and assistance has made this study somewhat palatable during many trying moments. Words of praise do not do justice to her contribution to the completion of this dissertation.

TABLE OF CONTENTS

TABLE OF CONTENTS (Continued)

LIST OF TABLES

LIST OF TABLES (Continued)

LIST OF TABLES (Continued)

LIST OF FIGURES

CHAPTER ONE

INTRODUCTION

The purpose of this study is to examine the extent to which different types of firms have formalized and institutionalized energy management. The study entails two overall foci. One, an attempt is made to examine what differences exist, if any, in the approaches to energy management adopted by (a) growth and non-growth firms, (b) energy intensive and non-intensive firms and, (c) divisions of large multidivision firms and independent firms. Two, energy management decision making processes are explicated in different contexts, e.g., energy intensive firms and divisions as opposed to non-energy intensive firms and independent firms, and at the headquarters level of large multidivisional firms as opposed to that at the division level of these firms.

Significance of Study

The significance of this study has its origins in at least six (6) sources:

1. The complexity, uncertainty and turbulence of the energy problem;

2. Current federal efforts to formulate a national energy policy;

3. The large volume of government resources devoted to the development and diffusion of more energy efficient industrial processes, techniques and behaviors;

4. The significance and potential for energy efficiency improvement in industry.

1

5. The energy environment as a recent source of problems/threats and/or opportunities for business; and

6. The relationship of this study to a broad range of studies in a number of disciplinary and inter-disciplinary areas.

Following is a summary review of each of these six (6) sources.

1. Abundant, cheap energy has been a decisive element in the industrial development of the United States. More specifically, fossil energy provided the impetus for the industrial revolution (Berg, 1978) and has increasingly replaced human labor in the marketplace, and contributed to spectacular growth in economic productivity and higher standards of living.[1] In fact, it can be argued that the entire stock of capital goods--industrial plants, commercial buildings, private dwellings, automobiles, etc.,--is the output of an era of unrestricted and cheap energy (Mancke, 1974; Schumacker, 1973; Commoner, 1976).

However, most analysts of the energy situation in America today would contend that the 1970s have witnessed a departure from the era of abundant and cheap energy. As shown in Figure I-1, for over two decades, the price of energy sources has declined in real terms.[2] The decrease in the real price of electricity was particularly substantial during this period.[3] U.S. energy prices in general, and imported oil prices in particular, have advanced much faster than consumer prices (see Figure I-2). It will be noted from Table I-1, that although the 1973 Arab Oil embargo was one of the

FIGURE I-1

FOSSIL FUEL PRICE TRENDS, 1950-1977

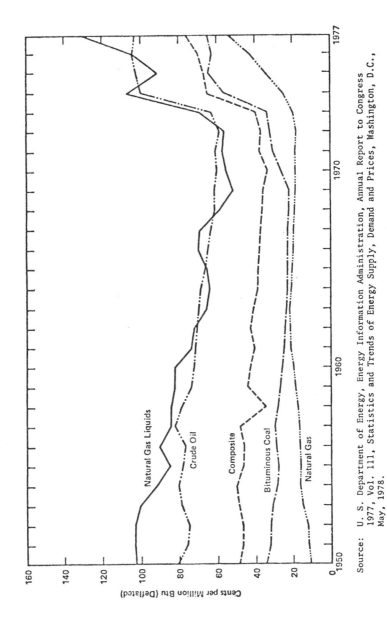

Source: U. S. Department of Energy, Energy Information Administration, Annual Report to Congress 1977, Vol. 111, Statistics and Trends of Energy Supply, Demand and Prices, Washington, D.C., May, 1978.

FIGURE I-2

COMPARISON OF ENERGY PRICE INDICES WITH

CONSUMER PRICE INDEX, 1970-1976

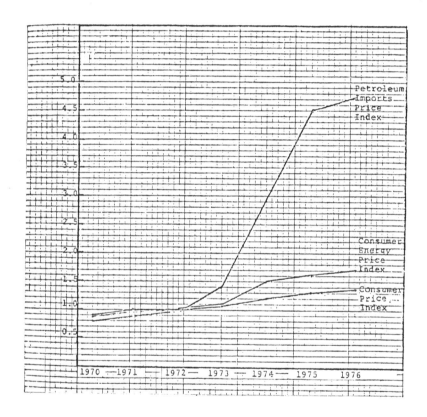

Note: Energy Price Index (1972 = 1.00)

Source: 1977 National Energy Outlook, Federal Energy Administration, Washington, DC, Janaury 15, 1977, Draft.

TABLE I-1

PRICES OF DOMESTICALLY PRODUCED MINERAL FUELS, 1950-77

Year	Crude Oil		Natural Gas Liquids		Natural Gas		Bituminous Coal		Anthracite Coal		Composite[a]		GNP Implicit Price Deflators[b]
	Current	Deflated	Current	Deflated	Current	Deflated	Current	Deflated	Current	Deflated	Current	Deflated	
1950	43.3	80.7	55.0	102.5	6.0	11.2	18.5	34.5	35.0	65.2	26.3	49.0	53.64
1951	43.6	76.1	59.0	103.0	7.1	12.4	18.8	32.8	37.4	65.3	26.9	47.0	57.27
1952	43.6	75.2	59.9	103.3	7.5	12.9	18.7	32.2	36.9	63.6	27.3	47.1	58.00
1953	46.2	78.5	59.8	101.6	8.9	15.1	18.8	31.9	38.1	64.7	28.7	48.7	58.88
1954	47.9	80.2	65.0	92.1	9.8	16.4	17.3	29.0	33.5	56.1	29.1	48.8	59.69
1955	47.8	78.4	52.4	85.9	9.8	16.1	17.2	28.2	30.9	50.7	28.5	46.7	60.98
1956	48.1	76.5	56.7	90.1	10.4	16.5	18.4	29.3	32.2	51.2	29.2	46.4	62.90
1957	53.3	82.0	54.8	84.3	10.9	16.8	19.4	29.8	35.4	54.4	31.3	48.1	65.02
1958	51.9	78.6	55.7	84.3	11.6	17.6	18.6	28.2	35.0	53.0	24.8	37.5	66.06
1959	50.0	74.1	56.2	83.2	12.5	18.5	18.2	27.0	32.4	48.0	29.9	44.3	67.52
1960	49.7	72.4	56.7	82.6	13.6	19.8	17.9	26.1	30.8	44.9	29.8	43.4	68.67
1961	49.8	71.9	51.4	74.2	14.6	21.1	17.5	25.3	31.7	45.8	28.0	40.4	69.28
1962	50.0	70.9	50.9	72.1	15.0	21.3	17.1	24.2	31.3	44.4	29.9	42.4	70.55
1963	49.8	69.6	47.4	66.2	15.4	21.5	16.8	23.5	33.1	46.2	29.4	41.1	71.59
1964	49.7	68.4	46.7	64.2	15.0	20.6	17.0	23.4	34.1	46.9	28.9	39.7	72.71
1965	49.3	66.3	49.0	65.9	15.1	20.3	16.9	22.7	33.5	45.1	28.6	38.5	74.32
1966	49.7	64.7	53.3	69.4	15.2	19.8	17.3	22.5	31.8	41.4	29.1	37.9	76.76
1967	50.3	63.7	54.5	69.0	15.5	19.6	17.6	22.3	32.1	40.6	29.8	37.7	79.02
1968	50.7	61.4	48.6	58.9	15.8	19.1	17.8	21.6	34.6	41.9	29.8	36.1	82.57
1969	53.3	61.5	45.2	52.1	16.2	18.7	19.0	21.9	39.0	45.0	30.8	35.5	86.72
1970	54.8	60.0	50.0	54.7	16.6	18.2	23.9	26.2	42.6	46.6	30.4	33.3	91.36
1971	58.4	60.8	54.6	56.9	17.7	18.4	29.1	30.3	46.7	48.6	35.7	37.2	96.02
1972	58.4	58.4	56.2	56.2	18.0	18.0	31.9	31.9	47.2	47.2	36.5	36.5	100.00
1973	67.0	63.3	72.9	68.9	21.0	19.8	35.5	33.5	52.0	49.1	41.9	39.6	105.80
1974	116.2	100.2	124.2	107.1	29.5	25.4	65.6	56.5	86.1	74.2	75.7	65.1	116.02
1975	130.3	102.5	116.4	91.5	43.6	34.3	81.8	64.3	127.2	100.0	85.4	67.2	127.18
1976	140.3	104.8	139.6	104.3	56.0	42.3	84.1	62.8	136.6	102.0	94.6	70.6	133.88
1977[c]	146.6	103.8	187.3	132.6	76.4	54.1	92.1	65.2	142.0	100.5	108.0	76.4	141.29

All fuel prices taken as close as possible to the point of production.
[a] Weighted by relative importance of individual fuels in total mineral fuels production.
[b] GNP implicit price deflators are used in computing the deflated prices shown.
[c] Preliminary.

Source: U. S. Department of Energy, Energy Information Administration, Annual Report to Congress, 1977, Vol. III, Statistics and Trends of Energy Supply, Demand and Prices. Washington, D.C., May, 1978.

major factors in the initiation of major increases in energy prices,
the prices of U.S. domestically produced energy sources (in real
terms) had begun to level off in the early 1970s.

These price trends are a reflection of a more basic trans-
formation that was occurring in the U.S. energy situation--a growing
imbalance between supply and demand for the major energy sources
(i.e., natural gas and oil) at prevailing prices.

U.S. domestic oil production peaked in 1970; between 1971 and
1976, petroleum production declined annually by 2.9 percent. Production of natural gas reached its zenith in the 1971-1973 period and has
declined since then at a rate of 3.2 percent per year. Consequently,
for the first time since 1958, total U.S. energy production declined
in the period 1973-1975 by 1.4 percent per year, but it has leveled
off during 1976 and 1977 (see Figure I-3) due to increased production
from the Elk Hills Field in California and from the North Slope in
Alaska.[4]

As shown in Figure I-4, energy consumption in the United States,
reflecting declining energy prices and increasing economic activity,
had increased at an annual rate of 3.2 percent between 1947 and 1973.
The decline in U.S. domestic production of oil and natural gas, in
conjunction with (among other factors) the Arab oil embargo in 1973,
aforementioned increases in real energy prices, and the economic depression of 1974-1975, contributed during 1974-1975 to the first decrease in total U.S. energy consumption since the early 1950s. During
1974 and 1975 total U.S. energy consumption fell 2.7 percent per year,
but then increased in 1976 and 1977 by 5.3 percent and 2.0 percent,

FIGURE I-3

TOTAL US ENERGY PRODUCTION, 1947-77

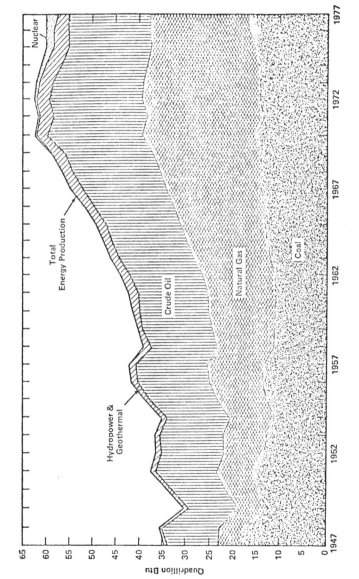

Source: U. S. Department of Energy, Energy Information Administration, Annual Report to Congress, 1977, Vol. III, Statistics and Trends of Energy Supply, Demand and Prices. Washington, D.C., May, 1978.

FIGURE I-4

TOTAL US ENERGY CONSUMPTION, I947-77

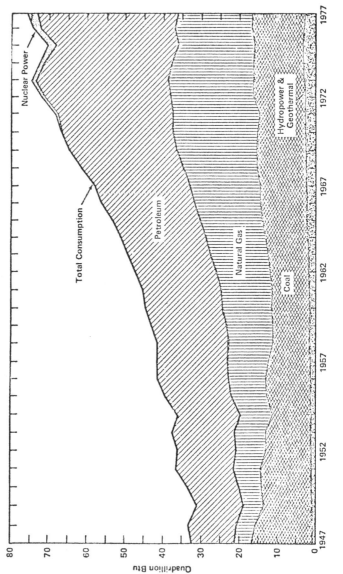

Source: U. S. Department of Energy, Energy Information Administration, Annual Report to Congress, 1977, Vol. lll, Statistics and Trends of Energy Supply, Demand and Prices. Washington, D.C., May, 1978.

respectively, despite annual real price increases of 1.2 percent for crude oil and 7.4 percent for natural gas during the 1975-1977 period.

Given the leveling off in U.S. domestic production of oil and natural gas and the increase in total U.S. energy consumption since 1975, it is not surprising to find that the domestic supply-demand imbalance at prevailing price levels is made up by an increasing dependence on imports as shown in Figure I-5. Imports of refined petroleum products have more than doubled during the last fifteen years.[5] The increasing dependence of the U.S. on foreign sources of petroleum supplies is illustrated in Figure I-6.

In view of these changes in the supply-demand-price relationships for the major conventional energy sources (i.e., oil and natural gas) it is difficult to dispute the contention that consumption of them cannot continue to grow at the pace and price levels to which American consumers have become accustomed unless major new supplies of energy become available and/or major efficiencies in energy utilization are realized.

Further weight is added to this contention (and thus to the complexity and uncertainty inherent in the U.S. energy situation) when the projected domestic resources of oil,[6] natural gas and coal and the costs of exploiting them are considered, as well as the difficulties involved in developing non-conventional energy sources. U.S. oil reserves are estimated at 29.5 billion barrels, where reserves are defined to be "the amount of oil in the ground that the petroleum industry believes is now available for production and can be recovered economically under existing prices and technology"

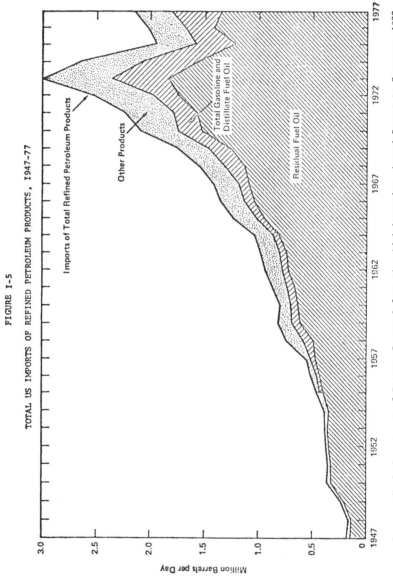

FIGURE I-5

TOTAL US IMPORTS OF REFINED PETROLEUM PRODUCTS, 1947-77

Source: U. S. Department of Energy, Energy Information Administration, Annual Report to Congress, 1977, Vol. III, Statistics and Trends of Energy Supply, Demand and Prices. Washington, D.C., May, 1978.

11

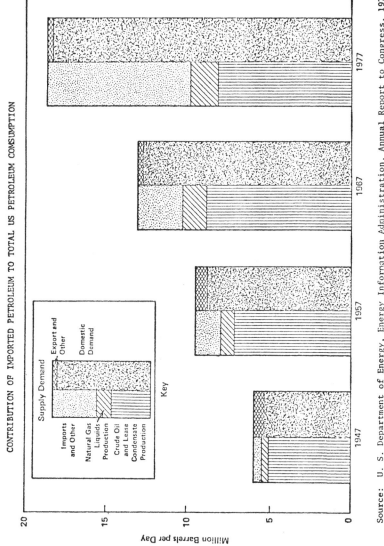

FIGURE I-6

CONTRIBUTION OF IMPORTED PETROLEUM TO TOTAL US PETROLEUM COMSUMPTION

Source: U. S. Department of Energy, Energy Information Administration, Annual Report to Congress, 1977, Vol. III, Statistics and Trends of Energy Supply, Demand and Prices, Washington, D.C., May, 1978.

(Press, 1978). In 1977, the U.S. produced 2.9 billion barrels of crude oil but only 1.4 billion barrels were added to the reserves through field discoveries, revisions and extensions. A similar story applies to natural gas. With the exception of the Prudhoe Bay reserves added in 1970, the total natural gas reserves have dropped each year for the past nine years (Press, 1978).

Counterbalancing the increased drilling and exploration for oil and natural gas, due to increased energy prices, "is the overall downward trend of oil and natural gas discoveries per foot or per hole drilled in new field wildcats" (Press, 1978). Thus, the stream of energy supply due to new oil and natural gas exploration may be moving toward the point of diminishing marginal returns. At the international level the picture is no better.[7]

Although the U.S. has sufficient coal reserves to satisfy all its energy requirements for at least 500 years,[8] the environmental costs of large scale coal production, the associated transportation problems and the costs of converting present facilities to coal utilization,[9] place major obstacles in the path of any rapid movement to coal to relieve the U.S.'s dependence on oil and natural gas.

The long lead times involved in developing non-conventional sources of energy (i.e., solar, geothermal, nuclear), in deriving oil from non-conventional sources (e.g., coal) and in exploiting unconventional gas resources (e.g., tight sands, Devonian shale, coal seam methane and geopressured aquilers) render the expected contribution of these energy sources to the total U.S. energy supply as negligible for the remainder of the century.

In view of the U.S.'s current and expected dependence on two energy sources (i.e., oil and natural gas) which are projected to decrease in availability, and the difficulties inherent in the development of alternative energy sources, it is not surprising that the energy situation in the U.S. has been popularly labeled "the energy crisis" or "the energy problem." What is remarkable is that the problem or crisis received such scant attention prior to the Arab oil embargo despite a multitude of evidence to suggest that the escalating demand for energy in the U.S. (and, indeed, the world) could not go unabated without evoking substantial price increases due to a shrinkage in potential supply[10] (Darmstadter and Landsberg, 1975; Penrose, 1975; Brooks, 1975).

The transition to a new energy era as reflected in these demand-supply-price relationships to a large extent masks the complexity, turbulence and uncertainty of the energy problem. The energy crisis is a multidimensional phenomenon: it affects all segments of society and has linkages to major events and their interactions in the social, economic and political arenas. The energy supply-demand-price relationship can critically affect the rate of economic growth[11] (Darmstadter, 1972), inflation, the balance of payments,[12] governmental fiscal and monetary policies, national security, international relations (Reifman et al., 1976) and domestic politics.[13] Similarly, proposed solutions to the impact of the energy problem on any one of these areas can often create or intensify existing problems in other areas (The Ford Foundation, 1974; Mancke, 1974).

A reflection of the fact that the energy problem has diverse, and often conflicting implications, is that it is as much a social and political problem as it is an economic problem since economic solutions to the energy crisis can have major social implications. Major conflicts in economic, social, and political goals emerge within the context of proposed solutions to the energy problem. For example, major increases in coal production may jeopardize previous efforts to safeguard the environment; energy self-sufficiency may be an admirable goal from a political perspective, but the economic costs of achieving this goal may result in social and economic dislocations; deregulating natural gas may be prudent economically, but its consequences may conflict with the socio-political goal of ensuring that rising energy prices do not place extra hardships on the poor and fixed income sectors of the population.[14] Additionally, regional disparities in the location of U.S. energy supplies can lead to differential social, economic, and political implications of alternate energy policies and events.[15]

Given the changing energy supply-demand-price relationships, the extent to which the energy problem is interwoven into social, political and economic affairs and the unavoidable conflicts inherent in potential remedial actions, it is little wonder that there are major differences in opinion as to the source(s) of our present energy predicament and the most desirable and equitable solution to it. One body of opinion believes that the energy problem is largely a non-problem and certainly not a crisis: if market forces were allowed to operate freely, the market mechanism, through inevitable

price increases, would serve both to reduce consumption and induce
energy supplies where it is presently unprofitable to do so (McAvoy
and Pindyck, 1975). At the other extreme, the energy situation is
viewed as a multiplicity of interacting problems which demand a
variety of public policy and private (market) initiatives (Ford
Foundation, 1976; Mancke, 1974; Freeman, 1974).[16] The time-frame
within which policy prescriptions are addressed also affects the
definitions of the energy problem and the associated solutions
(Brooks, 1976).

Confusion on the part of energy consumers as to the source
of the energy problem is evidenced in consumer surveys and public
opinion polls which show that the Middle-East oil-producing countries,
the multinational oil corporations and the U.S. government are variously seen as the major sources of the energy problem.[17]

Despite rising energy prices there is little evidence that
individual consumers have adopted energy conserving behavior.[18]
There is also some evidence that industry is moving to greater dependence on oil despite its higher cost.[19] This apparent non-rational
or aberrant behavior of energy consumers is somewhat understandable
when viewed against a background of uncertainty with regard to available and potential energy reserves; to the sources of and solutions
to the energy problem; and the conflicting nature of pronouncements
by public representatives and officials.

Perhaps a partial explanation for the confusion and uncertainty which pervades the energy issue can be found in the expectation that inevitably technology will solve the problem. Historically,

the U.S. has depended on technological solutions to solve many of its problems (Ferkiss, 1969; Freeman, 1974): thus, energy is just another area for which scientific knowledge and its application (i.e., technology) can be expected to come to the rescue.[20]

Few experts agree as to the extent to which technology can contribute to solving the energy problem, i.e., provide major supplies of old or new energy sources at reasonable prices in this century. A major study by the Ford Foundation (1974) on the energy choices facing the U.S. suggests that technological developments alone may be insufficient to avoid rising real energy prices.[21] However, what is clear is that technological "solutions" can give rise to economic, political, social and technological problems (Ackoff, 1974; Freeman, 1974a; Freeman, 1974b, Drucker, 1969; Churchman, 1968).

Thus, if we assume that technology cannot provide sufficient energy supplies to meet demand at constant real prices or the means by which considerable efficiencies in energy utilization can be realized, then, individuals and organizations will unavoidably have to adapt to increasing energy prices in real terms. Indeed, this is a task which has faced energy consumers since the early 1970s and has resulted in cries for the establishment of a "conservation ethic" from many quarters.[22]

This study is an attempt to examine how one set of organizations (i.e., industrial firms) have adapted to such variables as rising energy prices, occasional interruptions in energy supply and the general complexity, uncertainty and turbulence of the energy situation.

2. It is evident from the discussion on the complex nature of the energy issue that energy problems exist in many time-frames, on many levels (national security, economic stability, etc.) and affect all segments of the population. Consequently, it makes sense for energy problems to be addressed on a national scale.

In an attempt to reduce some of the uncertainty which had enveloped the energy situation, President Carter unveiled the U.S.'s first National Energy Plan in April, 1977. The Plan proclaims that the U.S. is in an era of energy transition; it asserts that cheap and abundant energy is a thing of the past; that the American society faces sobering new energy realities. The Office of Technology Assessment's (1977) review of the Plan points out that one of its most important messages is that even if the U.S. could afford to import unlimited amounts of oil indefinitely, unlimited amounts of oil do not exist anywhere in the world. The Plan acknowledges the hard energy choices the U.S. must make and the high cost of these choices.

The President's National Energy Plan attempts to set forth a comprehensive and consistent set of policies that will permit the U.S. to begin to manage its energy supplies before conflicting claims on diminishing world oil supplies reach crisis proportions. Central to the strategies and specific programs proposed in the Plan are three overriding energy objectives:

1. As an immediate objective that will become even more important in the future, to reduce dependence on foreign oil and vulnerability to supply interruptions.

2.   In the medium term to keep U.S. imports sufficiently
     low to weather the period when oil production
     approaches its capacity limitation; and

3.   In the long term, to have renewable and essentially
     inexhaustible sources of energy for sustained economic
     growth.

Although the Plan recognizes that there are no easy solutions
to the U.S. energy situation, it does propose specific goals so that
the progress of American society in reorienting itself "to the newly
recognized energy realities" can be monitored and assessed.

The proposed goals, to be achieved by 1985 are:

1.   Reduce the growth rate of energy consumption to
     below 2 percent per year;

2.   Reduce gasoline consumption by 10 percent below
     1976 level;

3.   Reduce oil imports to less than 6 million barrels per
     day, about one-eighth of total energy consumption;

4.   Establish a strategic petroleum program of one billion
     barrels;

5.   Increase coal production by about two-thirds, to more
     than one billion tons annually;

6.   Bring ninety percent of existing American homes and
     all new buildings up to minimum energy efficiency
     standards; and

7.   Use solar energy in more than 2.5 million homes.

The salient features of this Plan (or the means by which these goals can be attained) can be derived from an examination of the previously mentioned objectives and of the goals outlined above: (1) conservation and fuel efficiency; (2) rational pricing and production policies; (3) reasonable certainty and stability in government policies; (4) substitution of abundant energy resources for those in short supply; and (5) development of non-conventional technologies for the future.

The Plan describes the public policies that will be required and the demands that would be placed upon various socio-economic sectors in order to achieve the proposed goals. Of particular significance for this study is the emphasis placed upon the establishment of effective conservation programs in all sectors of energy use and the specific proposals directed toward industry.

Conservation is described as "the cornerstone of the National Energy Plan" and as "the cleanest and cheapest source of new energy supply." The Plan proclaims that America needs to embrace the conservation ethic: the attitudes and habits developed during the era of abundant, cheap energy are no longer appropriate in an era of declining supplies of America's predominant energy sources.

The Plan also proposes a major reorganization of federal energy agencies. The Department of Energy now incorporates all of the independent energy agencies which existed prior to October 1st, 1977 as well as the energy related functions of the other executive departments.

The interrelationship of the energy problem to financial and monetary policies, economic growth, the balance of payments, the interests of different political constituencies (e.g., individual consumers seeking lower energy prices, natural gas producing states seeking higher prices, etc.) and indeed, the political ideologies of different political groupings, is clearly evidenced in the Congressional response to the package of proposals contained in the Plan. The entrenchment of the differences of opinion with respect to the appropriate means to tackle the energy problem has been such, that the energy bill as finally passed by Congress in October, 1978, bears little resemblance to the Plan as sent to it by President Carter.

3. President Carter's National Energy Plan represents the major thrust of the federal government's efforts to develop a coherent and systematic national energy policy; however, there exists a large volume of additional governmental resources which are specifically geared to stimulate energy conservation, and in particular, energy conservation in industry.

The Department of Energy (DOE) had a total budget of $10.2 billion for its first year (FY 1978) which represented approximately a 70 percent increase over the President's National Energy Program FY 1977 budget of $6,053 million. Table I-2 shows the estimated FY 79 DOE budget and a comparison by major program areas with FY 78 budget.

It will be noted that the budget increase for "Conservation and Grants" (from $692 million in FY 78 to $1010 million in FY 79) is in keeping with the National Energy Plan's promulgation of conservation as the cornerstone of national energy policy as opposed to previous emphasis on increased energy supply. The expanded conservation and

TABLE I-2

TOTAL DOE BUDGET, FY 1978 AND FY-1979

	Budget Authority (In Millions)		
	1978	1979	Change
Strategic Petroleum Reserve	$ 3,595	$ 4,255	+ $ 660
Conservation and Grants	692	1,010	+ 318
Energy Supplies	2,696	2,670	- 26
Production and Delivery	908	692	- 216
Regulatory & Information	131	167	+ 36
Defense Activities	2,512	2,892	+ 317
Environment & Basic Sciences	615	635	+ 20
Policy & Management	388	505	+ 117
	$11,537	$12,763	+ $1,226
Less Supplementals/Other Adjustments	-1,254	-70	
Total DOE Funding	$10,283	$12,593	+ $2,310

grant programs are intended to decrease end-use demand and improve efficiency of energy utilization across a broad range of socio-economic sectors (e.g., schools, hospitals, low-income groups, state and local governments, etc.).

DOE's Division of Industrial Energy Conservation is directly concerned with stimulating energy conservation in industry. The FY 79 budget for DOE's Industrial Energy Conservation Program is $49 million, an increase of $20 million over the previous year. These programs

> are directed toward cost-shared research, development and demonstration to improve the efficiency of energy intensive processes, monitoring of progress and the implementing of new and existing energy technologies in the private sector.[23]

Projects funded under this program focus only on industrial energy conservation technologies which are not being pursued at all or which are receiving relatively little support by industry.

However, the federal government's efforts to stimulate industrial energy efficiency go much beyond DOE's $49 million industrial energy conservation research, development and demonstration program. The Department of Commerce began to sponsor in 1974 the Voluntary Industry Energy Conservation Program. This program is now organized under the auspices of DOE. Trade and industry associations monitor the progress of their members toward the attainment of voluntarily established energy efficiency improvement goals and report the results to the DOE.

A mixture of financial and economic incentives and measures are also employed to motivate industrial energy conservation efforts. Within the National Energy Plan's proposals, conservation in industry

would be stimulated through: (1) alterations in the pricing system
for oil and natural gas (i.e., "the price of oil and natural gas should
reflect the economic fact that the true value of a depleting resource
is the cost of replacing it"); (2) the placement of taxes on use of oil
and natural gas in certain situations (e.g., where coal can be used to
replace oil and natural gas); (3) financial incentives to reduce energy
usage (e.g., an additional 10 percent investment tax credit would
generally be available for investments in energy saving equipment).
As part of its responsibilities under the Energy Policy and Conservation Act, DOE has established specific energy efficiency targets for
the ten most energy consumptive industries,[24] as well as a specific
reporting system for the fifty most energy consumptive firms in each
of these ten industries.

    4. The significance and potential for energy efficiency
improvement in industry is paramount, since industry is the largest
energy using sector in the economy, accounting for 37 percent of total
energy use in 1975. Primary Metals, Chemical and Related Products and
Stone, Clay and Glass industries (all of which are well represented in
the sample of firms investigated in this study) account for over 50
percent of total industry use.

    Industrial energy consumption largely reflects the pattern for
total U.S. energy consumption reported earlier. As shown in Table I-3,
during the period 1960-1972, when energy prices in real terms were
declining, and economic growth continued to advance, total industrial
energy consumption increased at an annual average rate of 4.1 percent.

TABLE I-3

HISTORICAL GROWTH RATES FOR NET INDUSTRIAL

ENERGY CONSUMPTION AND PRICES

	1960-72		1972-75	
	Consump-tion	Price	Consump-tion	Price
Electricity	5.3	-0.9	1.1	6.2
Natural Gas	6.6	-0.3	-4.7	13.0
Distillate Oil	4.5	0.0	1.2	11.7
Residual Oil	-0.5	0.2	-4.8	22.5
Coal	-2.0	-0.7	-10.6	0.1
Oil (Misc.)[a]	6.1	-0.5	-1.9	15.2
TOTAL	4.1	-0.5	-4.3	11.2

[a]Includes liquid gases, naphthas, lubes and waxes and other miscellaneous products.

In the period 1972-1975, with rapidly increasing energy prices and the economic depression of 1974-1975, an average annual decrease of 4.3 percent in total industrial energy consumption took place.

A number of studies have indicated that with currently available and expected advancements in technology, potentially large energy savings could be realized in industry. For instance, the final Project Independence report projected that between 1971 and 1980 for the six industries studied (food and kindred products, paper and allied products, chemicals, petroleum and coal products, stone clay and glass and primary metals) energy consumption per dollar of value added would decrease by 1.93 percent per year--a 22.7 percent increase on the long run historical rate of decrease of 1.57 percent per year recorded during the period 1954 to 1971.[25] The Thermo-Electron Corporation, as part of its study for the Ford Foundation's Energy Policy Project, estimated that a one-third savings could be effected in much of industry.[26] That such projected energy savings are realistic is evidenced by the energy efficiency improvements which have already been reported by many industry and trade organizations as part of the DOE's Voluntary Industry Energy Conservation Program.

However, despite improvements in energy efficiency, the uncertainties and complexities of the energy problem are manifest in industry's consideration of and response to the energy situation. In fact, many business pronouncements on the energy problem address themselves directly to the uncertainties which business sees as dominating energy issues, thus inhibiting a rational response on the part of industry.[27] A reflection of these uncertainties is the movement of some firms towards greater dependence on oil and alternate fuel despite its rapidly increasing cost and greater likelihood of major supply interruption (due to increasing dependence on foreign imports). Also, a tendency has been noted among some medium and small manufacturing businesses to install electricity as the primary energy source in new buildings and plants despite the fact that it can be three or four times more expensive than oil or natural gas.[28]

5. Thus, industry is faced with the task of interpreting and responding to an environment where many of the critical variables (e.g., specific government policies and energy supply projections) are characterized by uncertainty and where (as is the case with many other issues which impact business) many of the vital decisions affecting the energy issue are enacted in the political arena and not in the economic market place. The energy issue can therefore be viewed as one of the major socio-political phenomena with which business must be concerned.

A number of literatures have examined the importance of the ongoing processes of change in society to the management problems and opportunities faced by industrial organizations. This relationship has been delineated by (among others) organization theorists (Drucker, 1969; Lawrence and Lorsch, 1969), systems theorists (Ackoff, 1974; Churchman, 1968), social commentators (Toffler, 1970; Fromm, 1969; Bell, 1973), "Business and Society" authors (Steiner, 1977; Davis and Bloomstrom, 1977; Chamberlain, 1973; Lodge, 1975) and corporate planning practitioners (Sawyer, 1973; Wilson, 1974). An important question for business firms which has been raised by many of these authors, is whether anything can be done by business management to anticipate, adapt to, or even to shape extant and/or emerging socio-political trends and concerns.

Although many of the trends and social changes discussed by these authors are continuing and pervasive, they can develop from time to time into major social issues generating public and legislative controversy. From all that has been said above, it is clear that a recent example of such a discontinuity is the emergence of the energy problem. This study examines the manner in which business firms have responded to an environment (i.e., the energy situation) where major changes have occurred in the last few years and where many important variables (e.g., the specific content of a national energy policy) are clouded in uncertainty.

6. Although empirical studies on energy management (as defined in this study) are relatively few, this research is related to the theory and ongoing empirical research in at least three areas: (1) the process of strategic planning; (2) the innovation adoption process; and (3) the economics of technical change. The linkages between these three literatures and this study are developed in chapters three and four.

Summary

This study is concerned with the extent to which differences exist in the approach to energy management by different types of firms (large multidivisional firms at corporate headquarters level and division level and independent firms; energy intensive and non-energy intensive firms; and, growth and non-growth firms).

The significance of this study is reflected by the timeliness and urgency for national energy management and energy conservation, per se, and the diversity of opinions and perspectives which characterize the energy issue; the complexity of the energy problem as represented by the ongoing efforts to formulate a national energy policy; the potential for improvement in energy efficiency and conservation in industry; the large volume of governmental resources devoted to the development and diffusion of more energy efficient industrial processes, techniques and behaviors; energy-related events in the last few years as a source of discontinuity and change in firm's environment; and finally, the study's relationship to a long line of inquiries in a number of disciplinary and interdisciplinary areas.

With regard to the last reason, from a scholarly research perspective, this study has ties to and potential implications for the academic fields of study generally referred to as the process of strategic management (planning), the innovation adoption process and the economics of technical change.

Overview of Study

This study is concerned with the response patterns of firms to the complex and uncertain energy environment. Specifically, this study focuses upon the approaches adopted by different types of firms to the management of their energy resources. The purpose is to determine the extent to which energy management is a formalized component of the process of management in industrial firms.

Energy management is defined as consisting of six (6) separate and independent dimensions: (1) organization for energy management

(e.g., extent of assigned energy management responsibilities);
(2) energy data generation and analysis; (3) energy management accountability (e.g., is energy management a part of line management's formal
accountability?); (4) energy efficiency improvement investments and
programs; (5) R and D programs (i.e., the extent to which firms' R and
D programs are oriented toward improving energy efficiency); and
(6) the development and marketing of energy efficient products and
services.

As conceptualized in this study, energy management is investigated from the perspective of business strategy and the processes involved in adopting organizational and/or technological innovations.
The energy management approach employed by each firm can be regarded
as its strategy to manage its energy resources. The concept of
strategy facilitates examination of specific components of energy management (e.g., to what extent is the firm's R and D strategy oriented
to energy efficiency improvement?). Specifically, energy management
strategy is defined as the combination of a firm's response along each
of the six (6) energy management dimensions mentioned above, i.e., the
decision making procedures and processes, investments and technologies,
and other behavior or practices which are intended to improve the
firm's own level of energy efficiency or energy efficiency in other
organizations.

Energy management can also be viewed in a number of ways as a
manifestation of innovative behavior. The decision by a firm to systematically manage its energy resources can be regarded as an organizational innovation (Knight, 1967; Wilson, 1966). Technological

innovation is represented by the consideration and adoption of energy conserving technologies (Rubenstein et al., 1974; Utterback, 1974; Mansfield, 1975).

Energy management along each of the six dimensions is investigated in two groups of firms: (1) eleven large multidivisional firms (i.e., annual sales in excess of $250 million) and (2) twenty-four small to medium sized firms (i.e., annual sales between $10 million and $100 million).

In view of the exploratory nature of the research, both quantitative and qualitative methodologies are employed in analyzing the energy management approaches of the sample firms. The intent of the study is as much to generate questions and hypotheses for further investigation as it is to test specific, a priori, hypotheses. This is especially so with respect to the qualitative analysis of the energy management decision making processes in the case of large multidivisional firms where the sample size and the nature of the data do not permit rigorous quantitative analysis.

Three characteristics of the smaller sized firms are examined to determine whether they are related to firms' energy management responses. These firm characteristics are: (1) growth (i.e., the annual average growth rate in sales in the five year period 1971-1976); (2) energy intensity (i.e., total energy consumption as a percentage of total costs); and (3) structure (i.e., whether the firm is a division of a multidivisional firm or an independent firm). In order to facilitate quantitative analysis of the relationships between growth, energy intensity and structure and the firms' energy management responses, the following tentative hypotheses are established and tested.

Hypothesis 1: Growth firms will demonstrate a greater degree of strategic responsiveness in their approach to energy management than non-growth firms.

Hypothesis 2: Energy intensive firms will demonstrate a greater degree of strategic responsiveness in their approach to energy management than non-energy intensive firms.

Hypothesis 3: Divisions of large multidivisional firms will demonstrate a greater degree of strategic responsiveness in their approach to energy management than independent firms.

Testing these hypotheses alone tells us relatively little about the process(es) of energy management decision making in industrial firms. This study attempts to explicate the following aspects of energy management decision making processes: (1) the kinds of decisions that are involved in energy management; (2) the major economic, behavioral, and organizational factors which influence these decisions; and (3) the nature of the roles played by the key participants in energy management decision making. These facets of energy management decision making are examined in the context of both multidivisional firms and small to medium sized firms.

Outline of Study

With the purpose, significance and a brief overview of the study contained in this chapter, the remainder of the dissertation proceeds according to the following outline.

Chapter Two provides a detailed statement of how energy management is defined and investigated. The specific hypotheses and propositions are set forth and explained at this point. To facilitate clarification and interpretation of the hypotheses/propositions, a set of definitions of the key terms which are used in this study are set forth in the beginning of this chapter. The chapter concludes with an explication of the variables of interest in energy management decision making.

Chapter Three develops the conceptual foundations of the study; the linkages between the study and the business policy/planning and organizational and technological innovation literatures are identified.

Chapter Four is a review of previous empirical research relevant to this study. This review includes empirical studies in the following academic fields: (1) business policy/strategic planning; (2) the innovation adoption process; and (3) the economics of technical change. Their relationship to the overall research approach adopted in this study (i.e., the testing of general hypotheses and specific propositions as well as the explication of energy management decision making processes) are considered in this chapter.

The overall research design guiding this study is presented in Chapter Five. The principal elements of the research design and methodology (study population and sample, data collection approach and data analysis techniques) used to confirm or refute the hypotheses/ propositions and explicate energy management decision making processes are delineated.

Chapter Six contains the first section of data analysis and interpretation of results with regard to the smaller sized firms in the sample (i.e., the hypotheses/propositions testing). For expository purposes with regards to the hypotheses testing, the approach adopted is to test each proposition separately.

Chapter Seven provides the analysis of energy management deci- sion making in the smaller sized firms. An overview of the major findings with respect to interaction among the energy management dimen- sions is presented. Energy management decision making procedures and processes in two groups of firms with distinct characteristics (high growth and highly energy intensive firms as opposed to low growth and very low energy intensive firms) are compared and contrasted. Finally, an attempt is made to identify and examine the factors (both economic and non-economic) which influence the emergence and evaluation of energy conservation investment ideas.

In Chapter Eight, an overview of the major characteristics of energy management in large multidivisional firms is presented. The energy management decision making processes in the two firms with the most systematic and comprehensive approaches to the management of energy resources is also detailed.

In Chapter Nine, conclusions from the previous chapters are drawn, and the limitations of the study are noted. Implications of these conclusions for corporate energy management programs, federal energy policy programs and extant theories of innovation and corporate planning are discussed. Recommendations pertaining to the above conclusions are suggested as well as potential areas for future investigation.

FOOTNOTES

[1]That energy availability and its utilization is closely
associated with our economic and social well-being is taken for granted
by almost all authors and analysts specializing in the study of energy
and its impact on society.

[2]Almost all of the data given here on energy prices, supply and
demand are taken from U.S. Department of Energy, Energy Information
Administration, Annual Report to Congress, 1977 Vol. 111, Statistics
and Trends of Energy Supply, Demand and Prices. Washington, D.C., May,
1978.

[3]In the 1960s, electricity was more than three times cheaper
and oil was more than twice as cheap as it had been in 1946.

[4]The imbalance between supply and demand for oil and natural
gas at the price levels which have prevailed during the 1970s is well-
documented and illustrated in 1977 National Energy Outlook, Federal
Energy Administration, Washington, D.C., January 15, 1977 and in
Analysis of the Proposed National Energy Plan, Office of Technology
Assessment, Washington, D.C., June, 1977.

[5]The previously mentioned increase in total energy consumption
in 1977 is reflected in the increase in oil imports from an average of
7.3 million barrels per day in 1976 to 8.7 million barrels per day in
1977.

[6]The criticality of the assumptions inherent in projections of
energy reserves is reflected in the geological uncertainties within
the official U.S. geological survey estimates of the U.S. energy resource base which could cause domestic oil production projections to
range from 8 billion to 12 billion barrels per day in 1985. See, 1977
National Energy Outlook, op. cit., p. 16.

[7]President Carter's National Energy Plan points out that the
world consumes over 20 billion barrels of oil per year. To maintain
even that rate of consumption and keep reserves intact the world would
have to discover another Kuwait or Iran roughly every three years or
another Texas or Alaska every six months.

[8]According to the Bureau of Mines, the demonstrated coal re-
serve base of the U.S. (i.e., in place coal that is technically and
economically mineable) on January 1, 1976, was estimated to total

438 billion tons. The bastness of the total potential U.S. coal resources is reflected in the U.S. Geological Survey estimate of 1,700
billion tons of coal at less than 3,000 feet.

[9]Most analyses of greater utilization of coal cite these problems, among others. For a discussion of the technical difficulties
involved, see U.S. Department of Energy, Coal Conversion and Utilization Division, Washington, D.C., November, 1976. For a more general
discussion of these problems, see S. David Freeman, Energy: The New
Era. (New York: Vintage Books, 1974).

[10]For example, an interagency study published under the auspi-
ces of the Office of Science and Technology in 1966 pointed to energy
as a public policy concern but only one of relatively low urgency.
The report said quite explicitly that domestic supplies of petroleum
and natural gas, supplemented by coal and nuclear power, would be
sufficient to meet U.S. energy needs for the balance of the century
with stable or declining prices.

[11]A positive relationship is often portrayed between increases
in energy consumption and increases in Gross National Product. However, the energy/GNP ratio may be of limited usefulness as a predictor
of energy usage, unemployment, etc. A detailed discussion of these
relationships can be found in Sam H. Schurr, ed., Energy Economic
Growth and Environment. (Baltimore: Johns-Hopkins University Press,
1972).

[12]Preliminary estimates for 1977 suggest that oil imports cost
the U.S. about $45 billion.

[13]The extent to which energy can critically affect political,
social and economic affairs is well illustrated in "The Oil Crises
in Perspective," Daedalus, Fall, 1975 and "Middle and Long Term Energy
Policies and Alternatives," Parts 1-6, Appendix to Hearings Before the
Sub-committee on Energy and Power of the Committee on Interstate and
Foreign Commerce, House of Representatives, 94th Congress, 2nd session
on Energy Choices Facing the Nation and Their Long Range Implications:
Mobilizing for Social Goals, March 25 and 26, 1976.

[14]The arguments supporting these contentions may be found in
U.S. Energy Research and Development Administration, Managing the Social
and Economic Impacts of Energy Development, Washington, D.C., July 1976.
Elliot L. Richardson and Frank G. Zarb, Perspectives in Energy Policy,
Energy Research Council, Washington, D.C., December 16, 1976 and
Federal Energy Administration, Project Independence: A Summary,
Washington, D.C., November, 1974.

[15] Many discussions of the U.S. energy situation fail to take into account the major regional differences that exist with respect to energy supply and consumption. For a general discussion of the significance of these regional differences in analyses of the energy problem, see, Philip F. Palmedo, "Approaches to Regional Energy Analysis," Growth and Change, October, 1976; and William H. Miernyk, "Regional Energy Prices and Regional Economic Development," Growth and Change, July, 1977.

[16] The scope of the differences and perspectives and the conviction with which they are propounded with respect to the nature of the energy problem and the possible solutions to it, are well illustrated in the distance between the viewpoint elaborated by the Energy Policy Project of the Ford Foundation, A Time to Choose (Cambridge, Mass.: Ballinger Publishing Co., 1974) and a collection of critiques of the report entitled, No Time to Confuse, Institute for Contemporary Studies, 1975.

[17] This state of confusion and uncertainty on the part of energy consumers is amply illustrated in a series of studies conducted by the Opinion Research Corporation for the Department of Energy. See for example, General Public Attitudes and Behavior Regarding Energy Saving, Highlight Report, Volume IX, April, 1975.

[18] Ibid.

[19] See Regional Energy Policy Alternatives: A Study of the Allegheny County Region, Carnegie Mellon Institute of Research, Final Report, Phase 1, 1977.

[20] The assumption and hope that technology can solve the energy problem has been evident in the federal government's approach to seeking an energy solution. The Secretary of The Department of Energy, James Schlesinger, in a presentation to the Subcommittee on Advanced Energy Technologies and Energy Conservation, Research Development and Demonstration of the Committee of Science and Technology, January 30, 1978, admitted that historically "ERDA budgets emphasized technology development solutions to energy supply and conservation efforts."

[21] The Ford Foundation (1974) study suggests that even if "zero energy growth" were realized by the year 2000, higher energy prices would occur then if the "Historical Growth" or "Technical Fix" scenarios were to prevail. The "Historical Growth Scenario" assumes that energy use in the United States would continue to grow until the end of the century at about 3.4 percent annually, the average rate of growth of the years from 1950 to 1970. The "Technical Fix Scenario" assumes that by putting to use the practical, economical energy saving technology that is either available now or soon will be, energy consumption would be one-third less than the Historical Growth rate. See, The Ford Foundation, 1974, op. cit.

[22]A delineation of some of the reasons for the establishment of a "conservation ethic" can be found in "A National Plan for Energy Research, Development and Demonstration: Creating Energy Choices for the Future," Volume: The Plan ERDA, 1976.

[23]This is how the focus of DOE's Industrial Energy Conservation Program was described by Dale D. Myers, Under Secretary, Department of Energy, in a presentation to the Subcommittee on Advanced Energy Technologies and Energy Conservation, Research Development and Demonstration of the Committee of Science and Technology, January 30, 1978.

[24]The proposed improvement targets range from 10 percent for SIC 33, Primary Metals, to 27 percent for SIC 22, Textile Mills Products.

[25]"Energy Conservation in the Manufacturing Sector," Federal Energy Administration, Project Independence Blueprint, Final Task Force Report, November, 1974.

[26]Guftopoulos, Elias, Lazaros Lazaridis and Thomas Widmer, Potential Fuel Effectiveness in Industry, A Report to the Energy Policy Project of the Ford Foundation, 1974.

[27]This is clearly seen in the presentation of many industrial spokespersons at various Congressional hearings.

[28]See "Regional Energy Policy Alternatives: Study of the Allegheny County Region," op. cit.

CHAPTER TWO

ENERGY MANAGEMENT: DEFINITIONS, HYPOTHESES AND PROCESSES

Definitions

A number of terms which are central to this study demand precise definition. The terms which will be defined in this manner are: corporate headquarters; divisions and independent firms; energy intensive and non-energy intensive firms; growth and non-growth firms; energy management; energy management dimensions, and finally, strategic responsiveness and non-responsiveness.

Corporate Headquarters, Divisions And Independent Firms

The types of firms or operating units which constitute the focus of this study fall into three categories: (1) the corporate headquarters of large (i.e., annual sales in excess of $250 million) multidivisional firms; (2) individual divisions of such large, multidivisional firms, and (3) independent firms (firms which do not have financial or managerial ties or relationships to any other firm).

The investigation of the energy management approach of two organizational levels within large multidivisional firms (i.e., corporate headquarters and individual divisions) recognizes the necessity of distinguishing between corporate strategy and business planning at these levels (Hofer, 1975; Vancil and Lorange, 1975; Hofer and Schendel, 1978).

Energy Intensive versus Non-energy
Intensive Firms

Two approaches are adopted to aid in categorizing corporate headquarters, divisions and independent firms as energy intensive or non-energy intensive. First, all three organization types are classified as energy intensive or non-energy intensive using the SIC (Standard Industrial Code) classification code, in conjunction with federal and private studies which have identified and categorized the degree of energy intensiveness of two-digit and four-digit SIC classification codes. Divisions and independent firms are defined as energy intensive or non-energy intensive according to their four-digit SIC classification code. The headquarters of large multidivisional firms are defined as energy intensive if more than fifty percent of their sales are in the six two-digit SIC classification codes which the Department of Energy has defined as the most energy consumptive.[1]

Second, as a check on the use of the SIC classification code system as a surrogate for energy intensiveness, firms were asked to determine their total energy costs as a percentage of their total operating costs. Although this is a more precise measurement of a firm's energy intensity than dependence on the SIC classification system,[2] not all firms were able to determine and/or willing to disclose the percentage of total operating cost represented by total energy costs.[3] However, to the extent that these figures were obtained, they helped ensure consistency in the groups of firms defined as energy intensive and non-energy intensive.

Growth versus Non-growth Firms

For the purposes of this research, the growth rate of firms refers to the average annual growth in sales in the five financial years prior to this research (i.e., 1971-1976). In all cases, firms provided their growth figures for these years. Where it is necessary to segment the sample firms into "growth" and "non-growth" firms, the median of the growth rates exhibited by the sample firms is utilized.

It should be pointed out that a number of other definitions of "growth" could also be employed (e.g., growth as measured by profit-ability, increase in the number of employees, etc.). However, as was the case in this study (especially with regard to the independent firms and some of the divisions) firms are generally reluctant to disclose profitability figures. Also, a growth firm as measured by sales need not necessarily be a "growth" firm as measured by profitability.

Energy Management

No generally accepted definition of industrial energy manage-ment (i.e., what energy management in industry entails), appears to exist. For the purposes of this research, energy management is defined as the activity involved in managing the combination of strategies, pro-grams, procedures, processes and/or products which the firm has adopted and/or developed to improve its own level of energy efficiency and/or the level of energy efficiency in its customers' operations. It is important to note (as was indicated in the previous chapter) that energy management is considered not only as a set of energy related strategies, programs and procedures, but it also includes the decision making processes which relate and integrate these activities. The

specific activities or dimensions which are investigated in this study
will now be defined.

Energy Management Dimensions

The general energy management dimensions and the specific components of each dimension are shown in Table II-1. The choice of energy
management dimensions was dictated by four factors: (1) the desire to
examine a range of energy management activities which would allow for
a determination of the extent to which energy management has been
institutionalized by firms in different contexts (i.e., growth and
non-growth firms, energy intensive and non-energy intensive firms,
corporate headquarters, divisions and independent firms); (2) the
need to investigate energy management activities and programs which
would be consonant with generally accepted notions of organizational
or technological innovation (see Chapter 3); (3) the insights which
would be gained by investigating both internally and externally focused facets of energy management; and (4) the insights which would
be gained by examining organizational, managerial, technological and
informational aspects of the process of managing firms' energy resources. The relationship between (1) and (2) will be explicated in
the next chapter. The relationship between (3) and (4) is shown in
Table II-2.

Strategic Responsiveness versus
Non-responsiveness

The energy management dimensions and their components are the
criteria by which the strategic responsiveness of firms to the energy
environment is measured. Table II-2 shows the distinction between

TABLE II-1

ENERGY MANAGEMENT DIMENSIONS AND THEIR COMPONENTS

ENERGY MANAGEMENT DIMENSIONS	ENERGY MANAGEMENT DIMENSION COMPONENTS[1]
(EMD 1) Organization for Energy Management	a. Assigned Responsibility for energy management b. Full time and/or part-time positions c. Energy Management Committee d. Specific targets/objectives
(EMD 2) Energy Data Base and Monitoring Process	a. Energy data availability b. Development of energy efficiency measures c. Existence of energy audits d. Frequency of energy audits
(EMD 3) Management Accountability	a. Management Accountability b. Energy Efficiency Improvement Plan
(EMD 4) Energy Efficiency Improvement Programs/ Investments	a. "Housekeeping" programs (e.g., Insulation, thermostat control, etc.) b. Production/manufacturing process changes c. Energy conservation investment evaluation criteria
(EMD 5) Research and Development Programs	a. Orientation of R & D program to improving production/manufacturing process energy efficiency b. Adoption of more energy efficient technologies/techniques produced by R & D
(EMD 6) Development and Marketing of Energy Efficient Products and Services	a. Development of new, more energy efficient products/services b. Modification of existing products/ services to improve their energy efficiency c. Utilization of energy efficiency considerations in marketing/sales activities

---

[1]The energy management dimension components thus provide the operational definition of each energy management dimension.

TABLE II-2

FOCUS OF ENERGY MANAGEMENT DIMENSIONS

E.M. Facets 1/E Focus	Organization	Management	Technology	Information
Internal	EMD 1[1]	EMD 3 EMD 4 c	EMD 4 a,b,c EMD 5	EMD 2
External	————————————————EMD 6————————————————			

---

[1]For a description of the components of each EMD, see Table II-1

TABLE II-3

STRATEGIC RESPONSIVENESS AND NON-RESPONSIVENESS

IN THE CONTEXT OF ENERGY MANAGEMENT

Degree of Responsiveness / EMDs	Non-Responsiveness	Responsiveness
Organization for Energy Management (EMD 1)	Lack of assigned responsibilities, and energy management efficiency objectives.	Clearly assigned responsibilities, use of task forces/committees, specified objectives.
Energy Data Base and Monitoring Process (EMD 2)	Little collection and analysis of energy data, and/or auditing of energy objectives.	Continuous and systematic data gathering and analysis, specific energy efficiency measures developed energy audits frequently conducted.
Management Accountability (EMD 3)	"Housekeeping" efforts (i.e., insulation, controlling energy waste, reducing unnecessary idling of equipment, etc.)	Production/process changes: generally investments which require substantial capital outlay.
Energy Efficiency Improvement Programs/Investments (EMD 4)	Little, if any, R&D effort devoted to energy conservation technologies.	Specific R&D projects to develop energy conservation technologies.
Research and Development Programs (EMD 5)	Minimal considerations of energy efficiency.	Energy management a prescribed part of management's functions.
Development and Marketing of Energy Efficient Products/Services	Little, if any, concern with incorporating energy efficiency considerations into product/market strategies.	More energy efficient products developed. Energy efficiency considerations in marketing and sales programs.

strategic responsiveness and non-responsiveness along each energy management dimension. Thus, a firm is said to have responded to its environment in a strategic manner if it has operationalized (i.e., institutionalized) the energy management activities implicit in each energy management dimension as shown in Table II-3.

Of particular interest from the perspective of the concept of strategy is whether firms which show a strategic response along internally focused dimensions of energy management also demonstrate a strategic response along the externally focused dimensions of energy management, i.e., do the firms which try to improve their own levels of energy efficiency, also attempt to develop and market more energy efficient products, processes and/or services from an energy efficiency perspective?

These definitions provide the background which allows us to understand the relationships in the hypotheses and propositions which are now stated.

Hypotheses/Propositions

The central hypotheses guiding part of this research are stated in broad terms, and, thus, cannot be directly tested. The set of sub-hypotheses or propositions tested are directly derivable from these hypotheses.

Hypothesis 1

Growth firms will demonstrate a greater degree of strategic responsiveness in their approach to energy management than non-growth firms.

A number of studies (Thune and House, 1970; Eastlack and McDonald, 1970; Gerstner, 1972; Herold, 1972; Ansoff et al., 1971) have shown a positive relationship between formalized approaches to strategy formulation and implementation and economic performance (in terms of increased sales, profits and return on capital). Thus, it can be expected that firms which show superior performance in terms of increased sales will have formalized and institutionalized their approaches to energy management.

In many respects, a growth firm, as the term is utilized in this study, is a synonym for a well-managed firm--a firm which is responsive to signals from its environment. Growth firms owe their success (in terms of sales) to good management practice rather than fortuitous circumstances.

Such good management practice might be the ability to bring to fruition in terms of marketable products, the firm's own research output, or the ability to carry out market and engineering development of inventions derived from sources other than its own research output (Schon, 1967). Such good management practices resulting in growth firms might also be the creation of an organizational climate conducive to the development of internal entrepreneurs (Roberts, 1969), or product champions (Doctors, 1969), or the ability to attract technical expertise or government contracts (Shimshoni, 1966). The maintenance of an appropriate relationship between a firm's strategies and its organization structure (Rumelt, 1974), between a firm's structure and both its external environment (Burns and Stalker, 1961; Lawrence and Lorsch, 1967), and the authority relationships within the firm (Wilson,

1966), may also result in a higher growth rate than if such is not the case.

However, from the point of view of this research, what factors cause a firm to exhibit a higher than average growth rate, is not directly of interest. What is of interest is whether or not these firms manifest a higher degree of strategic responsiveness in their approach to energy management, than less than average growth firms or non-growth firms.

Hypothesis 2

Energy intensive firms will demonstrate a greater degree of strategic responsiveness in their approach to energy management than non-energy intensive firms.

This hypothesis has its basis in the micro-economic theory of the firm which suggests that firms, in order to maximize their profits, will seek that combination of inputs which produces a given level of output at minimum cost (Baumol, 1977; Eckaus, 1972). Thus the higher the relative level of energy costs incurred by a firm, the more likely it is that the firm will attempt to control its energy costs.

The micro-economic and/or econometrically based studies of Mansfield et al. (1975), Enos (1962), and Schmookler (1966), generally support the thrust of this hypothesis, i.e., that the increase in energy costs since the early 1970s will generate some degree of compensating response by industrial firms. Based on the above research findings, these authors suggest that when the cost of a particular input rises, firms may be expected to initiate and implement innovations aimed at reducing the cost of that factor in producing an end-product.

Hypothesis 3

Divisions of large multidivisional firms will demonstrate a greater degree of strategic responsiveness in their approach to energy management than independent firms.

The corporate headquarters in a large, multidivisional firm is usually described as setting the corporation's overall objectives, policies, and plans, a major component of which is evaluating and in-fluencing the strategic choices and strategies of the corporation's individual divisions (Vancil and Lorange, 1975; Berg, 1965).

These authors, among others (e.g., Bower, 1972) point out that corporate divisions will usually receive support (including, if neces-sary, capital funds) from the firm's headquarters, for products which satisfy the firm's investment criteria and management's own goals. Divisions of large multidivisional firms, are, therefore, apt to have greater discretionary investment resources at their disposal than independent firms.

There is also a body of empirical research which suggests that large multidivisional firms are becoming more concerned with their response to major social problems and changes (Ackerman, 1972, 1975; Ackerman and Bauer, 1975; Murray, 1976; Wygal, 1977). Since social responsiveness must ultimately be implemented at the division level, this suggests that divisions of large, multidivisional firms may be actively engaged in developing and implementing a response to the energy problem.

Since these hypotheses are not stated in testable form, the following are the sub-hypotheses or propositions which it is proposed to test. Each proposition focuses on a single energy management dimension (see Table II-1). By testing each proposition separately, it is possible to examine which dimensions of energy management have received the most attention (and, by implication, are considered the most important) by the sample firms.

EMD1: ORGANIZATION FOR ENERGY MANAGEMENT

Proposition 1A: Growth firms will show a greater propensity than non-growth firms to organize themselves to manage their energy affairs.

Proposition 1B: Energy intensive firms will show a greater propensity than non-energy intensive firms to organize themselves to manage their energy affairs.

Proposition 1C: Divisions will show a greater propensity than independent firms to organize themselves to manage their energy affairs.

EMD2: ENERGY DATA BASE AND MONITORING PROCESS

Proposition 2A: Growth firms will show a greater propensity than non-growth firms to develop an energy data base and monitoring process.

Proposition 2B: Energy intensive firms will show a greater tendency than non-energy intensive firms to develop an energy data base and monitoring process.

Proposition 2C: Divisions will show a greater tendency than independent firms to develop an energy data base and monitoring process.

EMD3: MANAGEMENT ACCOUNTABILITY

Proposition 3A: Growth firms will be more inclined than non-growth firms to make energy management a formal part of line management's accountability.

Proposition 3B: Energy intensive firms will be more inclined than non-energy intensive firms to make energy management a formal part of line management's accountability.

Proposition 3C: Divisions will be more inclined than independent firms to make energy management a formal part of line management's accountability.

EMD4: ENERGY EFFICIENCY IMPROVEMENT PROGRAMS/INVESTMENTS

Proposition 4A: Growth firms will make production/process changes as well as "housekeeping" improvements (in order to become more energy efficient) whereas non-growth firms will implement "housekeeping" efforts only.

Proposition 4B: Energy intensive firms will make production/process changes as well as "housekeeping" improvements (in order to become more energy efficient) whereas non-energy intensive firms will implement "housekeeping" efforts only.

Proposition 4C: Division will make production/process changes as well as "housekeeping" improvements (in order to become more energy efficient) whereas independent firms will implement "housekeeping" efforts only.

EMD5: RESEARCH AND DEVELOPMENT PROGRAMS

Proposition 5A: Growth firms will demonstrate a greater propensity than non-growth firms to devote their R and D resources to the improvement of their firm's energy efficiency.

Proposition 5B: Energy intensive firms will demonstrate a greater propensity than non-energy intensive firms to devote their R and D resources to the improvement of their firm's energy efficiency.

Proposition 5C: Divisions will demonstrate a greater propensity than independent firms to devote their R and D resources to the improvement of their firm's energy efficiency.

EMD6: DEVELOPMENT AND MARKETING OF ENERGY
EFFICIENT PRODUCTS AND SERVICES

Proposition 6A: Growth firms will show a greater tendency than non-growth firms to develop and/or market more energy efficient products/services.

Proposition 6B: Energy intensive firms will show a greater tendency than non-energy intensive firms to develop and/or market more energy efficient products/services.

Proposition 6C: Divisions will show a greater tendency than independent firms to develop and/or market more energy efficient products/services.

Energy Management Decision Making Processes

The tests of the hypotheses and propositions constitutes but
one part of this study. The hypotheses/propositions testing affords
us relatively little insight into the processes by which energy-related
decisions are actually made in industrial organizations. Thus, the
other segment of the study which is separate from, though related to,
the hypotheses testing, is the examination and delineation of energy
management decision making processes.

A large number of authors have developed conceptualizations
of organizational decision making (Lindblom, 1959; Simon, 1947; Cyert
and March, 1963; Thompson, 1967; Allison, 1972; Galbraith, 1973).
Decision making in a wide number of organizations has been described:
educational institutions (March and Olsen, 1976; Butler et al., 1978),
utilities (Hickson et al., 1978), and industrial firms (Carter, 1972;
Pettigrew, 1973). Mintzberg et al. (1976) have conducted the most
systematic study of strategic management decisions across a range of
different organizational settings.

The focus of most empirical studies on decision making in
industrial organizations has been a specific decision or a set of
specific decisions (Hickson et al., 1978). This study focuses on
the explication of certain aspects of decision making in a particular
area of management activity, i.e., energy management.

The specific purposes of explicating energy management decision making are the following:

1. to provide a qualitative understanding of the phenomena and processes which may underlie relationships that become evident in the hypotheses/propositions testing;

2. to examine the procedures, processes, investments and practices by which energy management is institutionalized along each of the six (6) EMD;

3. to identify the organizational influences which impact energy related decisions, and

4. to generate hypotheses and questions which can be examined in future research studies.

A principal focus of the study of energy management decision making processes is the extent to which energy management is institutionalized along each EMD and the processes by which the EMD are related within the context of energy management decision making. Firms will have institutionalized energy management to the extent that energy management responsibilities are clearly assigned, energy data collection and analysis processes have been established, etc.

Each EMD reflects a different facet of energy management decision making. Indeed, widely different approaches to energy management could be adopted along each EMD. For instance, with respect to EMD1: organization for energy management, a firm need not have an energy management committee or even a full-time energy management position and yet have clearly assigned energy management responsibilities (e.g., a plant manager might assume such responsibilities). By examining the differences within each EMD and interactions among EMD it is hoped to provide insights into the organizational approaches which firms have developed to implement energy management.

Another major focus of the investigation of energy management decision making is to provide a qualitative understanding of quantitative relationships which may be evident in the tests of the hypotheses. A qualitative description of the rationale underlying energy related decisions (or non-decisions) and the specific processes involved in making these decisions may generate explanations of the results of the hypotheses/propositions testing. It may be of little theoretical value to know that energy intensive firms demonstrate a higher degree of strategic responsiveness in their approach to energy management than non-energy intensive firms if we cannot suggest reasons why this is so.

Energy management decisions (and specifically energy conservation decisions) are often portrayed as if they are almost exclusively determined by economic forces. A substantial empirical body of literature suggests that behavioral and organizational factors influence organizational decision making (Cyert and March, 1963; Bower, 1972; Guth, 1973). This study attempts to identify and examine the influence of non-economic (i.e., behavioral/organizational/political factors) on energy management decision making. Such behavioral/organizational/political factors might be the role of managerial perceptions of the energy situation in general, or specific energy conservation investments in particular, or interdepartmental or functional power and influence (e.g., plant management may be able to veto energy efficiency proposals generated by the engineering function).

Finally, the description of energy management decision making by itself is of limited significance: it is the in-depth analysis of energy management decision making directed toward the identification of questions and hypotheses, which may be fruitful areas for future research studies. Only in this way, can research truly be cumulative.

Summary

This chapter identified the hypotheses and propositions which are tested in this study. A number of key concepts which are critical to understanding these hypotheses/propositions were defined. Energy management decision making as the term is employed in this study was also discussed.

It was pointed out that the hypotheses/propositions testing and the delineation of energy management decision making processes are separate though related foci of this study. The examination of energy management decision making is intended to explicate phenomena and processes which may underlie relationships manifested (or not manifested) in the hypotheses testing. Given the exploratory nature of this research, a major reason for focusing on the processes of energy management decision making is the generation of hypotheses and research questions which can be examined more systematically in future research studies.

With the focus of the study detailed in this chapter, the next chapter provides the conceptual foundations for the direction of the research.

[1]The six (6) two-digit SIC industries in decreasing order of energy intensiveness are:

1. SIC 28, Chemical and Allied Products

2. SIC 33, Primary Metals Industries

3. SIC 29, Petroleum and Coal Products

4. SIC 32, Stone, Clay and Glass Products

5. SIC 26, Paper and Allied Products

6. SIC 20, Food and Kindred Products

[2]Although extensively utilized by economists and corporate strategy researchers (e.g., Rumelt, 1974), among others, dependence on the SIC classification scheme has a number of limitations. It provides a crude measure of firms' product-markets and manufacturing processes, but the management styles and behaviors of firms can be very different among firms within a given 4-digit SIC code. Thus, a 4-digit SIC classification code tells us relatively little about the strategies which individual firms might pursue (e.g., firms might pursue very different strategies with respect to improving their energy efficiency.

[3]All but five of the twenty-four firms in the 4-digit SIC classification codes investigated in this study tendered some approximation of energy costs as a percentage of total operating cost. At least one firm in each 4-digit SIC classification code reported some estimate of this percentage.

CHAPTER THREE

LITERATURE REVIEW: CONCEPTUAL FOUNDATIONS OF STUDY

The previous two chapters identified and discussed some of the major reasons for the significance of this research and provided the purpose and scope of this study of energy management. This chapter examines the theoretical foundations of the study; its relationship to the business policy/strategy and organizational innovation literature is particularly stressed. Energy management strategy and programs as a component of corporate strategy is first discussed; then, the linkage between energy management and organizational innovation is elaborated.

Corporate Strategy and Energy Management

Definition of Strategy

Review of the business policy and strategic planning literature shows a continuously growing and evolving consideration and definition of business strategy from the time Chandler (1962) first used the term "strategy" in conjunction with business policy questions to recent developments of the notion of strategic management (Ansoff, Declerck, and Hayes, 1976).

A wide variety of conceptual approaches to the concept of strategy have been developed (Ansoff, 1965; Ackoff, 1969; Steiner, 1969; Katz, 1970; Andrews, 1971; Newman and Logan, 1971; Cooper and Schendel, 1972; Hofer, 1975). Representative of the contemporary broad view of

58

strategy is the definition proposed by Christensen, Andrews and Bower
(1973).

> . . . strategy is the pattern of objectives, purposes
> or goals and major policies and plans for achieving
> these goals, stated in such a way as to define what
> business the company is in or is to be in and the kind
> of company it is or is not to be.

A more narrow definition of strategy which focuses on the means which

a firm employs to achieve its objectives is found in Hofer and Schendel

(1978) who define an organizational strategy as the

> fundamental pattern of present and planned resource
> deployment and environmental interactions that indi-
> cates how the organization will achieve its objec-
> tives.

Irrespective of the breadth and focus of the definition of strategy

which is employed, it is clear that strategy is the synthesizing con-

cept (Grant, 1975) which relates the firm to its environment through

the formulation and implementation of the firm's mission (King and

Cleland, 1978), goals and objectives (Ackoff, 1969; McNichols, 1972;

Uyterhoeven, Ackerman, and Rosenblum, 1973) and policies, plans and

programs (Andrews, 1971; Paine and Naumes, 1973; Steiner and Miner,

1977). ·

Types of Strategies

A number of the different types of strategies identified by

Steiner and Miner (1977) and Hofer and Schendel (1978), among others,

are relevant to this study.

Strategies may be defined in terms of organizational level:

Lorange and Vancil (1975) distinguish between corporate strategy

(headquarters strategy), business strategy (division strategy) and

functional strategy (e.g., marketing or engineering strategy). This
study examines certain facets of energy management strategy at all
three organizational levels.

The relative emphasis among the common components (scope,
resource deployment, competitive advantage and synergy) of strategy
at each organizational level as identified by Hofer and Schendel (1978)
differs markedly (Lorange and Vancil, 1975). Resource deployment will
receive the major attention in this study, i.e., how do firms allocate
their resources to achieve effective and efficient energy management?

Another major classification of strategy that is relevant to
this study is the concept of product-market strategies. Product-
market strategy can be defined as the development of new products for
existing or new markets and/or the development of new markets for
existing products. Product-market strategy is one of the principal
elements in a firm's strategic posture vis-à-vis its environment
(Katz, 1970; Luck and Prell, 1968). The impact of energy conservation
on firms' product-market strategies is examined, i.e., have firms
modified existing products specifically to make them more energy
efficient? have firms emphasized energy efficiency considerations
in their marketing activities?

A number of authors (e.g., Newman and Logan, 1971; Glueck,
1976, King and Cleland, 1978) distinguish between corporate strategies
and programs. As is evident from the Christensen, Andrews and Bower
(1973) and Hofer and Schendel (1978) definitions of strategy quoted
above, strategies are seen as broad guides to action and as "specific
major actions or patterns of action for attainment of objectives"

(Paine and Naumes, 1973). Programs are considered as elements of strategies; they are the means by which strategies are operationalized. In this sense, programs are very close to the notion of functional level (e.g., production, marketing, etc.) strategies. For example, a set of marketing activities (e.g., advertising and physical distribution programs) are formulated and implemented to achieve a product-market strategy (e.g., introduction of a new product into new and existing markets). A number of energy related functional strategies or programs are investigated in this research: has the R and D function initiated programs to develop more energy efficient products or more energy conserving production/manufacturing technologies? have firms established investment programs to improve production/manufacturing process efficiency? (The distinction between strategies and programs is elaborated upon further in the next section).

The final type of strategy relevant to this study is the concept of strategies specifically designed to manage material or non-material resources (Steiner and Miner, 1977). Energy management strategies and programs can be considered as the integration of firms' efforts to manage their energy (physical) resources. Thus, "energy management strategy" as the term is used in this study includes energy strategies at different organizational levels, product-market strategies and functional strategies or programs which are designed to manage the firm's energy resources.

Strategic versus Operational Management

Using the definitions of strategy and the different types of
strategy identified above, a useful approach to the analysis of business policy and planning can be developed by considering the activity
of managing strategy, i.e., the process of strategic management
(Frankenhoff and Granger, 1971; Schendel and Hatten, 1972; Ansoff,
1972; Irwin, 1974; Ansoff, Declerck and Hayes, 1976). Schendel and
Hatten (1972) define strategic management as

> . . . the process of determining (and maintaining)
> the relationship of the organization to its environ-
> ment expressed through the use of selected objectives,
> and of attempting to achieve the desired states of
> relationships through resource allocations which allow
> efficient and effective action programs by the organi-
> zation and its subparts.

The process of energy management, i.e., the organizational activities,
procedures and resource deployments involved in managing firms' energy
strategy is the focal point of this research.

Fundamental to these definitions of strategy and strategic
management is the distinction between operating and strategic variables. Strategic variables are generally referred to as those dimensions along which a firm expresses its relationship with its environment (Christensen, Andrews, and Bower, 1973), while operating or
tactical variables express in precise detail the action elements or
programs (Paine and Naumes, 1975), or the means by which strategic
goals are pursued (Ackoff, 1969). Katz (1970) illuminates the distinction between strategic and operating management considerations
when he suggests that "strategic variables give the enterprise
direction (and) operating variables provide its control." Thus,

it is evident that operational or tactical management is a subset of
strategic management.

Both energy management strategic and operating variables are
considered in this study. The major strategic variables examined are
energy management objectives, R and D strategies, and the impact of
energy efficiency considerations on firms' product-market strategies.
Examples of major operating (resource deployment) variables (programs)
examined are the extent to which personnel are engaged in energy management activities and the nature of the energy investment programs
which firms have undertaken.

Organization Processes, Rationality And Strategic Management

Strategy is the output of a decision making process. Strategic
management is not something which just happens; as is evident in
Schendel and Hatten's definition, as quoted above, it must be actively
managed.

Two approaches to the nature of the managerial processes involved in strategic management are evident in the business policy and
planning and related literatures. The first approach which is heavily
normative in nature, has its basic in classical economic theory and
capital budgeting: it typically treats strategic management (or, more
specifically, strategy formulation) as a sequential process of scanning
the environment for opportunities and threats, assessing the firm's
strengths and weaknesses, and then matching the two (Ansoff, 1965;
Cannon, 1968; Katz, 1970; McNichols, 1972; Vancil, 1976). In this
approach, strategy formulation is largely an intellectual process;
it implies agreement on goals and the means to attain them.

The thrust of classical economic theory is that firms operate "rationally" when they seek to maximize profits. Classical economic theory provides a criterion for decision making, i.e., profit maximization, but it does not tell us how organizations make decisions.

There is a body of literature which suggests a different definition of rationality in organizational decision making. March and Simon (1958), Cyert and March (1963), Thompson (1967) and Child (1972) suggest that organizations can best be viewed as coalitions of participants with different motivations and limited ability to solve all problems simultaneously. Objectives are formulated in the light of such constraints and achieved through a bargaining process. It is not surprising then to discover that empirical evidence exists to suggest that there is not always agreement on goals and the means to achieve them (Lindblom, 1959; Bower, 1970; Allison, 1971).

This study attempts to shed some light on both economic and non-economic rationales in energy management decision making.

Strategy and Environment

A wide range of authors from a variety of business related disciplines such as Dill (1958), Cyert and March (1963), Emery and Trist (1965), Perrow (1967), Mansfield (1968), Galbraith (1973), Kast and Rosenzweig (1974) and Beurgeois (1977) have emphasized firm environment interaction or more specifically, that firms must adapt to external forces in order to maintain viability. The empirical studies of Dill (1958), Burns and Stalker (1961), Lawrence and Lorsch (1967), Duncan (1972) and Neghandi and Reimann (1973) show the differential response patterns of firms or (segments of the same firm) to their environment(s).

In the business policy and planning literature, the environment is generally conceived as a source of problems and threats and/or opportunities for the firm. Many of the authors identified above have not only emphasized the need to respond to environmental change, but also the need to anticipate and plan for such change. In other words, firms can take initiating actions towards the environment as well as responding to changes within it. Thus, many commentators on firm-environment interaction (see, for example, Ansoff, DeClerck and Hayes, 1976) see organizations becoming more concerned with the process of managing the appropriate responses to and/or anticipation of, environmental changes.

Corporate Strategy and Energy Management

As discussed in Chapter 1, a number of reasons can be cited why the energy environment which firms face has become increasingly turbulent in the 1970s: (1) the United States' domestic production of oil and natural gas is no longer capable of meeting demands at prices to which the U.S. public has become accustomed; (2) the consequent supply deficiency in oil must be met by increased dependence upon foreign sources of supply--the Middle East--thus, adding to the potentially deleterious consequences of a supply interruption as occurred with the Arab oil embargo in Fall, 1973; (3) the increasing Executive and Congressional involvement in energy matters, often as a response to very diverse constituencies (which, of course, have different and often directly conflicting interests) represents for the industrial sector a highly complex and uncertain set of variables which it must take into account in its decision making; (4) the geographic location of energy supplies within the United States and the problems inherent in distributing energy supplies to non-producing regions (e.g., the higher rate structure for natural gas in producing states than in the interstate market) has meant that firms increasingly are not facing a single energy environment but rather a range of regional energy environments which demand different corporate responses; (5) partly as a consequence of the above factors, the prices and availabilities of oil and natural gas are no longer as predictable as they were prior to the early 1970s.

Thus, firms are facing a wide range of environmental stimuli and indicators which are indicative of a high degree of change and uncertainty in the energy environment. The underlying assumption in this study is that firms as entities which respond to and initiate upon their environment, will demonstrate some measure of response to this uncertain environment in both their internal operations and their interface with the environment.

Institutionalization of the Strategic Management Process

Most of the studies which have examined the relationships between formalized approaches to strategy formulation (i.e., strategic planning) and the economic performance of firms have indicated that the former significantly affects the latter in terms of superior performance in sales, profits and return on assets (Thune and House, 1970; Eastlock and MacDonald, 1970; Gerstner, 1972; Herald, 1972; Ansoff et al., 1971).

Almost all of the normative literature on strategy formulation/ strategic planning emphasizes the necessity to conduct a broad environmental analysis. The purpose of such an analysis is generally described as the identification of changes in a firm's broader social, political, legal, regulatory, demographic, and technological environments which may create opportunities and/or threats which would be missed by confining environmental analysis to the firm's narrow economic environment, i.e., its own industry (Katz, 1970; Christensen, Andrews, and Bower, 1973; Steiner and Miner, 1977). The incorporation of broad environmental factors and trends into corporate strategy formulation has also been described by a number of corporate planners (Wilson, 1976; Lipson, 1971; Newgren, 1976).

However, an area which has received considerably less attention in the business policy/planning literature are the methods, procedures and processes employed to institutionalize firms' responses to major socio-political and other broad environmental threats and/or opportunities. For instance, how well are such issues integrated into firms' formal planning systems? What specific decision making processes have firms established to consider such issues? What types of firms are most likely to institutionalize a response process to such questions?

Ackerman and Bauer (1976) and Ackerman (1973 and 1975) have built upon the earlier work of Selznick (1957) in their examination of the institutionalization of corporate social policy in large decentralized multidivisional firms and Murray (1976) has also investigated the same process in a sample of small commercial banks which are generally characterized by highly centralized decision making processes.

As described by these authors, the "social response process" (i.e., the manner in which a firm responds to socio-political issues and demands) consists of three phases: (1) the recognition of the social concern or issue by top management; (2) the appointment by the president of a staff specialist or group of specialists to coordinate the corporate activities in the area of concern; and (3) institutionalization of the policy, i.e., working into the decision making process by which resources are allocated. Table III-1 is the schematic model presented by Ackerman to illustrate how a (corporate-social) policy planning problem is converted into a managerial problem through the process of institutionalization. However, only Murray has attempted to identify and trace out the sequence of operating procedures, changes in management evaluation criteria, and resource allocation decisions which are major components of the institutionalization phase.

This research can be viewed as a logical extension of the above studies in a number of ways: (1) it attempts to delineate the institutionalization process in considerably more detail along specific dimensions; (2) the institutionalization process is examined in a variety of settings: at the headquarters level of large multidivisional firms, in the divisions of such firms; and in independent firms; (3) not only are the manifestations of an institutionalization response process examined (e.g., the extent to which energy management is a component of management accountability, the kind of energy efficiency improvement investments that have been made) but the decision

TABLE III-1

THE SOCIAL RESPONSE PROCESS SUMMARIZED

Organizational level		Phases of organization involvement		
		Phase 1	Phase 2	Phase 3
Chief executive	Issue:	Corporate obligation	Obtain knowledge	Obtain organizational commitment
	Action:	Write and communicate policy	Add staff specialists	Change performance expectations
	Outcome:	Enriched pur- pose, increased awareness		
Staff specialists	Issue:		Technical problem	Provoke response from operating units
	Action:		Design data system and interpret environment	Apply data system to performance measurement
	Outcome:		Technical and informa- tional groundwork	
Division management	Issue:			Management problem
	Action:			Commit re- sources and modify proce- dures
	Outcome:			Increased responsiveness

making processes involved in establishing and maintaining an institutionalized response process are also investigated.

Energy Management Strategy and Innovation

The evolution of strategic management and, specifically, the
emergence and implementation of a social response process as described
by Ackerman (1973 and 1975) and Murray (1976) can be viewed from an
organizational innovation perspective. Although the concept of organizational innovation did not contribute to the conceptual or empirical
foundations of the above studies, a major research question posed by
Murray was how business enterprises can effectively administer innovations, i.e., the institutionalization of organization change such as
energy management.

The capacity of organizations to engage in successful innovation has become a major focal point among organization theorists and
practitioners. As with the concept of corporate strategy, organizational scholars began to develop, during the 1960s, the basic ideas,
concepts and models which would be needed for a theoretical framework
for organizational innovation (Becker and Whisler, 1967; Knight, 1967;
Shepard, 1967; Thompson, 1969; Wilson, 1966). A growing list of
studies have been conducted to identify the organizational and environmental attributes most associated with innovation (Aiken and Alford,
1967; Evan and Black, 1967; Sapolsky, 1967; Myers and Marquis, 1969;
Rubenstein, Chakrabarti and O'Keefe, 1975). The conceptual and empirical body of knowledge concerning the process of innovation in organizations has been formulated largely by economists (Griliches, 1957;

Mansfield, 1968 and 1971; Hirsch, 1956; Arrow, 1962; Nelson, Peck, and Kalachek, 1967), sociologists (Rogers, 1962; Rogers and Shoemaker, 1972; Zaltman, Duncan and Holbek, 1973) and political scientists (Mohr, 1969; Wilson, 1966; Walker, 1969; Gray, 1973). Although many important questions with respect to organizational innovation remain to be answered (Row and Boise, 1977) and the various disciplines studying the innovation process have tended to focus on different aspects of innovation, and have employed a variety of operational definitions (Werner, 1976), thus, limiting the comparability of studies, the perspectives of organizational and technological innovation are relevant to this study, i.e., the institutionalization of energy management in business firms.

Definitions of Organizational Innovation

A definition of organizational innovation has not yet fully emerged (Rowe and Boise, 1975); reference to definitions employed in a number of studies illustrates the applicability of the concept to this study.

Gross, Giancquinta and Berstein (1971) define an organizational innovation as "any proposed idea or set of ideas, about the organizational behaviors of members should be changed in order to resolve problems of the organization or to improve its performance." Evan and Black (1967) seeking the correlates of successful and unsuccessful staff proposals, define organizational innovation "as the implementation of new procedures or ideas." Wilson (1966) defines innovation as "a fundamental change in a significant number of tasks." In the

context of these definitions of organizational innovation, the decision
of a firm to systematically manage energy affairs is, itself, an innovation. This application of the concept of organizational innovation
is also very close to the thrust of the definitions found in Zaltman,
Duncan and Holbek (1973) and Rogers and Shoemaker (1971).

Thompson's (1969) definition of organizational innovation as
"the generation, acceptance and implementation of new ideas, processes,
products and services" perhaps best reflects the three phase social
response process described by Ackerman (1973) and Murray (1976).

The broad definition of innovation employed by Myers and
Marquis (1960) with its focus on technological development, but with
due recognition of the organizational processes involved, provides a
framework within which we can view a firm's consideration and adoption
of energy management practices and behaviors and energy conserving
technologies.

> A technical innovation is a complex activity which
> proceeds from the conceptualization of a new idea
> to a solution of the problem and then to actual
> utilization of a new item of economic and social
> value. [Alternatively] innovation is not a single
> action but a total process of interrelated sub-
> processes. It is not just the conception of a new
> idea, nor the invention of a new device, nor the
> development of a new market. The process is all
> of these things acting in an integrated fashion.

The definitions of innovation proposed by Myers and Marquis
and Thompson highlight the sequential and integrated nature of the
elements or subprocesses involved in organizational innovation from
the conception of an idea through its implementation. Thus, a firm's
decision to actively manage its energy affairs is only a first step;

it must formulate and institutionalize procedures and practices to do so.

Types of Innovation

Another way in which energy management and, specifically, the linkage between strategic management and organizational innovation can be conceptualized and synthesized is to consider the different types of innovation which have been identified.

Knight (1967) has identified four innovation categories: people, organizational/structure, production/process and product/ services innovations. Each innovation class represents an energy management dimension or element of firms' energy management strategy which is investigated in this study: (1) people innovations--have full-time energy management positions and/or energy management committees been established? (2) organization/structure innovations-- are energy data generation and analysis procedures established? is energy management a component of management's accountability? (3) production-process innovation--have firms developed and/or adopted from other sources more energy efficient technologies? (4) production/ service innovations--have firms introduced (or are they planning to introduce) products which can be more energy efficient?

It appears that these four types of innovations are highly interrelated. Thus, in an area which has received little systematic research attention such as energy management in industry, it would seem appropriate to explicitly examine these four types of innovation activity in conjunction with each other.

Another important area of organizational innovation has been added to Knight's classification scheme by Zaltman, Duncan and Holbek (1973) namely, policy innovations, defined as major changes in the organization's strategies for achieving its major objectives. A firm's decision to systematically manage its energy affairs (as opposed to being unconcerned with energy as a cost item or factor impacting the firm's strategic or tactical choices) would fall within the domain of a policy innovation. It should be noted that a policy innovation is a sufficient but not a necessary condition preceding the types of innovation discussed by Knight.

The relationships between types of organizational innovations and types of energy management strategies is shown in Table III-2. A number of observations on Table III-2 are central to this study:

1. It is evident from Table III-2 that innovation in the context of energy management (as defined in this study) includes both organizational innovations (e.g., the development of energy data gathering and evaluation procedures) and technological innovations (e.g., the adoption of energy conserving technologies). Energy management innovation is not simply the adoption of energy conserving technologies but also includes the consideration of organizational changes which may be required to facilitate the adoption of such technologies. Thus, energy management as a form of organizational innovation which requires the acquisition of new skills, knowledge and techniques and their implementation within the organization, may be viewed as broadly similar to the adoption of strategic planning processes or organizational development techniques.

TABLE III-2

RELATIONSHIP BETWEEN TYPES OF STRATEGY
AND TYPES OF ORGANIZATIONAL INNOVATION[1]

Type of Strategy \ Type of Innovation	Policy	People	Organization/ Structure	Production/ Process	Product/ Service
Product/ Market Strategy	Decision to modify Product/ Market Strategies				R&D: New Product/ Service Development. Modification of existing Products.
Strategic Programs/ Functional Strategies	Decision to modify "Programs" or function-al strategies	Have E.M. responsibil-ities been assigned? Has an EMC been estab-lished?	Are energy data generation and analysis pro-cedures estab-lished? Are E.M. targets/ objectives for-mulated? Is E.M. a component of management's accountability?	Investments to improve produc-tion/manufactur-ing energy efficiency. R&D efforts to improve produc-tion/manufactur-ing energy effi-ciency.	

Note: E.M. = Energy Management
EMC = Energy Management Committee

1. Only the cells which are examined in this study are shown in the table.

2. The different types of energy management strategies can each be conceived as varieties of organizational innovation. For the purposes of this study, we thus define organizational innovation in the context of energy management as the adoption and/or implementation of decision making procedures and/or processes, technologies (investments) and/or other practices to improve firms' own level of energy efficiency (including energy conservation) or energy efficiency levels in other organizations.

3. Table III-2 and our definition of organizational innovation clearly indicate that the emphasis in this study is on the institutionalization of energy management strategy, i.e., the procedures, processes, technologies and other behaviors which firms have adopted or implemented to make energy management an ongoing part of the strategic management process. Thus, we are primarily investigating energy management after firms have made a "policy innovation" decision to formally manage their energy resources.

4. This study does not follow many organizational theorists who draw a major conceptual distinction between "imitation" (the adoption of an idea, technology, etc., which has already been implemented in another organization) and "innovation" (the development of the original idea, technology, etc.). Energy management as defined in this study (i.e., the EMD) is a set of interrelated activities: each firm can develop its own approach to energy management. Thus, the notion of imitation is considerably less applicable in the context of energy management than in the case of strictly technological changes.

5. All of the strategies/programs and/or organizational innovations are relevant to divisions and independent firms. In large,
multidivisional firms the people and organization/structure types of
innovation are relevant at both the corporate headquarters and division levels. While production/process and product/service innovations
are relevant only to divisions, they may be influenced by energy management decision making procedures which reflect a high degree of
interaction between corporate headquarters and divisions.

Process Versus Event Approaches to Studying Organizational Innovations

This study attempts to combine the two major approaches which
have characterized the investigation of organizational and technological innovation. The more traditional of these approaches is the
event or result approach to innovation, i.e., the result of an innovation (e.g., rate of diffusion, date of adoption, etc.) is related
to characteristics of the organization or its members. This approach
is characteristic of the organizational innovation studies conducted
by economists (e.g., Mansfield, 1971, 1963, 1975; Blackman, 1971;
Griliches, 1957; Bungaard-Nielson and Fiehn, 1974). The second method
of investigating organizational and technological innovation is the
process approach to innovation, i.e., the identification and examination of the stages or phases in an innovation decision ordered along
temporal dimensions of their anticipated sequence. The process
approach to organizational innovation is well exemplified in the

studies of Myers and Marquis (1969), Utterback (1969), Robertson, Achilladelis and Jervis (1972), and Rubenstein, Chakrabarti and O'Keefe (1974).

The event/result approach is reflected in this study's attempt to determine whether divisions or independent firms, growth or non-growth firms, and energy intensive or non-energy intensive firms show a greater propensity to adopt energy management strategies and programs. The emphasis of this study on the investigation of energy management decision making processes in a variety of organizational contexts reflects the process approach to the study of organizational innovation.

The manner in which the linkage between these two methods of studying organizational and technological innovations and the notion of energy management strategies and programs are conceptualized and implemented in this study is shown in Figure III-1.

Summary

This chapter has indicated how this study is related to the conceptual and empirical work in two distinct though related fields of inquiry: (1) business policy/planning and (2) organizational/technological innovation. The integration of these academic fields provides the conceptual framework within which energy management is investigated.

Energy management strategy, as the term is used in this study, includes energy strategies at different organization levels, functional strategies and programs, and product-market strategies which are designed to improve the firm's level of energy efficiency or the energy efficiency level in other organizations. The emphasis in this study

FIGURE III-1

CONCEPTUAL MODEL INTEGRATING APPROACHES TO STUDYING INNOVATION
AND THE CONCEPT OF CORPORATE STRATEGY/PROGRAMS IN THE
CONTEXT OF ENERGY MANAGEMENT

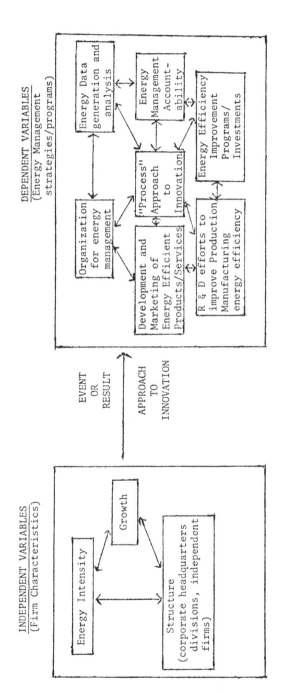

is on the extent to which energy management is institutionalized, i.e., the extent to which energy management decision making procedures and processes, energy conserving technologies and other behaviors and practices have been adopted or implemented to make energy management an ongoing part of the strategic management process.

The two related approaches employed in this study to investigate the institutionalization of energy management (i.e., the testing of tentative hypotheses which relate firms' characteristics and whether specific innovations have been adopted, and the explication of energy management decision making processes) reflect the two major approaches which have been utilized in the study of innovation adoption.

The next chapter focuses on specific empirical researches which provide support for this study's conceptualization and research approach to the investigation of energy management.

CHAPTER FOUR

LITERATURE REVIEW: EMPIRICAL RESEARCH

Empirical research studies in a number of areas can be examined for their support of the general hypotheses and specific propositions of this study, as well as choice of energy management dimensions. These studies are also investigated for descriptions and analyses of decision making processes in a variety of contexts which may aid in the analysis of energy management decision making processes. The general literatures examined are: (1) the process of strategic planning; (2) the innovation adoption process; and, (3) the economics of technical change.[1]

The Process of Strategic Planning

Bower

The overall objective in Bower's study (1970) was to identify and examine the forces which influence the capital investment process in a large private corporation. Bower's study is the most comprehensive treatment of this subject in the strategic planning process literature. The particular factors examined by Bower which are of relevance to this study are:

1. Organization structural context, i.e., formal hierarchy, the systems of measurement and evaluation, and the systems of reward and punishment.

81

2. The "definition" phase of the capital investment process, i.e., the process by which the basic technical and economical characteristics of a proposed investment project are determined.

3. The "impetus" phase of the investment process, i.e., the process which determines which proposals will be supported by persons with the necessary credibility to insure funding.

Bower found in the large corporation which he studied that planning and investment decisions are made by managers at many levels of the firm: corporate, division and business or department. New strategic ideas are generally developed at the business level. As the strategic idea takes shape and emerges into a specific investment proposal, it proceeds upwards through many management levels, and each level of management influences the ones above and below it.

The nature of the influence process is critical both to planning and investment. The managers who make the individual investment and/or planning decisions respond to unique and personal sets of incentives. These incentives are not necessarily or likely to be the same as those of managers at any other level within the organization. Bower's major finding with regard to the impact of the influence process is that when systems of measurement and reward are not integrated with the planning and investment process, problems result: investment projects serve the needs of managers and not of the business; the choice and timing of projects reflects organizational politics and not market consideration; and coordination among projects is lost.

What Bower defined as organization structure--definition of jobs, hierarchical relationships, management information systems and management reward systems--played a large role in shaping the "definition" phase of the investment process, i.e., the technical and economic content of plans and project proposals and the "impetus" phase, i.e., the determination of which proposals will be funded. Particularly critical was the need to bring to bear well-developed general management skills on capital allocation or capital budgeting questions.

Bower's work is predominately descriptive since it focuses on only one corporation; it is comparative only to the extent that divisional activities are contrasted. However, it does provide a conceptual basis for some of the propositions and energy management dimensions which are investigated in this study.

It is evident that an organization's social and political processes are just as important as economic and financial considerations in the planning and investment activities of capital intensive firms. Thus, how a firm organizes itself to plan for and implement energy management (propositions 1A, 1B and 1C) is rightfully a question of primary concern.

The finding that the criteria applied by a manager in the determination of which investment proposals would be funded was dependent upon the measures which the manager perceived as being applied to his judgment and management skills suggests the need to be concerned with the extent to which energy management phenomena, per se, are an express component of management's accountability (propositions 3A, 3B and 3C).

Finally, Bower's prescriptive conclusions based on his research findings are worth noting. He suggests that the firm's strategy should provide the criteria for the design of the structural context of planning and investment decisions. Since it is the role of corporate headquarters to set corporate-wide strategies and objectives (a major component of which is the evaluation of divisional plans) it is expected that the stimulus for and direction of corporate energy management is located at corporate headquarters. Thus, in large multidivisional firms it is necessary (as is done in this study) to examine energy management decision making processes at corporate headquarters level as well as at the division level.

Berg

The purpose of Berg's research (1965) was to investigate the process of strategic planning in conglomerate companies. Specifically, Berg was concerned with the identification of those factors leading to different policies, plans and procedures between corporate headquarters and division.

Berg's conclusions add validity to those of Bower. Berg suggests that an essential prerequisite to understanding strategic planning in a conglomerate company is to view the process as a multilevel activity, which cannot be separated from, or made independent of, short range planning and current profit goals. In other words, pressure on current profits will tend to work against investments designed to lay the groundwork for future corporate growth.

Berg also predated another of Bower's principal findings when he suggests that the strategic planning process in a conglomerate company involves non-economic as well as economic goals at each organizational level.

As indicated from the above, a major variable which must be examined in the context of energy management concerns the kinds of energy efficiency improvement investments which are made (propositions 4A, 4B and 4C) as well as the complex of factors (both economic and non-economic) which influence the emergence and evaluation of energy conservation investment proposals.

A major finding which supports Hypothesis 1 (i.e., that growth firms will demonstrate a greater degree of strategic responsiveness in their approach to energy management than non-growth firms) underlying this research is that growth divisions are more likely than non-growth divisions to obtain funds from corporate headquarters and, thus, are more likely to have a larger volume of discretionary capital. It could, therefore, be anticipated that growth divisions would be more likely than non-growth divisions to make capital investments with a view to improving energy efficiency.

Litschert

Litschert (1973) attempted to measure the effect of the technological environment, company size, and organization structure on firms' long range planning (i.e., the nature of their strategic and operational plans) within a single industry (the paint and varnish industry, SIC 2851).

Companies were classified as facing a rapidly changing environment if 70 percent or more of their sales were accounted for by the product category which respondents testified had a very high rate of technological product change.

Almost without exception, companies operating in technological environments characterized by rapid change employed research-oriented strategies. Although Lischert's study is concerned with product-related strategies, it does suggest that firms facing technological change with respect to their production processes will be more likely to engage in R and D directed toward the improvement of energy efficiency (propositions 5A, 5B and 5C).

Lischert also found that companies employing research-oriented strategies developed more sophisticated operating strategies than firms with market-oriented strategies. If it is accepted that research-oriented firms in the long run (through the development and introduction of new products, processes, etc., or the modification of existing products, processes, etc.) are likely to be closer to our notion of growth firms than marketing-oriented firms, then, Lischert's findings supports one of the hypotheses underlying this study: i.e., that growth firms will be more likely than non-growth firms to demonstrate strategic responsiveness in their approach to energy management.

Ackerman

Ackerman (1973) has conducted the most comprehensive study regarding processes by which large multidivisional firms integrate into their regular operating procedures responses to major social

changes. Ackerman has termed the institutionalization of these responses "the social response process" which he describes as a "response
process through which issues can be recognized and formed into policy,
implications and possible solutions explored, and, finally, plans
generated to govern action."

Table IV-1 is the result of Ackerman's efforts to capture and
depict the underlying order and logic in the social response process:
it illustrates how any major socio-political issue or problem (e.g.,
changes in the energy environment) becomes a corporate policy/planning
concern and is then converted into a managerial problem through the
process of institutionalization.

As indicated in Chapter 3, this study is concerned with a more
systematic and comprehensive examination of Phase Three of Ackerman's
model in the context of energy management. The institutionalization
of energy management is measured, along each of the six (6) energy
management dimensions.

Ackerman does not define the organizational procedures which
constitute the institutionalization phase; neither does he detail the
process of institutionalization with respect to any major social issue.
Although many of his observations relate implicitly to the decision
making process involved in the "social response process," no attempt
is made to detail the interaction between different management levels
or groups, or to identify the sources of and evaluation criteria applied
to investment proposals to implement firms' desired response pattern
to social issues.

TABLE IV-1

THE SOCIAL RESPONSE PROCESS SUMMARIZED

Organizational level		Phases of organization involvement		
		Phase 1	Phase 2	Phase 3
Chief executive	Issue:	Corporate obligation	Obtain knowledge	Obtain organizational commitment
	Action:	Write and communicate policy	Add staff specialists	Change performance expectations
	Outcome:	Enriched purpose, increased awareness		
Staff specialists	Issue:		Technical problem	Provoke response from operating units
	Action:		Design data system and interpret environment	Apply data system to performance measurement
	Outcome:		Technical and informational groundwork	
Division management	Issue:			Management problem
	Action:			Commit resources and modify pro-procedures
	Outcome:			Increased responsiveness

Murray

Murray's study (1976) attempts to apply Ackerman's model of the
social response process in a context other than that of large, multidivisional firms. The research setting chosen by Murray was a sample
of small commercial banks.

The major contribution of Murray's findings is the division of
Ackerman's Phase Two into a "technical learning" phase and an "administrative learning" phase. Technical learning is defined as the acquisition of new knowledge or skills related to a particular social issue
or problem by a task force or specialist staff appointed by senior
management. Administrative learning is described as the knowledge and
skills acquired by different management levels in their attempts to
develop specific procedures and programs which would constitute the
institutionalization phase. Both phases are critical in the evolution
of the social response process and both can be examined within the
context of energy management decision making.

The general criticisms of Ackerman's study are relevant to
Murray's research. The present study provides a more precise context
(i.e., the specification of energy management dimensions) within which
to examine the institutionalization phase of the Ackerman-Murray model.

Other Studies

Ackerman (1970), building on the previous work of Bower and Berg,
studied the resource allocation process in a small sample of integrated
and diversified firms. Ackerman's findings generally supported those
of Bower. Of particular interest to this study is Ackerman's conclusion

that the authorization of investment proposals is a function of the availability of funds and political power in the organization in both integrative and diversified firms. This again suggests that both economic and non-economic factors must be considered in examining firms' approaches to energy management.

In one of the earliest research efforts devoted to the analysis of the way corporations organize for planning, Wrapp found that one of the four common dimensions was the creation of a planning committee comprised of top management which had responsibility for both planning and operations.

Karger (1973), in a paper on integrated formal long-range planning, reported that 93 percent of high growth companies rated "the setting of basic objectives" and "the setting of goals for the years ahead" as important factors, whereas low growth companies rated these items 81 and 88 percent, respectively. Thus, growth firms may be expected to show a greater propensity than non-growth firms to establish energy efficiency objectives.

In a survey of current planning practices and experiences of 40 widely diversified "Fortune 500" firms, most of which had multi-divisional structures and decentralized management philosophies, Ringbakk (1968) found that traditional accounting data alone is inadequate for planning processes. This may be especially so in the case of energy, where most of the major concerns are external to the firm, and accounting functions have not historically treated energy costs as a separate item.

Summary

The strategic planning process literature provides a considerable basis for the hypotheses developed in this study as well as the
energy management dimensions which are investigated. Of particular
consequence for this study is the recognition that planning and investment decisions (both their formulation and implementation) are imbedded
in organizational processes that are highly political and behavioral in
nature. Thus an appraisal of the extent to which energy management is
institutionalized in corporations must take into account factors other
than those which are directly amenable to economic analysis.

However, there is a noted absence of empirical studies in the
business policy-strategic planning literature which attempt to utilize
organizational innovation concepts in research on strategy formulation
and implementation processes. For this reason, the next literature
which will be examined for its contributions to this study is the
literature on the innovation adoption process.

The Innovation Adoption Process

A large number of descriptive studies focus on the process of
innovation, i.e., the sequential stages in the decision process involved in innovation and an examination of the phenomena and events
which affect each of these stages. These studies, for the most part,
focus on the process involved in the adoption of technological innovations and, only secondarily, investigate the impact of firms' characteristics (e.g., size and growth rate of the firm) on the innovation
process. (The latter represents the event or result approach to

innovation and will be dealt with in the review of the next body of
literature--the economics of technical change.)

The outcome of these studies at the level of individual innovations is a useful and widely shared paradigm of the innovation process.
Three stages are often distinguished in the innovation process: idea
generation, adoption, and implementation (Shepard, 1967). A more in-
clusive delineation of the process of innovation is put forward by
Utterback (1974): generation of an idea, problem-solving or development, and implementation and diffusion. Utterback's depiction of the
significant stages in the innovation process is basically that which
was employed by Myers and Marquis (1969) in their study of the major
factors impinging on the adoption of technological innovations.

Myers and Marquis

A study conducted by Myers and Marquis (1969) for the National
Science Foundation is typical of the focus, methodology and conclusions
of many empirical efforts to describe the process of technological
innovation. The overall objective of their study was to examine the
process by which process or product innovations take place in industrial organizations, the major factors involved in the initiation of
such innovations and the nature, sources, and means of obtaining information significant in creating the innovations. The industries studied
were railroad companies, railroad suppliers, housing suppliers, computer manufacturers and computer suppliers.

The innovation model employed by Marquis and Myers consists of
three stages: (1) idea generation and formulation; (2) problem solving

(i.e., setting specific technical goals and designing alternative solutions to meet them), and (3) implementation (i.e., the manufacturing/ engineering, tooling, and plant and market start-up required to bring an original invention or solution to its final use or market introduction).

It will be noted that, although this study is at least partially concerned with each of these three innovation stages in an organizational (and not merely technological) context, the primary emphasis is on the last phase, i.e., the implementation (or in Ackerman's terms, the institutionalization) stage (for example, the integration of energy efficiency considerations into firms' product-market strategies or the adoption of more energy efficient technologies in the firm's own manufacturing/production processes which were developed by the firm's R and D group).

Specifically, Myers and Marquis examined the role of information in each stage of their innovation model. No consistent differences were apparent between large and small firms, across all five industries studied with respect to the proportion of innovations for which the information input evoked the idea or contributed to the solution of the problem. In 27 percent of the projects, the major information input evoked the idea for the innovation. These firms were not actively working on the problem at the time the information was received, although half of them were working on a related problem.

Robertson, Achilladelis and Jervis

One of the most ambitious efforts to explicate the most influential administrative factors within the innovation process is the study of success and failure in industrial innovation (SAPPHO)

conducted at the University of Sussex. Significantly, from the point

of view of this research, the SAPPHO investigators observe in the

introduction to their findings:

> typically, studies of innovation have highlighted the
> "single factor" in the process, on which the ultimate
> success is believed to have hanged. Accepting that
> innovation is a complex sequence of events, involving
> scientific research as well as technological develop-
> ment, management production and selling, it was felt
> that those single factor interpretations were less
> than satisfactory. . . .

Project SAPPHO identified and evaluated 29 pairs of innovations

in two industries--chemical and scientific instruments. Each pair was

selected to provide one successful and one unsuccessful attempt to in-

troduce comparable innovations. Interviewers documented 201 character-

istics of each case and then compared the members of each pair to es-

tablish whether and in what way they differed on each characteristic.

The SAPPHO study offered five principal conclusions concerning

factors contributing to successful innovation. Three pertain to the

innovating organization's relations with its external environment;

successful innovators had significantly better understanding of user

needs, paid more attention to marketing tasks and made more effective

use of external technical resources. Two other organizational charac-

teristics seemed consistently and strongly associated with success:

more efficient performance of development tasks and the assignment

of responsibility to a more senior executive.

Both the Myers and Marquis and the "SAPPHO" studies provide

little direct support for this study's hypotheses, but they do lend

empirical support for the choice of energy management dimensions which are investigated [e.g., the assignment of energy management responsibilities (EMD1), energy data generation and analysis (EMD2) and product-market considerations (EMD6)].

Allan

In a series of related studies, Allan (1967, 1969) has examined a critical element in the innovation process--information flow between the firm and its environment, and information flow within the firm. Small research organizations were the subject of Allan's studies.

Allan foreshadowed the findings of Myers and Marquis when he observed that most of the information used in problem-solving comes from within the firm. Information about advanced technology is primarily communicated through external discussion sources and technical literature.

However, this information is usually brought into the firm by a few individuals, termed "technical gatekeepers," who have more extensive contact than do others with colleagues outside the firm or with technical literature or both. Technological gatekeepers, Allan contends, are effective mechanisms for bridging organization boundary impedence.

Although Allan's studies do not provide us with any explanatory insights as to what kinds of organizations will display a high degree of innovativeness under different circumstances, they do emphasize the necessity to pay particular attention to the use of information in the innovating process (propositions 2A, 2B and 2C).

Rubenstein, Chakrabati and O'Keefe

As part of their ongoing work in the Program of Research on the Management of Research and Development at Northwestern University, Rubenstein et al. (1974), conducted a study to identify those factors that act as barriers or facilitators to the Research and Development/ Innovation process.

In à major departure from many previous studies, Rubenstein et al., chose the project as the unit of analysis rather than the firm, the function (e.g., marketing, R and D, etc.), the individual executive, or the decision. The concept of a project was defined as "a unit that identifies a goal-directed effort with a readily identified end in view, although this end may change frequently or gradually as the work progresses."

Although most of the factors investigated had already been presented in the literature as conclusions about what causes success and failure in the innovation process, a relatively small number of the variables (less than 25 percent) achieved a "high" level of significance over the set of research sites and projects.

Of particular significance to this study is Rubenstein et al.'s summary conclusion in which they "urge greater concentration on the kind of internal management factors resulting from the study that could have impact on the success of the RD/I process." They single out (1) the need for improved communication between the functional areas and (2) major improvements in the methods of data gathering, analysis, and decision making on which projects to initiate, modify, or terminate as the internal management areas requiring more detailed attention. Energy data gathering and analysis constitute the dependent variable in Proposition 2A, 2B and 2C while coordinated communication is implicit in the positions with specific responsibilities for energy management (propositions 1A, 1B and 1C). Of course, many of the management factors which Rubenstein et al. consider so significant in the innovation process will be considered in explications of energy management decision making processes.

Other Studies

Baker et al. (1967), Carter and Williams (1957), Tannenbaum et al. (1966), and Utterback (1969) all found that from 60 to 80 percent of important innovations were stimulated by market needs as opposed to those which emerged in response to new scientific or technological advances and opportunities. This result suggests the desirability of investigating whether firms are responding to the present concern with energy scarcity and utilization through the production and marketing of more energy efficient products and processes (propositions 6A, 6B and 6C).

Summary

These studies provide a representative sample of the kinds of the empirical efforts which have helped explicate the process of technological innovation. As is evident from the above entries, almost all the studies which have investigated the process of technological innovation have been predominantly descriptive in character. Little systematic attention has been devoted to the development of explanatory models of firms' propensity to adopt technological innovations.

Some economists, through the use of econometric models, have attempted to develop explanatory models of technological change in industrial firms. It is these studies which will be examined now.

The Economics of Technical Change

In their investigation of the process of the technological change economists have largely focused their efforts on

> a certain class of successful innovations namely,
> basically unchanging innovations (or more accurately,
> innovations treated as such analytically) which re-
> place similar but less efficient inputs in a produc-
> tion process or outputs in an industry's product mix
> assuming a conventional market profit orientation
> (Warner, 1974).

For such innovations,[2] economists have developed a body of knowledge which can be applied with reasonable success to explain and predict the pattern, speed and direction of the diffusion process both within firms and among firms in the relevant industries.

This review will focus on economists' depiction of technolog-ical change at the "micro-level" (the level of the firm) and not the "macro-level" (the level of the economy) oriented studies of (for example) Schmookler (1952), Solo (1957), Hogan (1958) and Beckman and Sato (1969). The latter kind of studies pay considerably less atten-tion to firms' characteristics and their relationship to the innova-tion process.

The Mansfield Studies

The work of Mansfield and his associates constitutes the most comprehensive economic analysis of the phenomena of technical change

and the diffusion of technical innovations. Many of the research findings of the Mansfield studies have a direct bearing on the overall research approach which is adopted in this study and the specific propositions which are tested.

In one of Mansfield's (1961) earlier studies, he observed that
no organization was forever, either a leader or follower in innovation.
Nevertheless, he concluded that "the successful innovators grew more
rapidly than others." This directly supports one of the main hypotheses
underlying this research, namely, that growth firms can be expected to
be more innovative than non-growth firms with respect to energy management.

Mansfield's findings generally indicate no significant advantages concerning inventive and innovative performance for the largest
firms in many industries over smaller firms. In some industries (e.g.,
ethical drugs, Mansfield, et al., 1971; the steel industry, Mansfield,
1968) the largest firms did not carry out the largest number of innovations (weighted or unweighted) relative to their size. Also, firms
half as large as the largest firms in Mansfield's (1971) most comprehensive study undertook proportionately as much of the more basic,
risky and long term research and development as the largest firms.

Through the use of econometric models, a general hypothesis
supported in the Mansfield studies is that the more profitable the
innovation and the smaller the required investment, the greater the
rate of imitation. Other factors--whether or not the innovation re-
places durable equipment, the rates of expansion of the relevant firms,
the point of history (the assumption being that the rate of diffusion

has increased over time, owing to improved channels of communication, etc.) and the phase of the business cycle--had apparent effects in the expected direction but their inclusion in the regression analysis did not significantly improve explanations of variations in the rate of imitation. Determination of the significance of these factors, Mansfield observed, requires more data than he had available.

Mansfield's econometric approach has, at best, succeeded in explaining about fifty percent of the variation in firms' propensity to innovate (Mansfield et al., 1975). In an earlier work, Mansfield (1968) was forced to conclude:

> Perhaps these (additional economic) variables are less important than other more elusive and essentially non-economic variables. The personality attributes, interests, training and other characteristics of top and middle management may play a very important role in determining how quickly a firm introduces an innovation.

Mansfield's conclusion that economic and non-economic variables must be considered simultaneously in any explanatory model of firms' innovativeness supports the research approach adopted in this study of combining the process and event or result approaches to the study of organizational or technological innovations.

Nabseth and Ray

Nabseth and Ray's work (1974) is highly relevant to this research. They organized a series of joint international studies of the diffusion of new industrial processes "because less is known about this than about the diffusion of new products."

Although the analysis was primarily economic in nature, many of the studies attempted to identify and measure the impact of such non-economic variables as information flow, management attitudes and perceptions, and institutional factors such as relevant legislative developments, as facilitative or inhibiting factors in the diffusion of new industrial processes. The general conclusions of the study were that: (1) information availability and flow; (2) profitability or relative advantage; (3) economic variables like internal rate of return, level of investment, etc., and (4) institutional factors were the most significant factors impinging on the acceptance of innovations.

Echoing the findings of the Mansfield studies, Nasbeth and Ray suggest that the threshold size at which firms respond rapidly to new technical processes need not be very big in any absolute sense. Also, the threshold size seems to be highly dependent on the technology in question. However, in most of the industries studied, it was not large firms, but rather medium-sized and small firms that were the first to introduce the new industrial processes.

One study found that the rate of expansion of available markets seemed to be the dominant influence in diffusion of the innovation (basic oxygen process in the steel industry). This would suggest that firms whose dominant product lines are in growth markets would be more inclined to adopt innovations than firms in non-growth markets.

Pavitt and Wald

Pavitt and Wald (1971) in an OECD (Organization for Economic Cooperation and Development) study examined empirical evidence developed during the 1960s, with regard to the role of both economic and non-economic factors in the process of technological change, and concluded that both large and small firms play an essential, complementary and interdependent role in the process of innovation.

Larger firms have tended to contribute most to innovation in areas requiring large scale R and D, production, and marketing. Smaller firms tend to concentrate on specialized but sophisticated components and equipment and have often made very major innovations when large firms let the opportunity slip by.

Large and small firms may, therefore, exhibit different emphasis in their approaches to energy management. Assuming a greater degree of discretionary capital, large firms (or divisions of large firms) may undertake a capital investment program to enhance energy efficiency whereas independent firms may emphasize "housekeeping" measures (improved maintenance, etc.) (proposition 4C).

Learning by Doing

Highly relevant to both intra-firm diffusion and inter-firm diffusion of new products and processes are the several studies on "learning by doing" (manufacturing process functions) dating from the mid-1950s. The thrust of these studies by a wide range of economists is that efficiency in the use of production of a novel item or technique increases with experience within the firm.

Hirsch (1956) and Alchian (1963) in their research on the aircraft industry have lent empirical support to the hypothesis that there is a negative linear relationship between the logarithm of labor effort expended and the logarithm of "experience" (i.e., number of units of output produced or number of uses of input).

Nelson, Peck and Kalachek (1967) contend that the long lead times from first use to widespread adoption of industrial innovation found by Enos (1962) and Mansfield (1961), among others, is partly because of the importance of learning by doing, on both the demand and supply side.

The "learning by doing" studies suggest that as firms gain experience in managing their energy affairs, they will become more innovative in their approach to energy management. This group of studies would also appear to suggest that growth firms because of their greater familiarity than non-growth firms with the need to innovate and adapt to change would exhibit a greater degree of strategic responsiveness in their approach to energy management.

Other Studies

A number of economists have addressed the question of "inventive activity" in industrial firms. Hamburg (1963) and Jewkes, Sawers and Stillerman (1958), among others, found that large research laboratories of industrial corporations were not responsible for the bulk of significant inventions.

Cooper's (1964) research suggests that a product would cost three to five times as much to develop in a large corporation as it would in a smaller firm. These studies indicate that smaller firms may be more innovative than larger firms with respect to some aspects of energy management.

The work of Enos (1962) and Schmookler (1966) is particularly relevant to the contention that the recent increases in energy costs will motivate some degree of compensating response by industrial firms (Hypothesis 2) i.e., that energy intensive firms will demonstrate a greater degree of strategic responsiveness in their approach to energy management than non-energy intensive firms. Both of these studies suggest that when the cost of a particular input rises, innovations may be expected to be aimed at reducing the use of that factor in producing an end-product.

In summary, economists are coming more and more to agree with the view of Langrish et al. (1972) that the events leading up to the adoption of an innovation often fail to conform to any simple linear model. The simple definitions of innovation employed by economists fail to tell us much about the decision making processes involved in firms' adoption or rejection of an innovation. In this study, therefore, as outlined in Chapter Two, we take a rather broad view of the concept of innovation as it relates to energy management.

Summary of Literature Review

A review of three bodies of literature (the process of strategic planning, the innovation adoption process and the economics of technical change) for their contributions to this study provide some empirical bases for the general hypotheses and specific propositions which it is proposed to test as well as the energy management dimensions which are investigated. A number of conclusions seem warranted.

1. Little empirical work has attempted to integrate some of the main themes in these literatures as we hope to do so in this study.

2. While the distinction between growth and non-growth firms is recognized in many business related literatures, few empirical studies have treated it as an explicit independent variable. Therefore, the concept of a growth firm as a determinant of firms' strategic choice or management behavior is largely untested.

3. It would appear that a negligible amount of research has been directed toward a comparison of the management process in divisions of large multidivisional firms and their independent competitors.

4. This study attempts to go beyond the "single factor" approach of the vast majority of research efforts concerned with the innovation process in industrial firms. Organizational type (i.e., headquarters of large multidivisional firms, division and independent firms) as well as major characteristics of these organizational entities (e.g., growth rate and energy intensiveness) are considered as independent variables.

5. In a similar vein, energy management (the dependent variable) is viewed as a group of events or activities (i.e., the six energy management dimensions) and not as a strictly dichotomous result or outcome as tends to be the case in economists' (and others') discussion of technological (organizational) change, i.e., a firm either adopts or does not adopt an innovation.

6. The choice of energy management dimensions (dependent variables) finds much support in the largely descriptive studies on the

innovation process and in the empirical studies which have focused on the implementation phase of corporate strategy and the "social response process."

Now that the conceptual and empirical foundations of this study have been discussed, the next chapter details the research design and methodology which is employed to explore the notion of energy management in industrial firms.

FOOTNOTES

[1]A number of other literatures might also have been reviewed for their contributions to this study. Among these literatures might be: (a) the literature on organizational change; (b) the literature on the response of firms to governmental regulations; (c) the literature on technology transfer.

[2]This comment is well reflected in Mansfield's definition of innovation as "the first application on a commercial scale of a new or improved product or process." See Edwin Mansfield, "The Economics of Industrial Innovation: Major Questions, State of the Art, and Needed Research, in Technological Innovation: A Critical Review of Current Knowledge. Advanced Technology and Science Studies Group, Georgia Tech, Atlanta, Georgia, January, 1975.

CHAPTER FIVE

RESEARCH DESIGN AND METHODOLOGY

The previous chapters have provided the conceptual and empirical framework for this study. This chapter will discuss the research
design and methodology of the study. First, the nature of the study
sample is described; second, the data collection process is delineated;
and third, the data analysis techniques to test the hypotheses/proposi-
tions and explicate energy management decision making processes are
detailed.

Study Population and Sample

For the purposes of this study, the population of firms is
defined as those firms or divisions which have their headquarters in
the Pittsburgh SMSA (Standard Metropolitan Statistical Area).

A stratified sample was selected using two levels of segmentation bases. Corporate structure (large multidivisional firms, individual 'ivisions of such firms, and independent firms) is the major
segmentation variable. Size of the firms (annual $ sales), SIC clas-
sification code and energy intensity are the secondary bases of segmentation (see Table V-1). The study sample consists of eleven large
multidivisional firms, twelve divisions and twelve independent firms.

Large multidivisional firms are defined as those firms with
annual sales in excess of $250 million. These firms are characterized
as energy intensive if more than 50 percent of their sales volume is

TABLE V-1

SAMPLE SEGMENTATION BASES

	Corporate Structure		
	Large Multidivi- sional Firms	Divisions	Independent Firms
Size	Greater than $250 million	$10 - 100 million	$10 - 100 million
SIC Classifica- tion Code	2 digit	4 digit	4 digit
Energy	Energy intensive if more than 50% of sales in the 6 most energy intensive industries	Based on SIC classification code	Based on SIC classifica- tion code
No. of Firms	11	12	12

in the six (6) most energy intensive industries (i.e., using the two-digit SIC classification code) as determined by the Department of Energy. Using these criteria, eleven large multidivisional firms were selected. Table V-2 shows the sales, growth, and energy intensity characteristics of these firms.

In order to provide a basis for comparability between divisions and independent firms, four-digit SIC classification codes are utilized. The SIC classification code is intended as a partial control for these firms' product lines and technologies; also, given that the division(s) and independent firm(s) within each SIC classification code are located in the same geographical region, it is expected that they face approximately the same competitive environment.

Table V-2 shows the ten SIC classification codes and the number of divisions and independent firms within each which constitute the study's sample with respect to divisions and independent firms. The sales level and growth rate of the sample's small sized firms is shown in Table V-4.

The choice of SIC classification codes was constrained by the decision to satisfy three conditions: (1) the desirability to develop a mix of energy intensive and non-energy intensive firms; (2) the necessity to locate within the SMSA, at least one division and at least one independent firm within each SIC classification code; and (3) the necessity to ensure that the division(s) and independent firm(s) selected in each SIC classification code were reasonably similar in terms of firm size (i.e., annual dollar sales).

TABLE V-2

LARGE, MULTIDIVISIONAL FIRMS: SALES, GROWTH

AND ENERGY INTENSITY CHARACTERISTICS

Firm	Sales[1]	Growth[2]	Energy Intensity[3]
A	Over 3000	10-15%	EI[4]
B	Over 3000	Over 20%	EI
C	250-500	10-15%	NEI
D	1000-2000	10-15%	EI
E	2000-3000	10-15%	EI
F	Over 3000	15-20%	NEI
G	2000-3000	10-15%	EI
H	1000-2000	10-15%	NEI
I	Over 3000	5-10%	NEI
J	1000-2000	10-15%	EI
L	500-1000	10-15%	EI

[1] Sales are expressed in millions of dollars

[2] Growth is defined as the average annual growth in sales between 1971 and 1976. (These figures are not in constant terms.)

[3] Firms are defined as energy intensive if more than 50 percent of their sales is in the six (6) SIC categories which the Department of Energy has defined as the most energy consumptive.

[4] EI donotes energy intensive; NEI denotes non-energy intensive.

TABLE V-3

SAMPLE STRUCTURE: SMALL SIZED FIRMS

	SIC No.	SIC Title	Division	Independent Firms
Energy Intensive	2821	Plastics, Materials, Synthetic Resins, Non-vulcanizable elastomers	1	1
	2851	Paints, Varnishes, Lacquers Enamels and Allied Products	1	1
	3221	Glass Containers	1	1
	3312	Blast Furnaces (including coke ovens) and Steel Works, and Rolling Mills	1	1
	3321	Gray Iron Foundries	1	1
	3325	Steel Foundries, NEC	1	1
			6	6
Non-Energy Intensive	3441	Fabricated Structural Metal	2	2
	3443	Fabricated Plate Work	1	1
	3561	Pumps and Pumping Equipment	1	1
	3621	Motors and Generators	2	2
			6	6

TABLE V-4

SMALL SIZED FIRMS: SALES AND GROWTH

SIC No.	Divisions		Independent Firms	
	Sales[1]	Growth[2]	Sales	Growth
2821	80-100	15-20%	50-100	20-25%
2851	50-60	15-20%	20-30	5-10%
3221	80-100	5-10%	50-70	10-15%
3312	50-60	0-5 %	50-60	15-20%
3321	30-40	5-10%	15-20	0-5 %
3325	30-40	0-5 %	15-20	10-15%
3441	20-30	20-30%	15-20	5-10%
	10-20	10-15%	20-30	5-10%
3443	40-50	5-10%	10-20	10-15%
3561	40-50	10-15%	10-20	10-15%
3621	20-30	5-10%	20-30	0-5 %
	10-20	20-25%	10-20	5-10%

[1]Sales are expressed in millions of dollars

[2]Growth is defined as the annual average growth in sales between 1971 and 1976. (These figures are not in constant terms.)

Data Collection

The primary data collection technique was in-person interviews with key executives involved in energy management. It was considered necessary to conduct in-person interviews since little of the data which was required to test the stated hypotheses and to explicate energy management decision making processes is publicly available. Also, the richness of the data which can be acquired through in-person interviews outweighs that which can be gained through the use of mailed questionnaires or telephone interviews alone. This is particularly true in a study such as this which is largely exploratory in nature.

A dependence on in-person interviews becomes inevitable when an effort is made to construct energy management decision making processes since it is very likely that major differences will be manifest among the sample firms. In-person interviews allow the pursuit of issues which appear particularly interesting or significant and/or which appear to be unique to individual firms.

To structure the in-person interviews, two questionnaires which are basically similar were developed (see Appendices A and B). One questionnaire was administered to the large multidivisional firms; the other questionnaire was administered to both the divisions and independent firms. The intent of the questionnaire was to ensure that the same topic areas were covered with each firm. Each questionnaire focused on the six (6) EMD defined and discussed in Chapter 2.

To facilitate analysis, the questionnaires were designed to include both close-ended and open-ended questions. In many instances, a number of questions were asked before it was felt that an adequate answer was received to many of the items on the questionnaires.

An effort was made to conduct the initial on-site in-person interview in each firm with the member of management who was charged with responsibility for energy management. A series of telephone calls were made to each firm (usually beginning with a call to the president's office) to identify the individual charged with the responsibility for energy management and to gain agreement to an initial in-person interview. This strategy proved successful with all of the sample firms.

The initial in-person interview was used to identify other management personnel whom it would be appropriate to interview. In none of the large multidivisional firms did any one individual have all of the required data. In many cases, interviews were initiated with other management personnel with the assistance of the initial interviewee.

At the headquarters level of all the sample's large multidivisional firms, a minimum of two individuals were interviewed and in some firms, interviews were conducted with as many as five different individuals.

In only two divisions and two independent firms were two or more separate in-person interviews conducted. For the remainder of the divisions and independent firms, one in-person interview was considered sufficient.

In order to clarify some points raised in the in-person interviews, follow-up phone interviews were conducted with at least one of the in-person interviewees in all of the large multidivisional firms and in many of the divisions and independent firms.

Data Analysis

The data analysis scheme is presented in Figure V-1. The approach to data analysis is different at the headquarters level of multidivisional firms compared to that at the level of the smaller sized firms. The general hypotheses and specific propositions underlying this study are tested in the case of the smaller sized firms. For reasons which will be specified shortly, the hypotheses and propositions are not tested at the level of large multidivisional firms; rather the emphasis is on a descriptive analysis of each EMD and the kinds of energy management decision making processes utilized.

Smaller Sized Firms: Statistical Analysis

The scheme for data analysis at the level of the smaller sized firms includes both quantitative (statistical) and qualitative (descriptive) segments. The quantitative segment comprises three phases: (1) a test for interrelationship among the independent variables; (2) each proposition (i.e., the propositions with respect to each EMD) are tested individually, and (3) the results of the proposition tests are summed to provide a test of the general hypotheses.

117

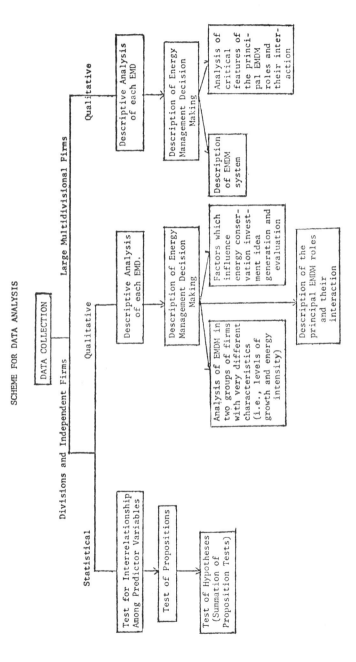

FIGURE V-1

SCHEME FOR DATA ANALYSIS

Note: EMD = Energy Management Dimension
EMDM = Energy Management Decision Making

Interrelationships Among Independent Variables

The first step in the data analysis is to test for interrelationships among the predictor (independent) variables. This is to ensure that the predictor variables utilized in the data analysis are not significantly correlated. A correlation matrix for the predictor variables is examined and when significant intercorrelations emerge, regression analysis is employed to further test the direction and strength of these relationships.

Tests of Proposisions

The set of propositions relating to each EMD are tested separately using multiple regression analysis and cannonical correlation analysis. Proposition testing consists of three separate phases:

1. The first phase of the analysis is at the level of the individual components of each EMD. The adoption of each EMD component can be represented as a function of growth, energy intensity and structure, i.e.,

EMD component = f(growth, energy intensity and structure)

The statistical model implicit in the above equation is established as follows:

Let $Y(i)$ (the dependent variable) denote the (i)th component in EMD(y)

Where

      $Y(i) = 1$ if the firm is engaged in the activity
                represented by the component;

      $Y(i) = 0$ if the firm is not engaged in the activity
                represented by the component.

      Let $X(1)$ denote growth (a continuous variable)

      Let $X(2)$ denote a dummy variable representing energy
                intensity

Where

      $X(2) = 1$ for energy intensive firms

      $X(2) = 0$ for non-energy intensive firms

      Let $X(3)$ denote a dummy variable representing structure

Where

      $X(3) = 1$ for divisions

      $X(3) = 0$ for energy intensive firms

Thus, the statistical model utilized for testing the relationship between each EMD component and the predictor variables can be written as follows:

$$Y(i) = a(i) + b(1i)*x(1) + b(2i)*x(2) + b(3i)*x(3) + e(i)$$

The relationships represented in the above equation can be tested by means of multiple regression where we accept the proposition if F is greater than Fcrit (Fcrit is the alpha value at 10 percent level of significance).

      The F ratio for the coefficients of the predictor variables (i.e., growth, energy intensity and structure) can also be examined to test more specifically the relationship between the individual

predictor variables and the EMD components (the dependent variables).
Again, if F is greater than Fcrit we accept that there is a relationship
between predictor and dependent variable.

2. The components of each EMD are integrated to constitute an
EMD index (EMDI). An EMDI can be represented as a function of the predictor variables, i.e.,

EMDIm = f(growth, energy intensity and structure)

The statistical model implicit in the above equation is established as
follows:

Let Y(I) (the dependent variable) denote an EMDI

It is operationalized as

$$Y(I) = Y(a) * Y(b) * Y(c)....Y(n)$$

where Y(a)... Y(n) represent the components in the EMD.

Y(I) is operationalized as a multiplicative function because any EMD
components which are utilized in the development of an EMDI are assumed
to be independent of each other, i.e., a firm can adopt or implement a
specific component irrespective of whether it has already adopted/
implemented the other EMDI components or plans to do so.

Thus, the statistical model utilized for testing the relationship between the EMDI and predictor variables can be written as follows

$$Y(m) = a(m) + b(1m)*x(1) + b(2m)*x(2) + b(3m)*x(3) + e(m)$$

Again, the relationships represented in the above model can be tested by means of multiple regression where we accept the proposition if F is greater than the Fcrit (Fcrit is the alpha value at the 10 percent level of significance).

3. Energy management as it is conceptualized and operationalized in this study is a multidimensional construct (i.e., the set of EMDs). Each EMD is also viewed as a multidimensional construct (i.e., the EMD components). Each of the latter constructs (i.e., the EMDs) can be hypothesized as dependent on the predictor variables (i.e., growth, energy intensity and structure). Thus cannonical correlation analysis is an appropriate test of the relationships between the predictor and dependent variables (i.e., the components of each EMD). The statistical model utilized in cannonical correlation analysis is represented as follows:

$$Y(m) \ (Y(1), \ Y(2), \dots Y(n)) = f \ (X(1), \ X(2), \ X(3))$$

where

$Y(1)$, $Y(2)$,...$Y(n)$ are the components of any EMD (the dependent variables)

and

$X(1)$, $X(2)$ and $X(3)$ are the predictor variables: growth energy intensity and structure, respectively.

Both the predictor and dependent variables have the same characteristics as those described in the case of multiple regression analysis. We accept the relationship posited in the cannonical

correlation model if $X^2 > X^2$ crit (where X^2 crit is the alpha value
at 10 percent level of significance).

Test of Hypotheses

The hypotheses which give a major portion of this study direction are not stated in testable form. The hypotheses are tested indirectly through a summation of the results of proposition testing.
Given the exploratory nature of this research, all that is sought from
this phase of the data analysis is a set of conclusions based on the
proposition testing which allows us to state which of the suggested
hypotheses best explains firms' propensity to demonstrate strategic
responsiveness in their approach to energy management.

Smaller Sized Firms: Qualitative Analysis

The proposition testing does not tell us how energy management
decisions are made or who is involved in making these decisions. The
qualitative analysis phase of the data analysis scheme attempts to shed
some light on these questions.

First, the major findings within each EMD are qualitatively
described. Particular emphasis is placed upon the EMD component relationships which are described as statistically significant within the
quantitative analysis of the energy management indices. The purpose
of this section of the analysis is to highlight features of energy
management along each EMD which would not be evident from the statistical analysis.

Second, the process of energy management decision making is
examined and described from three different perspectives:

1.   The overall approach to energy management which is taken
by two groups of firms with very different characteristics (i.e. high
energy intensity and growth compared to low energy intensity and low
growth) is compared and contrasted within the EMDs.   In particular, an
attempt is made to identify alleged and/or apparent reasons why these
groups of firms adopt similar and/or different approaches to specific
facets of energy management.

2.   The roles (as well as the interaction among them) of different individuals and management levels and/or functions in energy
management decision making in a small sample of firms which have
attempted to develop a systematic approach to energy management are
described and analyzed.   The specific focus of this section of the data
analysis is to identify and examine the organizational process by which
energy efficiency improvement investments are initiated, evaluated and
approved.

3.   The final phase of the description of energy management
decision making is an enumeration and analysis of the factors which
appear to influence the emergence and evaluation of energy conservation
investment ideas.   Specifically, an effort is made to identify both
economic and non-economic factors or criteria which facilitate and/or
impede the consideration and appraisal of energy efficiency improvement
investment proposals or ideas.

Large, Multidivisional Firms

Due to the small sample size and the exploratory nature of
this research, the hypotheses and propositions are not tested at the

level of the larger organizational units (i.e., large, multidivisional firms). Rather, the emphasis is placed upon the systematic examination of the extent to which these firms actively manage their energy resources as well as the explication of energy management decision making processes which have evolved to date.

First, the approaches to energy management of the sample's large multidivisional firms is described and analyzed along each EMD. Attention is paid to identifying differences in the energy management approaches adopted by these firms and the reasons why these differences exist. Also, where possible, questions for future research are identified.

Second, the energy management decision making process in a small sample of the large, multidivisional firms which have demonstrated the most systematic and comprehensive approaches to energy management is delineated and analyzed. It is divided into two segments: (a) The energy management decision making system (EMDMS) is described and analyzed. Specifically, the EMDMS consists of a sequence of decision making points which are involved in the formulation and implementation of energy management strategies and programs. The purpose of this section of the data analysis is to describe how energy management decisions are made in large multidivisional firms. (b) The critical features of the roles of the major individuals and committees (and their interaction) involved in the EMDMS are described and examined.

Summary

The study sample consists of 24 small to medium sized firms (i.e., annual sales between $10 and 100 million dollars) and 11 large (i.e., annual sales in excess of $250 million) multidivisional firms.

The primary data collection mode is in-person interviews using a structured questionnaire, with follow-up telephone interviews where necessary.

Both quantitative (multiple regression and cannonical correlation analysis) and qualitative analysis are employed to explicate energy management in the smaller sized firms. The data analysis at the level of the large multidivisional firms concentrates on examining the decision making processes by which energy management strategy is formulated and implemented. A major theme of the research design and methodology is the integration of quantitative and qualitative approaches to the analysis of energy management, with a view to the generation of future research questions.

The next chapter provides the quantitative (statistical) analysis of energy management in the smaller sized firms, i.e., the hypotheses/propositions testing.

CHAPTER SIX

HYPOTHESES/PROPOSITIONS TESTING

This chapter reports the statistical research results on energy management in the smaller sized firms. The chapter is divided into three sections. Section One reports the results of the tests of the propositions as stated in Chapter 2. In this section, each energy management dimension (EMD) is treated separately. Section Two summarizes the results of the tests of propositions to provide a test of the hypotheses. The third section examines the data in an effort to identify patterns of energy management response (and, if possible, energy management indices) when all of the energy management dimensions are considered simultaneously.

Tests of Propositions

This section reports the results of the tests of the propositions with regard to the smaller sized firms. The methodology employed in testing the propositions is that which was described in detail in Chapter 5. However, before these propositions could be tested, the independent variables (i.e., size of firm--sales level--growth rate, energy intensity and structure--division or independent firm) were tested for interdependence so that only independent variables which were not significantly related would be utilized in the data analysis.

Table VI-1 shows the correlation matrix for the four independent variables: size of firm (measured by sales volume), growth rate,

TABLE VI-1

INTERCORRELATION AMONG INDEPENDENT VARIABLES

	Firm Size	Growth	Energy Intensity	Structure
Firm Size		0.2486	-0.4836[*]	-0.3968[**]
Growth			-0.1796	0.0460
Energy Intensity				0.0000

[*] $p < .01$

[**] $p < .05$

energy intensity, and structure. The growth rate of the sample firms was dichotomized using the median growth rate as the segmentation level.

As can be seen from Table VI-1, energy intensity and structure are significantly correlated with firm size ($p < .01$ for energy intensity and $p < .05$ for structure). To further test the significance of the relationship between firm size and energy intensity and structure, energy intensity and structure were regressed against the firm size. Table VI-2 shows the regression results. Again, the relationship between energy intensity and firm size is significant at $p < .01$ and the relationship between structure and firm size is significant at $p < .05$. Firm size is, therefore, not an "independent variable"; it is statistically a function of energy intensity and structure.

This relationship may be purely a function of the sample. Another explanation may be that energy intensive firms are generally more capital intensive than non-energy intensive firms, and thus, might be expected to have a higher sales level to compensate for the added investment. In any case, the usefulness of firm size as an explanatory variable in firms' propensity to manage their energy affairs is limited, since it will be contaminated by its statistical relationship to energy intensity and structure. Any interpretation of firm size as an independent variable will be confounded by its relationship to energy intensity and structure. It is, therefore, dropped from further consideration as an independent variable.

It should also be noted that by dropping sales and retaining energy intensity and structure as independent variables, the explanatory power of the data analysis (i.e., multiple regression analysis)

TABLE VI-2

MULTIPLE REGRESSION RESULTS: ENERGY INTENSITY
AND STRUCTURE AGAINST FIRM SIZE

Criterion Variable	Predictor Variables	Coefficients	Fi[1]
Firm Size	Energy Intensity	-0.25083	8.068***
	Structure	-0.20583	5.433**
	Constant	0.12537	

$$R^2 = 0.39132$$
$$\text{Adj } R^2 = 0.33335$$
$$F(2.21) = 6.75048$$

1. Fi refers to F ratio for coefficients

***$p < .01$

**$p < .05$

is greater than if sales were retained as an independent variable and energy intensity and structure were dropped from further investigation. Energy intensity and structure provide us with two independent variables which are qualitatively different in character.

The growth rate of firms is not statistically significantly correlated ($p > .10$ in all cases) with firm size, energy intensity and structure (see Table VI-1). To further test these relationships, energy intensity and structure were regressed against the growth rate of firms. Table VI-3 presents the regression results. Again, no significant relationships exist below a 10 percent level of significance. Thus we can say that the growth rate of firms is a true independent variable.

TABLE VI-3

MULTIPLE REGRESSION RESULTS: ENERGY INTENSITY
AND STRUCTURE AGAINST GROWTH

Criterion Variable	Predictor Variables	Coefficients	F_i[1]
Growth	Energy Intensity	-0.22500	0.701
	Structure	0.58333	0.047
	Constant	-0.05755	

$$R^2 = 0.03441$$

$$\text{Adj } R^2 = 0.05755$$

$$F(2.21) = 0.37423$$

---

1. F_i refers to F ratio for coefficients

EMD1: Organization for Energy Management

Proposition 1A: Growth firms will show a greater propensity than non-growth firms to organize themselves to manage their energy affairs.

Proposition 1B: Energy intensive firms will show a greater propensity than non-energy intensive firms to organize themselves to manage their energy affairs.

Proposition 1C: Divisions will show a greater propensity than independent firms to organize themselves to manage their energy affairs.

Dependent Variable: Energy Management Dimension, No. 1: Organization for Energy Management.

Measurement: Questions 1 and 2 of Divisions and Independent Firms' Questionnaire.

The Data

The energy management dimension (EMD1), organization for energy management, consists of two major foci: whether individuals have been assigned specific energy management responsibilities and whether specific energy management targets or objectives have been established.

Table VI-4 shows the multiple regression results for the set of predictor (independent) variables (growth, energy intensity and structure) regressed against each of the four components (assigned responsibility for energy management, full-time or part-time position, energy management committee, and specific energy management targets or objectives) of the criterion (dependent) variable, EMD1 (organization for energy management).

TABLE VI-4

MULTIPLE REGRESSION RESULTS: GROWTH, ENERGY INTENSITY
AND STRUCTURE AGAINST EMDI COMPONENTS

Criterion Variables	Predictor Variables	Coefficients	F_i[1]	
Assigned Responsibility for Energy Management	Structure	0.2590	4.040*	R^2 = 0.2420
	Energy Intensity	-0.1552	2.206	Adj R^2 = 0.13184
	Growth	0.48391	0.137	$F_{(3,20)}$ = 1.60112
	Constant	0.3463		
Full-Time or Part-Time Position	Structure	0.1712	4.721**	R^2 = 0.25121
	Growth	-0.7861	1.511	Adj R^2 = 0.13665
	Energy Intensity	0.4897	0.375	$F_{(3,20)}$ = 1.61737
	Constant	-0.2298		
Energy Management Committee	Energy Intensity	0.2426	1.936	R^2 = 0.10769
	Structure	0.8529	0.246	Adj R^2 = 0.08461
	Growth	-0.3252	0.054	$F_{(3,20)}$ = 1.51145
	Constant	0.1918		
Specific Targets or Objectives	Structure	0.6737	18.956***	R^2 = 0.5085
	Growth	-0.1209	0.928	Adj R^2 = 0.29781
	Energy Intensity	0.1394	0.788	$F_{(3,20)}$ = 5.14711
	Constant	-0.5512		

[1]F_i refers to F ratio for the coefficients   * $p < .10$ ** $p < .05$ *** $p < .01$

If the four components of the energy management dimension, organization for energy management, can be integrated into a single criterion variable, entitled "organization for energy management," it could be interpreted as an index of the extent to which firms have organized themselves for energy management. An index assumes that an equal weighting can be assigned to each of its components and that the components are not interdependent. In this case, assigned responsibility for energy management and the existence of a full-time or part-time position are interdependent; assigned responsibility for energy management is a prerequisite to the existence of a full-time or part-time energy management position. Thus, assigned responsibility for energy management can be dropped from the index since it is implicit in the index element, full-time or part-time position. Each of the remaining index elements (full-time or part-time position, energy management committee and specific targets or objectives) are relatively independent of each other. The establishment of an energy management committee does not presume the existence of at least some part-time energy management positions, but a firm could have full-time and/or part-time energy management positions without considering it necessary to establish an energy management committee. A firm could also establish energy management or energy efficiency improvement objectives in the absence of specific full-time and/or part-time energy management positions or energy management committee and vice-versa.

The index for "organization of energy management" assumes each component of the index is of equal importance. Thus, we assume that full-time or part-time positions, or an energy management committee and specific targets or objectives are equally important in how a firm organizes for energy management.

Table VI-5 shows the multiple regression results for the set of predictor variables regressed against the "organization for energy management" index.

Whether or not the assumptions inherent in the organization for energy management index are accepted, the relations between the individual components of the energy management dimension, organization for energy management, and the predictor or independent variables can be tested simultaneously by means of canonical correlation analysis. The results of this analysis are presented in Table VI-6.

Analysis

As can be seen from Tables VI-4 and VI-5, energy intensity and the growth rate of firms show no significant trend or relationship with any of the four components of EMD1.

Structure is significantly correlated with assigned responsibility for energy management (p < .10), full-time or part-time position (p < .05) and specific targets or objectives (p < .01). Structure is also the significant predictor variable (p < .01) in the index regression (see Table VI-5) and in the canonical correlation results (see Table VI-6). Thus, the evidence supports the proposition that divisions will be more inclined than independent firms to organize themselves to manage their energy affairs.

When the individual components of the energy management dimension are examined at the collective level, (i.e., the organization for

TABLE VI-5

MULTIPLE REGRESSION RESULTS: GROWTH, ENERGY
INTENSITY AND STRUCTURE AGAINST EMD1 INDEX

Criterion	Predictor Variables	Coefficients	Fi^1
Organization for Energy Management Index	Structure	0.2581	8.275***
	Energy Intensity	0.1568	3.143*
	Growth	-0.3396	0.234
	Constant	-0.3642	

$$R^2 = 0.3967$$

$$\text{Adj } R^2 = 0.2902$$

$$F(3,17) = 2.74430$$

[1]Fi refers to F ratio for coefficients

*** $p < .01$
  * $p < .10$

TABLE VI-6

CANONICAL CORRELATION RESULTS: GROWTH, ENERGY
INTENSITY AND STRUCTURE WITH EMD1 COMPONENTS

Number	Eigenvalue	Canonical Correlation	Wilks Lambda	Chi-Square	DF	Signif.
1	0.45977	0.67806	0.31434	21.98841	9	0.090

Coefficients for Canonical Variables

Full-time Position	0.42158	Growth	0.07795
Energy Management Committee	0.01957	Energy Intensity	0.42426
Specific Targets or Objectives	0.81044	Structure	0.91716

energy management index) there is some evidence (see Table VI-5) that energy intensity is a significant factor ($p < .10$). The canonical correlation results (see Table VI-6) also show evidence that energy intensity may be a significant factor in determining a firm's approach to organizing for energy management.

Conclusions

The data generally support the proposition that divisions will show a greater propensity than independent firms to organize themselves to manage their energy affairs. There is some evidence, based on the energy management dimension index regression results and the results of the canonical correlation analysis, that energy intensity is related to firms' propensity to organize themselves to manage their energy affairs although not enough evidence to accept proposition 2B, i.e., that energy intensive firms will show a greater propensity than non-energy intensive firms to organize themselves to manage their energy affairs.

The data show no support for the proposition that growth firms will show a greater propensity than non-growth firms to organize them-selves to manage their energy affairs.

EMD2:   Energy Data Base and Monitoring Process

Proposition 2A: Growth firms will show a greater tendency than non-growth firms to develop an energy data base and monitoring process.

Proposition 2B: Energy intensive firms will show a greater tendency than non-energy intensive firms to develop an energy data base and monitoring process.

Proposition 2C: Divisions will show a greater tendency than independent firms to develop an energy data base and monitoring process.

Dependent Variable: Energy management dimension, No. 2:
                      Energy Data Base and Monitoring Process.

        Measurement: Questions 3 and 4, of Divisions and Independent Firms' Questionnaire.

The Data

        The Energy Management Dimension, energy data base and monitoring process (EMD2) was separated into two overall components: (1) whether or not the firm had sufficient and appropriate data to facilitate development of measures of its energy efficiency, and (2) the extent to which the firm conducted specific energy audits of its main operating units or of its principal energy consumption end-points (e.g., furnaces boilers, etc.) or audited efficiency of each energy source utilized.

        Table VI-7 shows the regression results for the set of predictor variables (growth, energy intensity, and structure) regressed against each individual component (energy data availability, development of energy efficient measures, and existence and frequency of energy audits) of the criterion variable EMD2.

TABLE VI-7

MULTIPLE REGRESSION RESULTS: GROWTH, ENERGY INTENSITY
AND STRUCTURE AGAINST EMD2 COMPONENTS

Criterion	Predictor Variables	Coefficients	F_i[1]		
Energy Data Availability	Structure	0.4148	4.907**	R^2 = 0.2533	
	Energy Intensity	0.2569	1.825	Adj R^2 = 0.1413	
	Growth	0.3069	0.041	$F(3,20)$ = 2.26240	
	Constant	-0.7453			
Development of Energy Efficiency Measures	Structure	0.2904	4.907**	R^2 = 0.2533	
	Energy Intensity	0.1978	1.825	Adj R^2 = 0.1413	
	Growth	0.2138	0.041	$F(3,20)$ = 2.26240	
	Constant	-0.65217			
Existence of Energy Audits	Energy Intensity	0.2686	1.871	R^2 = 0.0966	
	Growth	0.8291	0.279	Adj R^2 = 0.03886	
	Structure	0.7849	0.165	$F(2,20)$ = 0.71323	
	Constant	0.61954			
Frequency of Energy Audits	Energy Intensity	0.2387	4.737**	R^2 = 0.2098	
	Growth	0.6106	0.485	Adj R^2 = 0.09137	
	Structure	0.7143	0.437	$F(2,20)$ = 1.77098	
	Constant	-0.1945			

[1]F_i refers to F ratios for coefficients

**$p < .05$

The development of energy efficient measures and the frequency with which energy audits were conducted were the components of the energy management dimension utilized to establish an energy data base and monitoring process index. If the firm can develop measures of its energy efficiency, it is assumed (for the purpose of the index) that it has appropriate and sufficient information to do so. Also the existence of an energy auditing process is implicit in the response to the question, how often are energy audits conducted? The results of regressing the independent variables against the energy data base and monitoring process index are shown in Table VI-8.

The results of the canonical correlation analysis are shown in Table VI-9. For purposes of comparability, the same two energy management dimensions are employed in the canonical correlation analysis as were utilized in development of the energy data base and monitoring process index.

Analysis

From Table VI-7 it is evident that structure is significantly correlated ($p < .05$) with availability of energy information and its utilization in the development of energy efficiency measures. However, structure is not significantly correlated with the existence of an energy auditing process and/or the frequency with which audits are conducted. Energy intensity is significantly correlated ($p < .05$) to the frequency with which energy audits are conducted.

The energy data base and monitoring process index regression results (see Table VI-8) and the canonical correlation analysis results

TABLE VI-8

MULTIPLE REGRESSION RESULTS: GROWTH, ENERGY
INTENSITY AND STRUCTURE AGAINST EMD2 INDEX

Criterion	Predictor Variables	Coefficients	Fi[1]
Energy Data	Structure	0.15333	2.147
Base and Monitoring Process Index	Energy Intensity	0.13333	1.623

$$R^2 = 0.15219$$

$$Adj\ R^2 = 0.07145$$

$$F(2,21) = 1.88486$$

[1] Fi refers to F ratios for coefficients

TABLE VI-9

CANONICAL CORRELATION RESULTS: GROWTH, ENERGY
INTENSITY AND STRUCTURE WITH EMD2 COMPONENTS

Number	Eigenvalue	Canonical Correlation	Wilks Lambda	Chi-Square	DF	Signif.
1	0.25338	0.50336	0.61773	9.63392	6	0.141

Coefficients for Canonical Variables

Development of Energy Efficiency Measures	0.00332	Growth	0.07966
		Energy Intensity	0.52886
Frequency of Energy Audits	0.99775	Structure	0.85019

(see Table VI-9) are not statistically significant at p = .10. Thus, in looking at the energy management dimension as a whole, no significant relationships exist between it and any combination of the firm's characteristics (i.e., growth, energy intensity, and structure) under study, or any of these characteristics individually.

Conclusion

There is partial support for proposition 2C, i.e., that the divisions will show a greater tendency than independent firms to develop an energy data base and monitoring process. It is the first part of EMD2 (development of energy efficiency measures) that is significantly related (p < .05) to structure. A possible explanation of this relationship may be that divisions in general have better developed management information systems than independent firms. This is a proposition which could be the object of future research.

There is also partial support for proposition 2B, i.e., that energy intensive firms will show a greater tendency than non-energy intensive firms to develop an energy data base and monitoring process. However, it is the second part of EMD2 (frequency of energy audits) which is significantly related to energy intensity. It may be that energy intensive firms, because of their higher energy consumption levels have found it necessary to more fully develop processes to monitor energy utilization. A larger data base than is available for this study would be required to test this explanation.

EMD3: Management Accountability

Proposition 3A: Growth firms will be more inclined than non-growth firms to make energy management a formal part of line management's accountability.

Proposition 3B: Energy intensive firms will be more inclined than non-energy intensive firms to make energy management a formal part of line management's accountability.

Proposition 3C: Divisions will be more inclined than independent firms to make energy management a formal part of line management's accountability.

Dependent Variable: Energy Management Dimension, No. 3: Management Accountability.

Measurement: Question 7 of Divisions and Independent Firms' Questionnaire.

The Data

The Energy Management Dimension, management accountability, (EMD3) for the purpose of analysis is segmented into two components: whether or not energy management/energy efficiency is perceived as a formal part of line management's accountability and, secondly, whether or not management at any level is required to submit a plan or program to the firm's top management (i.e., the independent firm's or division's president) detailing achieved and proposed energy efficiency improvements.

Table VI-10 shows the multiple regression results for the two energy management dimension components.

When the two components are combined into an energy management accountability index, Table VI-11 presents the index regression

TABLE VI-10

MULTIPLE REGRESSION RESULTS: GROWTH, ENERGY INTENSITY
AND STRUCTURE AGAINST EMD3 COMPONENTS

Criterion	Predictor Variables	Coefficients	F_i[1]
Management Accountability	Structure	0.9367	4.820**
	Energy Intensity	0.8392	3.752*
	Growth	0.3440	0.988
	Constant	0.33861	

$$R^2 = 0.33861$$

$$Adj\ R^2 = 0.23490$$

$$F(3,20) = 3.41305$$

Criterion	Predictor Variables	Coefficients	F_i
Energy Efficiency Improvement Plan	Growth	-0.8103	2.742
	Structure	-0.7027	1.357
	Energy Intensity	0.2343	0.146
	Constant	0.4326	

$$R^2 = 0.1925$$

$$Adj\ R^2 = 0.0714$$

$$F(3,20) = 1.58982$$

[1]F_i refers to F ratios for coefficients

* $p < .10$
** $p < .05$

TABLE VI-11

MULTIPLE REGRESSION RESULTS: GROWTH, ENERGY
INTENSITY AND STRUCTURE AGAINST EMD3 INDEX

Criterion	Predictor Variables	Coefficients	F_i[1]
Management Accountability Index	Growth	-0.37225	2.590
	Energy Intensity	0.28290	0.955
	Structure	-0.17828	0.391
	Constant	0.14069	

$$R^2 = 0.19164$$

$$\text{Adj } R^2 = 0.09734$$

$$F(3,20) = 1.58052$$

[1]F_i refers to F ratios for coefficients.

TABLE VI-12

CANONICAL CORRELATION RESULTS: GROWTH, ENERGY INTENSITY
AND STRUCTURE WITH EMD3 COMPONENTS

Number	Eigenvalue	Canonical Correlation	Wilks Lambda	Chi-Square	DF	Signif.
1	0.34114	0.58407	0.53205	12.62019	6	0.049
2	0.19246	0.43870	0.80754	4.27529	2	0.118

Coefficients for Canonical Variables

Energy Efficiency Improvement Plan	0.13131	Growth	-0.24046
Management Accountability	1.00532	Energy Intensity	0.59878
		Structure	0.74062

results. Table VI-12 shows the canonical correlation analysis
results.

Analysis

As shown in Table VI-10, structure (p < .05) and energy intensity (p < .10) are related to whether or not firms have made some
member of line management accountable for energy management. However,
there is no relationship between any of the independent variables and
the submission of an energy efficiency improvement plan to firms' top
management.

It would seem that firms do make energy management a formal
part of line management accountability but that a separate plan detailing achieved and proposed energy efficiency improvements is not required (this point will be further discussed in the next chapter when
energy management decision making in selected firms will be detailed
and analyzed).

The canonical correlation results (see Table VI-12) also show
some evidence (p < .05) that structure and energy intensity are related
to the formal establishment of management accountability for energy
management but not for the submission of an energy efficiency improvement plan to the firm's top management (the coefficient for the canonical variable, energy efficiency improvement plan has a negative sign).

Not surprisingly, in view of the above results, when the two
components of EMD3 are integrated to form a management accountability
index, the index is not significantly related (p > .10) to any of the
independent variables (see Table VI-11).

Conclusion

There is some evidence to support the propositions that structure and energy intensity are related to the establishment of energy
management as an element of line management's formal accountability
(Proposition 3B and 3C) with Proposition 3C (i.e., divisions will be
more inclined than independent firms to make energy management a formal part of the line management's accountability) receiving the
stronger support.

EMD:4 Energy Efficiency Improvement Programs/Investments

Proposition 4A: Growth firms will make production/process changes as well as "housekeeping" improvements (in order to become more energy efficient) whereas non-growth firms will implement "housekeeping" efforts only.

Proposition 4B: Energy intensive firms will make production/process changes as well as "housekeeping" improvements (in order to become more energy efficient) whereas non-energy efficient firms will implement "housekeeping" efforts only.

Proposition 4C: Divisions will make production/process changes as well as "housekeeping" improvements (in order to become more energy efficient) whereas independent firms will implement "housekeeping" efforts only.

Dependent Variable: Energy Management Dimension No. 4:
        Energy Efficiency Improvement Programs/Investments.

        Measurement: Questions 5 and 6 of Divisions and Independent Firms' Questionnaire.

The Data

        To facilitate analysis, Energy Efficiency Improvement Programs and Investments were conceptualized as consisting of two types: (1) "housekeeping" programs which could be described as usually requiring relatively little expenditure of either management time or capital (e.g., controlling air conditioning or temperature levels, reducing unnecessary idling of equipment, insulation, etc.) and, (2) modifications of the firm's production/manufacturing process(es) which usually require considerably more management consideration and capital expenditures than "housekeeping" programs.

        Table VI-13 shows the regression results for each component of the firm's housekeeping activities as well as for changes in the

TABLE VI-13

MULTIPLE REGRESSION RESULTS: GROWTH, ENERGY INTENSITY AND STRUCTURE AGAINST EMD4 COMPONENTS

Criterion Variables	Predictor Variables	Coefficients	Fi[1]		
Production/Manufacturing Changes	Energy Intensity	0.38749	3.692*	R^2 = 0.20748	
	Growth	-0.12964	0.674	Adj R^2 = 0.08860	
	Structure	-0.15770	0.146	$F_{(3,20)}$ = 1.67432	
	Constant	0.84231			
Insulation	Structure	0.41466	5.328**	R^2 = 0.22065	
	Energy Intensity	0.91063	0.249	Adj R^2 = 0.10375	
	Growth	0.34357	0.056	$F_{(3,20)}$ = 1.88750	
	Constant	0.88208			
Thermostat Control	Energy Intensity	0.23051	1.776	R^2 = 0.12249	
	Growth	-0.86582	0.393	Adj R^2 = -0.00914	
	Structure	0.88383	0.269	$F_{(3,20)}$ = 0.93057	
	Constant	0.71771			
Lighting & Ventilation	Structure	-0.16549	1.094	R^2 = 0.10111	
	Energy Intensity	-0.17120	1.136	Adj R^2 = 0.03373	
	Growth	-0.20156	0.025	$F_{(3,20)}$ = 0.74988	
	Constant	0.18549			

(Continued next page)

[1]Fi refers to F ratios for coefficients

* $p < .10$ ** $p < .05$

TABLE VI-13 (Continued)

Criterion Variables	Predictor Variables	Coefficients	F_i[1]	
Control Equipment Idling	Structure	0.76141	1.727	$R^2 = 0.12543$
	Energy Intensity	0.53932	0.840	Adj $R^2 = -0.00575$
	Growth	-0.19561	0.173	$F_{(3,20)} = 0.95615$
	Constant	-0.74886		
Furnace/Boiler Maintenance	Growth	-0.23402	2.169	$R^2 = 0.09361$
	Energy Intensity	-0.52655	0.070	Adj $R^2 = 0.00729$
	Constant	0.16180		$F_{(2,21)} = 1.08442$

[1]F_i refers to F ratio for the coefficients

* $p < .10$

** $p < .05$

firms' production/manufacturing processes. All of the housekeeping components can be integrated to constitute an energy management "housekeeping" index. The regression results for this index are presented in Table VI-14. Table VI-15 shows the corresponding cannonical correlation analysis results.

In some cases, insulation and improvement of boilers and furnaces could require substantial capital expenditures. In any case it seems safe to suggest that they would demand more capital expenditures than other "housekeeping" components. These two components of the "housekeeping" index could be added to production/manufacturing process changes to constitute a capital improvements index. Tables VI-16 and VI-17 show the regression and canonical analysis results respectively for the consequent energy capital improvement index.

Analysis

As can be seen from Table VI-13, energy intensity is the only independent variable which shows a significant relationship ($p < .05$) with firms' propensity to modify their manufacturing/production process(es) specifically to improve energy efficiency. It may be that for energy intensive firms, their manufacturing/production process(es) account for a major proportion of their total energy consumption and thus, make modification of production/manufacturing processes a viable investment. This is a tentative explanation that requires further research.

Structure is significantly related ($p < .05$) with firms' propensity to make insulation investments (see Table VI-13). This is

TABLE VI-14

MULTIPLE REGRESSION RESULTS: GROWTH, ENERGY INTENSITY AND
STRUCTURE AGAINST ENERGY "HOUSEKEEPING" IMPROVEMENTS INDEX

Criterion	Predictor Variables	Coefficients	Fi[1]
Energy "Housekeeping" Improvements Index	Growth	-0.25569	1.835
	Energy Intensity	0.24824	1.102
	Constant	0.22084	

$$R^2 = 0.07177$$

$$\text{Adj } R^2 = 0.03405$$

$$F(2,21) = 1.40533$$

[1]Fi refers to F ratios for coefficients

TABLE VI-15

CANONICAL CORRELATION RESULTS: GROWTH, ENERGY INTENSITY AND
STRUCTURE WITH ENERGY "HOUSEKEEPING" IMPROVEMENT COMPONENTS

Number	Eigenvalue	Canonical Correlation	Wilks Lambda	Chi-Square	DF	Signif.
1	0.41488	0.64411	0.44807	14.45061	18	0.699

Coefficients for Canonical Variables

Insulation	-0.78522	Growth	-0.12057
Thermostat Control	-0.63610	Energy Intensity	-0.58390
Control of Air Conditioning	0.18280	Structure	-0.81282
Lighting & Ventilation	0.30292		
Control Equipment Idling	-0.12642		
Furnace/Boiler Maintenance	0.40360		

TABLE VI-16

MULTIPLE REGRESSION RESULTS: GROWTH, ENERGY INTENSITY
AND STRUCTURE AGAINST ENERGY CAPITAL IMPROVEMENTS INDEX

Criterion	Predictor Variables	Coefficients	Fi^2
Energy Capital	Growth	-0.68486	0.781
Improvements Index	Structure	0.78995	0.684
	Energy Intensity	0.76257	0.681
	Constant	0.27504	

$$R^2 = 0.10399$$

$$\text{Adj } R^2 = -0.01166$$

$$F(3,20) = 0.77375$$

^{2}Fi refers to F ratios for coefficients

TABLE VI-17

CANONICAL CORRELATION RESULTS: GROWTH, ENERGY INTENSITY
AND STRUCTURE WITH ENERGY CAPITAL IMPROVEMENTS COMPONENTS

Number	Eigenvalue	Canonical Correlation	Wilks Lambda	Chi-Square	DF	Signif.
1	0.28218	0.52121	0.51489	12.94425	9	0.165

Coefficients for Canonical Variables

Insulation	1.00596	Growth	0.44113
Furnace/ Boiler Maintenance	-0.48882	Energy Intensity	0.08707
		Structure	0.88059
Production/ Manufacturing Changes	-0.21087		

the only significant relationship which emerges between the independent variables and energy management "housekeeping" elements. Consequently, the absence of any significant relationships when the independent variables are regressed against the energy "housekeeping" improvements index (see Table VI-16) and in the corresponding canonical correlation results (see Table VI-15) is expected.

Neither do any significant relationships emerge in relation to the capital improvements index or in the corresponding canonical correlation analysis. (See Tables VI-15 and VI-17)

Conclusion

The data does not allow us to fully accept any of the propositions as stated. Analysis of the data does not show any evidence of any relationships between the firms' characteristics under study (i.e., growth, energy intensity, and structure) and firms' propensity to implement "housekeeping" efficiency improvements with the exception that divisions are more inclined to make insulation investments ($p < .05$) than independent firms.

However, there is strong supporting evidence to allow us to accept the thrust of proposition 4B, i.e., that energy intensive firms will make production/process changes to enhance energy efficiency whereas non-energy intensive firms will not.

In order to more adequately test propositions 4A, 4B, and 4C, both energy "housekeeping" and capital improvements (i.e., changes in manufacturing/production processes) need to be more clearly conceptualized and defined. A high degree of variance in terms of the kind and extent of manufacturing/production process modifications which firms have affected to improve energy efficiency was evident among the sample firms. (This point will be further discussed in the next chapter.)

EMD5: Research and Development Programs

Proposition 5A: Growth firms will demonstrate a greater propensity than non-growth firms to devote their R and D resources to the improvement of their firm's energy efficiency.

Proposition 5B: Energy intensive firms will demonstrate a greater propensity than non-energy intensive firms to devote their R and D resources to the improvement of their firm's energy efficiency.

Proposition 5C: Divisions will demonstrate a greater propensity than independent firms to devote their R and D resources to the improvement of their firm's energy efficiency.

Dependent Variable: Energy Management Dimension, No. 5: Research and Development Programs.

Measurement: Question 8 of Divisions and Independent Firms' Questionnaire.

The Data and Analysis

Not enough firms had R and D programs to facilitate statistical analysis of the propositions. What is provided in its place is a descriptive analysis of the extent to which firms with R and D programs devoted their R and D resources to the improvement of energy efficiency within their manufacturing or production process(es).

Five divisions (four energy intensive and one non-energy intensive) and two independent firms (one energy intensive and one non-energy intensive) had what they described as an "R and D program."

Three energy intensive divisions did not make any attempt to direct R and D resources toward the improvement of energy utilization. These firms asserted that their R and D programs were aimed exclusively toward the development and introduction of new products and/or the

modification of existing products and thus, were not directed toward
the improvement of internal operating efficiency. None of these divisions believed that their R and D expertise could be readily directed
toward the enhancement of energy utilization within their manufacturing
processes. One division pointed out in very strong terms that to
orient any of its R and D resources to improving manufacturing efficiency would be highly dysfunctional; the potential gains to be derived
from the successful introduction of a new product or modified versions
of existing products would far outweigh any conceivable gains in improved internal operating efficiency.

One energy intensive division and both the independent firms
reported that their R and D efforts had already resulted in the adoption of more energy efficient/energy conserving technologies. Each
of these firms indicated that there was a close parallel between the
kinds of product oriented R and D which they engaged in, and production
or process improvements which might result in enhanced energy efficiencies.

The energy intensive division and the energy intensive independent firm were in the chemical industry (SIC 2821, Plastics Materials, Synthetic Resins, Nonvulcanizable Elastomers). Although R and
D was described by both firms as being primarily product oriented (as
opposed to production and process oriented) and improvement in the
energy efficiency of the manufacturing process was seen, at best, as
a minor goal of their R and D programs, both firms ascribed specific
improvements in production/manufacturing energy efficiency as a direct
consequence of their R and D programs.

The non-energy intensive independent firm is in SIC 3443, Fab-ricated Plate Work. Its R and D program was described as "very small scale" (more development than basic research). Yet in its efforts to improve product design and quality, the firm's chief plant engineer claimed that the company's product development work "through new in-sights gained in metallurgy and heat control" led directly to changes in its manufacturing process which resulted in significant energy savings.

Conclusions

Although the data do not allow any statistical testing of the propositions, some evidence was produced that some firms with R and D programs had directed part of their R and D resources toward the improvement of energy utilization in their production/manufacturing processes. It is clear that firms' efforts (or lack of efforts) to improve production/manufacturing energy efficiency requires consid-erably more research before we will understand why firms direct (or do not direct) their R and D programs toward improving production/ manufacturing efficiency.

EMD6: <u>Development</u> and <u>Marketing</u> <u>of</u> <u>Energy</u> <u>Efficient</u> <u>Products</u>
and Services

<u>Proposition</u> 6A   Growth firms will show a greater tendency than non-
growth firms to develop and/or market more energy efficient products/
services.

<u>Proposition</u> 6B   Energy intensive firms will show a greater tendency
than non-energy intensive firms to develop and/or market more energy
efficient products/services.

<u>Proposition</u> 6C   Divisions will show a greater tendency than indepen-
dent firms to develop and/or market more energy efficient products/
services.

<u>Dependent</u> <u>Variable</u>: Energy Management Dimension, No. 6:
        Development/Marketing of Energy Efficient Products and Services.

        Measurement: Question 9 of Divisions and Independent Firms'
Questionnaire.

The Data and Analysis

        The intent of this proposition is to examine the extent to

which firms have attempted to turn the energy environment of the 1970s

to their own economic advantage. This proposition, unlike the previous

ones, focuses upon firms' efforts to directly impact their environment

through the medium of their product market portfolio.

        Not enough firms have attempted to incorporate energy efficiency

as an element in their product-market activities and/or have perceived

energy efficiency as relevant to their product-market scope to allow

statistical analysis of the propositions. What follows will be a de-

scriptive analysis of why firms have, or have not, attempted to inte-

grate energy efficiency considerations into their product-market

strategies.

The efforts of firms to impact their environment was conceptualized along the following three product-market dimensions: (1) the
modification of existing products/services to make them more energy
efficient; (2) the development of new products/services which would
be more energy efficient than the firm's existing products/services;
and (3) the use of energy efficiency as a selling point for any of
its products and/or services.

1. Only one firm (an independent firm) has attempted to modify
any of its products or services in order to make them more energy conserving for its customers. This firm is in SIC 3443, Fabricated Plate
Works.

As reported in the data analysis section of Propositions 5A,
5B, and 5C, this firm's R and D program placed heavy emphasis on
development (as opposed to basic research) in metallurgy and heat
control. It was as a consequence of this development work that the
firm was able to improve the energy efficiency of certain parts of
its (industrial) customers' operations. However, the mix of factors
which prompted the firm to focus upon improving the energy efficiency
of customers' operations is not clear; both of the individuals interviewed in this firm gave different reasons as to why the firm had
adopted this strategy. Clearly this is a question which requires
further research.

Another three independent firms indicated that they believed
at least a portion of their current product line was amenable to
modification which would enhance its energy efficiency from the
perspective of the firms' customers. These firms were in the

chemical (SIC 2822, Plastics Materials, Synthetic Resins, Nonvulcanizable Elastomers), primary metal (SIC 3325, Steel Foundries, N.E.C.)
and the machinery (SIC 3561, Pumps and Pump Equipment) industries.
Each of these firms considered that at least part of their product
line would have a direct impact on the energy efficiency of its
customers' operations.

All three firms spelled out quite clearly why they had not
attempted to alter their product line so that its energy efficiency
(from the vantage point of the firms' customers) would be improved:
(1) the energy efficiency of their products/services was perceived as
being of minimal importance to their customers, (2) no other firm in
their industry was attempting to exploit product/service energy efficiency as a competitive advantage, (3) the cost involved in modifying
their product/service line to improve its energy efficiency (i.e.,
changes in manufacturing process, changes in raw materials required
for manufacturing, etc.) were perceived as strongly outweighing any
sales increases.

The remaining eight independent firms and all the divisions
did not consider energy efficiency as relevant to their product line.
They did not see their products/services as energy consuming, in and
of themselves, or as possessing the potential to directly or indirectly
affect the energy efficiency of their customers' operations. Thus,
eighty-three percent of the sample firms did not see any relationship
between energy considerations and their product portfolio.

2. All of the four independent firms which recognized the
relevance of energy efficiency to their product lines intimated that

they already had or were in the process of examining the feasibility of developing new products or radically modifying some of their existing product lines with a view to conserving energy for the firms' customers. No such new products or services have as yet been developed and introduced by any of these firms. While these firms claim that energy efficiency is a consideration in their new product/service development, it is not clear what their commitment is to the improvement of the energy efficiency of their product/service lines or the weight which is assigned to product/service energy efficiency (compared to other factors) in new product/service decision making. Considerably more research is required before answers can be attempted for these questions.

3. None of the sample firms have attempted to use energy considerations as a selling point in their marketing activities for any products or services. Not even the four independent firms which recognize the relevance of energy to their product-market strategy have marketed any of their products/services from an energy efficiency standpoint. They all indicated they believed such a marketing tactic was becoming more relevant and potentially viable. Again, the factors which inhibit or induce firms to incorporate energy efficiency considerations into their marketing strategies are clearly in need of future research.

Conclusion

Clearly, energy efficiency considerations have not been incorporated into the sample firms' product-market activities. Only four

firms considered energy efficiency as at all relevant to their product/
service lines, and even those four firms did not attempt to market any
part of their product/service line from an energy efficiency perspective.

Test of Hypotheses

Hypotheses

Hypothesis 1A: Growth firms will be more actively engaged in energy management than non-growth firms.

Hypothesis 1B: Energy intensive firms will be more actively engaged in energy management than non-energy intensive firms.

Hypothesis 1C: Divisions will be more actively engaged in energy management than independent firms.

Independent Variables: Growth, energy intensity, and structure.

Dependent Variables: Firms' energy management response along each of the six energy management dimensions identified in Chapter 2.

The Data

The preceding propositions serve as the data for these hypotheses (the results of which are summarized in Table VI-18). The following serves as an analysis for the hypotheses/propositions testing section of this chapter.

Analysis

Table VI-18 summarizes the results of proposition testing. The results have been confined to three categories of conclusions: tentatively confirmed, tentatively unconfirmed and no support. The data for Propositions 1C, 2B, 2C, 3B, 3C, and 4B manifest statistical relationships in the anticipated directions at $p = .05$ or above. Propositions 1B and 4C (which are categorized as tentatively unconfirmed) received some statistical support but not sufficient for their

TABLE VI-18

RESULTS OF PROPOSITION TESTING

Proposition[1]	Tentatively Confirmed[2]	Tentatively Unconfirmed	No Support
1A			X
1B		X	
1C	X		
2A			X
2B	X		
2C	XX		
3A			X
3B	X		
3C	XX		
4A			X
4B	X		
4C		X	

[1]The data did not allow statistical analysis of propositions 5 and 6, and, thus, they are not shown in this Table.

[2]Where two segments of an overall proposition have received some measure of statistical support, two XX's indicate a higher degree of statistical support than one X.

acceptance or confirmation. Propositions 1A, 2A, 3A and 4A did not receive any statistical support.

Conclusion

This research has tentatively confirmed that energy intensive firms and divisions are more likely to be actively engaged in energy management than non-energy intensive firms and independent firms respectively. For each energy management dimension which is statistically testable there is some evidence to support the hypotheses related to energy intensity (Hypothesis 1B) and structure (Hypothesis 1C).

However, this research has not been able to produce any evidence to support the hypothesis that growth firms will be more actively engaged in energy management than non-growth firms (Hypothesis 1A). It would seem that growth (as defined in this study) is not related to firms' propensity to engage in energy management.

The small sample size in this study, which has already been noted, is the reason for the tentative nature of the study's conclusion. The tentative confirmation of many of the study's propositions suggests the validity of a study with a larger sample size which would serve to further refine this study's findings.

One method of going beyond the results of the proposition testing within the present study is to examine the data for patterns of energy management response which cut across the energy management dimensions rather than focusing on each energy management dimension individually. It is with this purpose in mind that we turn to the final section of this chapter.

Interaction Among Energy Management Dimension Components

The tests of the propositions and hypotheses reported in the previous sections of this chapter were confined to an examination of each EMD individually; no attempt was made to relate components of different EMDs. The purpose of this section is to determine if there are patterns of energy management response which cut across the energy management dimensions. Specifically, the intent is to determine if energy management indices (i.e., relationships among EMD components) can be developed which discriminate the extent of the energy management activities of the sample firms.

All of the EMD components were factor analyzed to test for the existence of a single energy management dimension or set of energy management dimensions which could be used to differentiate the energy management approaches of the sample firms. No significant or meaningful relationships among the EMD components emerged.

The components of the six EMDs were then examined for inter-correlations. The intercorrelations between any two components were considered statistically significant if $p < .05$. Divisions and independent firms were chosen as the basis for the examination of inter-relations among the six EMD components because in the proposition/hypothesis testing, structure (i.e., divisions versus independent firms) more significantly discriminated the energy management approaches of the sample firms than either energy intensity or growth.

Tables VI-19 and VI-20 show the correlation matrices for the components of the six (6) EMDs for divisions and independent firms

TABLE VI-19

INTERCORRELATION AMONG EMD COMPONENTS--DIVISIONS

	Energy Management Committee	R&D Initiated Energy Efficiency Improvements	Management Accountability	Production/ Process Changes	Energy Conservation Investment Criteria
Energy Management Committee	--	0.6431	0.5556	0.5774	0.5441
R&D Initiated Energy Efficiency Improvements		--	0.7058	0.8422	NS
Management Accountability			--	0.5774	0.7543
Production/Process Changes				--	NS
Energy Conservation Investment Criteria					--

TABLE VI-20

INTERCORRELATION AMONG EMD COMPONENTS--INDEPENDENT FIRMS

	Energy Mgt. Comm.	Data Avail- ability	Existence of Energy Audits	Mgt. Account- ability	Production Manufactur- ing Changes	Energy Mgt. Targets Object- tives	Energy Con- servation Investment Criteria	R & D Initiated Energy Efficiency Improve- ments	Modify Existing Product/ Services	Develop New Products/ Services
Energy Mgt. Committee	--	0.5292	NS	NS	NS	NS	NS	NS	NS	NS
Data Avail- ability		--	0.5976	0.8166	0.7143	NS	NS	NS	NS	NS
Existence of Energy Audits			--	0.5160	0.8367	NS	NS	NS	NS	NS
Management Account- ability				--	0.6697	NS	NS	NS	NS	NS
Production/ Manufactur- ing Changes					--	0.4880	NS	NS	NS	NS
Energy Mgt. Targets/ Objectives						--	0.5222	NS	NS	NS
Energy Con- servation Invest. Crit.							--	0.6742	NS	NS
R&D Initiated Energy Efficien- cy Improvements								--	0.6680	0.6655
Modification of Existing Products									--	0.9956
Develop New Products/Serv.										--

respectively.[1] All of the significant (p < .05) intercorrelations among EMD components for divisions and independent firms are represented in Tables VI-19 and VI-20, respectively. For instance, in the case of divisions (as shown in Table VI-19) production process changes are related to the existence of an energy management committee, management accountability for energy management, and whether or not the firms' R and D program has led to energy efficiency improvements. Thus, Tables VI-19 and VI-20 represent groups of energy management activities which are closely interrelated for divisions and independent firms.

However, the major question which must be examined is whether these groups of energy management related activities are significantly different for divisions and independent firms. Each set of interrelated energy management components was related to the predictor variables (i.e., growth, energy intensity and structure) by means of canonical correlation[2] analysis to determine if they discriminated between the energy management approaches of the sample firms.[3]

Only three of the eleven groups of energy management activities showed significant results[4] (p < .05). Not surprisingly, in view of the fact that these groups of energy management activities were derived from the EMD component correlations for divisions and independent firms separately, structure is the predictor variable which is significantly correlated with each of these groups of energy management activities. However, the close correlation between energy management targets/objectives and structure dominates these results[5]: thus, these findings must be interpreted with caution.

Summary/Conclusion

A larger data base than is available in this study is required to further test and clarify relationships among the energy management activities which are examined in this research. An overall energy management dimension is not evident in this study.

This chapter has examined quantitatively the relationships posited in the hypotheses/propositions. Structure is the variable most positively related to firms' approach to energy management, i.e., divisions demonstrate a higher degree of strategic responsiveness in their approach to energy management than independent firms. The following chapter examines qualitatively energy management decision making processes in the smaller sized firms.

[1]Tables VI-19 and VI-20 are of different sizes because only the EMD components which are significantly related are shown in these tables. A greater number of EMD components are related in the case of independent firms.

[2]Canonical correlation analysis is the data analysis technique employed to examine the relationships since it does not assume any relationship between the components in the dependent variable, i.e., the groups of energy management related activities. However, when multiple regression analysis is employed, the same results emerge.

[3]Although the divisions and independent firms were separated for the correlation analysis, the canonical correlation analysis relates the groups of energy management related activities resulting from the correlation analysis and the predictor variables (i.e., growth, energy intensity and structure) at the level of divisions and independent firms combined. Since it is our purpose to test whether the interrelated sets of energy management activities discriminate between the different types of firms being studied, it is only at the level of divisions and independent firms grouped together (i.e., the entire sample of small organizations) that this analysis makes sense.

[4]The groups of energy management activities which showed significant results were:

a. energy data availability, existence of energy audits, manufacturing process changes, management accountability and energy management targets objectives.

b. energy management targets/objectives, manufacturing process changes, energy conservation investment criteria.

c. energy management targets/objectives, energy conservation investment criteria R & D initiated improvements in energy conservation.

[5]The very close correlation between energy management targets/objectives and structure can be seen by reviewing the results of testing propositions 1A, 1B and 1C.

CHAPTER SEVEN

ENERGY MANAGEMENT DECISION MAKING IN THE SMALLER SIZED FIRMS

The previous chapter examined the data for support of the hypotheses which provided the guidelines for part of this study. An attempt to identify interrelationships among the components of the EMDs which would discriminate the energy management approaches of the different types of firms proved relatively unsuccessful.

This chapter provides a qualitative analysis of energy management in the smaller sized firms. It is divided into three sections: (1) some general observations are made on the energy management response patterns of these firms; (2) the energy management strategies of two different groups of firms are delineated; and (3) the energy conservation decision making processes in two (2) firms which have attempted to develop systematic approaches to energy management are described.

Energy Management Response Patterns: Some General Observations

In the last part of the previous chapter, an attempt was made to identify sets of related energy management components which could be used to discriminate the extent of the energy management activities of the sample firms. However, it was found that the sets of EMD components which were statistically related showed little significant correlation with the firm characteristics (i.e., growth, energy intensity and structure) of interest in this study.

This section provides a general discussion of energy management in the smaller sized firms along each EMD. Where appropriate, an attempt is also made to provide a qualitative analysis of the EMD component relationships shown in Tables VI-19 and VI-20 in the previous chapter. To facilitate the analysis in this section, the EMD component relationships shown in Tables VI-19 and VI-20 are reproduced in Figures VII-1 and VII-2.

Since structure is more significantly related to the energy management approach adopted by firms than either energy intensity or growth in the hypotheses/propositions testing, a particular point of attention in this section is to identify reasons why divisions may have developed more systematic approaches to energy management than independent firms.

EMD 1: Organization for Energy Management

The Role of Energy Management Committees

Although not many firms (three divisions and two independent firms) have established an energy management committee it would appear that energy management committees play a more central role in divisions than they do in independent firms. In divisions, energy management committees are correlated with production/manufacturing changes, management accountability, R and D initiated improvements in energy conservation and energy conservation investment criteria (see Figure VII-1).

FIGURE VII-1

INTERCORRELATION AMONG EMD COMPONENTS--DIVISIONS

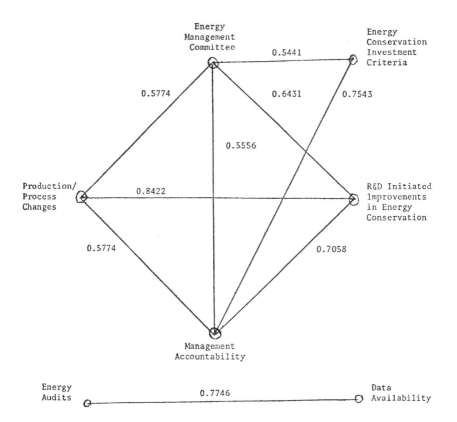

FIGURE VII-2

INTERCORRELATION AMONG EMD COMPONENTS--
INDEPENDENT FIRMS

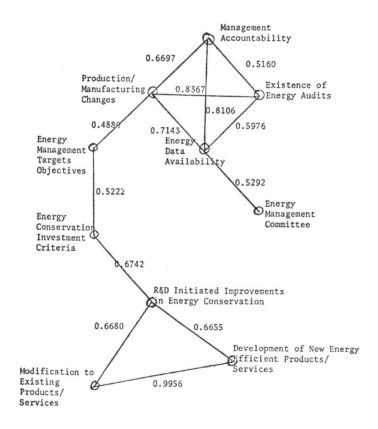

On the other hand, in independent firms energy management committees are only correlated with energy data availability (see Figure VII-2).

The above suggests that the role and scope of energy management committees is much greater in divisions than in independent firms; this is borne out by an appraisal of energy management committee activities. The two independent firms' energy management committees serve as firm-wide liaison groups for energy matters (i.e., providing ideas for energy efficiency improvements, disseminating energy conservation goals, providing support for controlling energy "housekeeping" costs, etc.), but none of those interviewed in either firm considered that the energy management committee is the locus of energy management decision making within their firms. Such decisions are made by plant and general management with "inputs from the energy management committee."

In two of the three divisions which have an energy management committee, a prescribed role of the committee is to formulate energy conservation investment proposals and also, to oversee the implementation of energy conservation programs as well as the appraisal of their effectiveness.

Though this research does not attempt to systematically compare the functions of energy management committees in divisions and independent firms, it is evident that energy management committees are more fully integrated into the process of decision making in divisions than in independent firms. Further research is required to detail the role of energy management committees in effective energy management decision making, and specifically, how these committees inhibit or induce investments to enhance energy efficiency.

Full-time Energy Management Positions

In relation to the institutionalization of energy management, it will be noted that assigned responsibility for energy management (full-time or part-time positions) does not appear in Figures VII-1 and VII-2. None of the twelve independent firms have a full-time energy management position; three of these firms do not assign responsibility for energy management at all. All of the twelve divisions indicated that they have clearly assigned energy responsibilities; two division (both energy intensive) have full-time energy management positions. Only one of the three divisions with an energy management committee has a full-time energy management position.

As with the case of energy management committees, further research is required to explicate the role of full-time and part-time energy management personnel and to measure their effectiveness in improving firms' energy efficiency.

Energy Management Objectives/Targets

All but one division have established specific energy management/efficiency objectives, but only three independent firms have done so. The nature of energy management/efficiency objectives in most cases consists of reducing energy utilization per unit of output, per man-hour, per process (or some other measure) by some percentage level over a certain period time.

Summary

The data strongly suggest that divisions have a more formalized approach to energy management than independent firms in terms of assigned responsibilities and the establishment of objectives. What we can not determine in this study is whether these organizational manifestations of concern with energy management have resulted in superior performance by divisions over independent firms in terms of improvements in energy efficiency.

EMD2: Energy Data Base and Monitoring Process

Not surprisingly, energy data availability and the conduct of energy audits are significantly related for both divisions and independent firms (see Figure VII-1 and VII-2). Nine (9) divisions and six (6) independent firms have conducted energy audits.

However, in the case of divisions, energy data is not significantly related with any energy management decision making activities (e.g., production/manufacturing changes), or energy management responsibilities (e.g., management accountability). Thus, from Figure VII-1, it would appear that in the case of divisions, energy management decision making and energy data generation are separate activities or, at least, are not well integrated. Figure VII-2 also suggests that the availability and appropriateness of energy information bears little relationship with the extent of independent firms' energy management activities.

A general review of the interview data with each division does not provide any convincing explanation for the apparent segregation of energy related data and energy management decision making. What is required to provide plausible explanations is a research study with a larger sample of firms which would focus on such questions as who

within the organization gathers energy related data? How is such data
disseminated within the organization? What kinds of energy (and other)
data are utilized in the process of making energy related decisions?
What differences exist between divisions and independent firms along
these dimensions? (Some of these and related questions are addressed
in the following two sections of this chapter.)

EMD3: Management Accountability

Even though the role of full-time and part-time energy management personnel is not evident from Figures VII-1 and VII-2, the importance of management accountability (i.e., energy management as a formal
part of some member of line management's accountability or evaluation)
is clearly manifest. In the case of both divisions and independent
firms, management accountability is related to production/manufacturing
changes; the evaluation of some member of management with regard to the
firm's effectiveness in managing its energy utilization/efficiency may
be a spur to investments in energy conservation/efficiency improvements.

In the case of divisions, management accountability is also
related to two other decision points: R and D initiated improvements
in energy efficiency and the criteria (i.e., ROI-return on investment)
employed in evaluating energy conservation investments. Thus, holding
some member of line management accountable for the firm's energy
management, may provide the necessary impetus for an organization-wide
effort to improve energy efficiency. The kinds of influence exercised
by a firm's "energy manager" (either a specific full-time or part-time
energy management position or a line manager who is charged with

responsibility for energy management) in his efforts to persuade other management personnel, functions and levels to contribute to improving the firm's energy management capability is clearly in need of further research.

EMD4: Energy Efficiency Improvement Programs/Investments

Seven divisions and five independent firms indicated they have clearly prescribed criteria (ROI--return on investment, payback period, etc.), which are applied to energy conservation investment proposals.

Only one division and one independent firm (both energy intensive) indicated that the ROI and payback criteria applied to capital intensive energy conservation/efficiency improvement investments were more lenient than for other capital investments. Both firms perceived a high degree of energy inefficiency within their operations; energy management had not long been a major management consideration and, thus, the potential return (ROI) on initial energy conservation investments might be expected to be high.

Many divisions and independent firms stressed that energy conservation/efficiency improvement investments were subjected to the same capital budgeting procedures and requirements as any other capital investment. Many interviewees pointed out that unless an energy related investment was "economically justified" it would not be implemented for "patriotic reasons," "because it was socially desirable or respectable to do so," "it would look good in the firm's end of the year statement," or "because President Carter had exhorted U.S. industry to become more energy efficient." Despite the professed economic rationale for energy related investments, an analysis of individual firms' investment processes and behavior reveals that other non-economic factors are also involved--this question will be addressed in the following section.

The importance of economic criteria were particularly stressed by smaller independent firms. Many of the sample firms in this category were under severe capital constraints. Unless an investment had an unambiguously high ROI it would not receive support. What is interesting from an investment behavior viewpoint and from the perspective of future research, is that these firms did not indicate that more stringent ROI/payback criteria were applied to energy related investments than to other capital investments. A major research question which needs to be addressed is how these firms apportion available capital resources between investment opportunities? For example, the president of one small firm indicated that the firm had not made a major investment in either energy conservation or energy supply/conversion even though it was his contention that such investments would be highly profitable because "the firm had to direct its investments elsewhere just to stay in business" (the firm was investing heavily in new plant and equipment).

EMD5: R and D Programs

EMD6: Development and Marketing of Energy Efficient
        Products/Services

The greater concern shown by independent firms to orient R and D to internal energy efficiency and toward the development of new products and modifications of existing products which were discussed

in relation to the test of Propositions 5A, 5B, and 5C and 6A, 6B, and
6C (see Chapter 6) is also evident in Figures VII-1 and VII-2.

The two independent firms whose R and D work had already resulted in improved internal energy efficiency had also demonstrated a
high degree of concern with the energy efficiency aspects of their
product/service lines--a concern which was manifestly absent in the
case of divisions (see test of Propositions 6A, 6B, and 6C).

Summary

The following are the principal findings which can be drawn
from this general discussion of energy management in the smaller sized
firms:

1. Although only three divisions and two independent firms
have established an energy management committee, it is evident that
energy management committees in divisions play a more significant role
in energy management decision making than they do in the independent
firms.

2. Only two divisions and none of the independent firms have
established a full-time energy management position. Only three firms
(all independent firms) did not assign responsibility for energy management at all.

3. Energy management objectives/targets are established by
all except one division but by only three independent firms.

4. A majority of the sample firms [nine (9) divisions and
six (6) independent firms] have conducted energy audits as a first
step toward a more comprehensive energy management data base.

5. Half the sample firms [seven (7) divisions and five (5)
independent firms] have clearly prescribed criteria (i.e., ROI, payback
period, etc.) which are applied to energy conservation investment proposals. Energy conservation investments are normally subjected to the
same capital budgeting process as any other potential investment. The
importance of a high rate of return on energy conservation investments
was particularly stressed by the smaller independent firms which may
be a reflection of their lack of capital and liquidity.

Energy Management in Contrasting Groups of Firms

With an overview of the energy management response patterns of
the smaller sized firms presented in the first section of this chapter,
the general purpose of this section is to provide a descriptive analysis of the energy management activity of both the divisions and independent firms in two SIC classification codes. It is not the intent
of this section to generate support for the study's hypotheses, but
rather to provide a detailed analysis of the energy management approach
of the firms in these two SIC classification codes (e.g., at what level
in these firms are different kinds of energy management decisions made?
What kinds of investments have been made to improve energy efficiency?
What kinds of energy related data do these firms generate and utilize?)

The two SIC classification codes (SIC 3221, Glass Containers
and SIC 3441, Fabricated Structured Metal) were selected because the
characteristics of the sample firms in terms of energy intensity, size
of firm (i.e., annual dollar sales) and generally with respect to their
growth rates differed greatly between the two SIC groups. As will

become evident, the approach to energy management of the firms in these two SIC categories is also distinctly different.

SIC 3221: Energy Intensive, and Growth Firms

SIC 3221, Glass Containers, includes "establishments primarily engaged in manufacturing glass containers for commercial packing and bottling, and for home canning."[1] The study sample contained one division and one independent firm in SIC 3221. Table VII-1 shows the sales, growth, energy intensity and employment levels of these two firms.

The selection of these two firms for a detailed examination of energy management is based on the following reasons: (1) both firms have been attempting for at least three years to develop a comprehensive approach to energy management; (2) as shown in Table VII-1, the two firms are reasonably similar in terms of annual sales, average annual sales growth and number of employees; (3) a dominant characteristic of the firms from the perspective of this study is their high level of energy intensity: both firms estimated that total energy costs as a percentage of their total operating costs was of the order of ten to fifteen percent.

Table VII-2 provides in summary fashion, a description of the energy management approach of the division and independent firm discussed. What follows is an appraisal of these firms' energy management efforts along four energy management dimensions: organization for energy management; energy data generation and analysis; management accountability and energy conservation and supply investment programs.

TABLE VII-1

SIC 3221 FIRMS: SALES, GROWTH, ENERGY INTENSITY
AND EMPLOYMENT LEVELS

	Sales[1] (1,000,000)	Growth[2]	Energy[3] Intensity	Number of[4] Employees
Divisions	80-100	8-10%	10-15%	900-1000
Independent Firms	50-70	10-15%	10-15%	500-600

---

[1]Both firms were reluctant to reveal their exact sales volume. The sales figures given above represent the most precise estimates that the interviewees in both firms were willing to make.

[2]The growth figures shown here are the actual estimates calculated by one interviewer in each firm. (These figures are in constant terms.)

[3]Both firms provided these energy intensity figures (i.e., total energy costs as a percentage of total operating costs) during the in-person interviews. The independent firm later provided actual energy costs which would seem to justify the energy intensity level shown above (10-15%) assuming a sales volume of $50-70 million.

[4]Number of employees as shown is the consensus estimate of the interviewees.

TABLE VII-2

ENERGY MANAGEMENT RESPONSE OF SIC 3221 FIRMS

		DIVISION	INDEPENDENT
ORGANIZATION OF ENERGY MANAGEMENT FUNCTION	Energy Management Responsibility	One full-time position, other assigned roles, responsibilities	Specific assigned roles, responsibilities
	Location of Responsibility	Energy Coordinator- part of engineering function	Chief plant engineer, technical director, general electrical engineer
	Energy Management Committee	No Committee	No Committee
ENERGY DATA GENERATION & ANALYSIS	Energy Conservation/ Efficiency Improvement Objectives	Overall objective specific project goals	No overall objective Specific project goals
	Monitoring of Energy Utilization	Establishing comprehensive program	Monitor main end-use point
	Energy Audits	Conducted detailed audit More focused audits in progress	Periodic audits on energy utilized by furnaces
MANAGEMENT ACCOUNTABILITY	Evaluation of Energy "Managers"/ Management	No personnel evaluated on their energy management efforts	
ENERGY CONSERVATION/ SUPPLY INVESTMENT PROGRAMS	"Housekeeping" Programs	Specific efforts to control space heating, and lighting usage/ costs	Sequential programs to control ventilation, space heating and lighting usage/costs
	Energy Conservation "Capital Expenditures"	Major investment program, rebuilt furnaces, insulation, modification of equipment	Major investment program, redesign of furnaces, replacement of inefficient equipment
	Energy "Conversion" Investments		Small scale effort

EMD1: Organization for Energy Management

Both firms have clearly delineated energy management tasks, roles and responsibilities. The engineering function is the hub of the energy management activity in both firms.

Assignment of Energy Management
Responsibilities

The division has established a full-time energy management position, entitled "Energy Management Coordinator." The original impetus for the establishment of this position was considered to be a combination of rapidly escalating energy prices, perceived energy inefficiencies within the firm and the desire to limit the deleterious consequences of potential energy supply interruptions. The fact that the energy implications of the firm's ongoing decision making do not clearly fall within the purview of any one previously existing position or function was mentioned by the present energy coordinator as a major reason for management's desire to locate within one position, specific responsibility for energy data collection and analysis, development and monitoring of energy conservation programs and identification and appraisal of the energy implications of decisions made by various departments or functions within the firm.

The Energy Coordinator described his chief functions and responsibilities as follows:

1. Monitoring and analyzing the consumption pattern of each energy source;

2. Designing, overseeing and evaluating audits of major energy consumption end-points;

3. Identification and development of specific energy
   conservation investment proposals;

4. Developing, monitoring and evaluating "housekeeping"
   programs, e.g., specific means to control space heating,
   ventilation, and lighting utilization;

5. Assessment of the energy implications of the firms'
   proposed and ongoing capital investment programs; and

6. Liaison with corporation headquarters (e.g., working
   with the office of the Director of Energy Affairs to
   establish divisional energy conservation strategy,
   energy efficiency improvement goals, etc.).

The position of Energy Coordinator is located within the
Engineering Department, and reports directly to the head of engineering.
Not much more will be said at this stage about the role of the Energy
Coordinator since many of the primary functions of the position will
be discussed later when a specific analysis will be made of the decision process involved in the initiation, development, evaluation,
approval and implementation of energy conservation investment proposals.

The independent firm did not consider it necessary to establish
a full-time energy management position. Rather it was suggested a
careful assignment of energy related tasks and responsibilities among
existing personnel was a more efficient means of managing the firm's
energy affairs. The establishment of a full-time energy management
position was strongly perceived as one which would largely duplicate
existing activities and responsibilities without necessarily entailing

any of the advantages of the present energy management arrangements. It was also suggested that a full-time energy management position would be one of many responsibilities but little influence: an Energy Coordinator would still have to work through the existing organizational hierarchy but would have little, if any, line authority. (This point is discussed in more detail later when considering the scope of the division Energy Coordinator's activities.)

The chief plant engineer, technical director and senior electrical engineer are the main figures involved in the independent firm's energy management activities. The technical director estimates that he spends approximately fifty percent of his time engaged in energy related activities, while the chief plant engineer believes energy related matters consume twenty-five percent of his time.

The technical director (who reports to the president) is the spearhead of the firm's energy management efforts. His role consists primarily of the technical evalution of potential and proposed energy conservation investments (e.g., what kinds of insulation would be compatible with the design and structure of the firm's furnaces) and the estimation of potential energy savings that might result from alternate energy conservation investments.

The chief plant engineer, working in close liaison with the technical director, assists in the identification and evaluation of energy conservation projects, particularly their impact on plant operations.

The senior electrical engineer has been charged with evaluating the efficiency of electricity utilization and transfer within the firm's plant; a specific element of his assigned function is to generate means by which the firm can reduce its electricity utilization and/or improve its electrical efficiency.

Energy Management Committees: Purpose and Practice

Both firms were highly critical of the concept of an energy management committee. The independent firm did not see any need for such a committee: the firm is sufficiently small that access to anybody involved in energy management is normally not a problem. The technical director also pointed out that the number of people consistently involved in energy decision making is so small that formalization of their efforts by means of a committee would be superfluous.

In the early stages of the development of its energy management efforts, the division created an energy management committee to ensure a diversity of perspectives in the evolution of its energy management programs. The energy management committee was also intended to function as a vehicle for coordination and consistency in energy management decision making; the present energy coordinator intimated that senior management saw the committee as a device which would inhibit any single department or individual from undue influence in the energy decision making process. However, the committee had a short-lived existence: due to its ineffectiveness in implementing energy decisions and increasing awareness of the complexity of the task of energy management, it was decided to establish in place of the committee, the full-time position of Energy Management Coordinator.

Energy Efficiency Improvement
Objectives

The two firms have adopted somewhat different approaches to establishing energy conservation or energy efficiency improvement objectives. The division has set an overall objective: to improve energy efficiency by five percent within a two year period. Specific goals were also set in terms of desired energy savings (btu's) or improved efficiency for each energy conservation investment (i.e., capital expenditure) or program (e.g., reduced utilization of lighting). The independent firm did not see any merit in setting an overall objective but set specific goals similar to those of the division.

The establishment of an overall division energy efficiency improvement target is not something which is entirely at the discretion of the division. Rather, it is established as part of a negotiation process with the energy management function at corporate headquarters. In most cases, the ultimately agreed upon target was described as a compromise between estimates of the division's energy personnel, and the expectations of corporate headquarter's personnel.

The division's Energy Coordinator pointed out that the level of the target itself, per se, may be less important than the existence of the target. In his view, the widespread dissemination of an energy efficiency improvement objective among division management was a major factor in motivating plant and general management, and production and operations personnel, to cooperate with the engineering function, in general, and his own efforts, in particular, in the formulation and implementation of energy management programs.

The absence of an overall energy efficiency improvement target did not seem to have any inhibiting impact on the independent firm's energy management efforts. Indeed, if measured by the total dollar investment in the improvement of energy efficiency, the independent firm has been more actively involved in energy management than the division. The independent firm has established very specific goals for various elements of its overall energy management program (e.g., the firm has estimated that over the past three years it has improved the average energy efficiency of its furnaces by approximately thirty percent but it is now examining specific possibilities to achieve another five percent efficiency which the firm considers close to the maximum attainable level). Thus, for the independent firm, specific project goals serve as a motivating force in much the same sense as the division Energy Coordinator described the role of the division's overall energy efficiency improvement target.

EMD2: Energy Data Base and Monitoring Process

Both firms are continuing to develop their procedures for more systematic monitoring of energy utilization, particularly at main energy consumption end-points. Both firms were quick to point out that their data on energy utilization was considerably less than adequate. Only within the previous year had either firm made a major effort to accurately determine the distribution of their total energy usage either by function (i.e., manufacturing/processing, space heating, ventilation, etc.), or by major end-use point (e.g., the energy efficiency of each furnace).

The division, under the direction of the Energy Coordinator, conducted a detailed audit of energy utilization. Prior to the audit, the Energy Coordinator indicated the firm had relatively little insight into how its total energy consumption was apportioned among and within different end-uses. The work entailed in conducting the detailed audit also laid the groundwork for ongoing monitoring of energy usage through the installation of meters, etc., and the familiarization of personnel with the concept of monitoring and analysis of energy usage patterns. The division has also begun a series of more focused audits to assess more accurately the areas of major potential energy savings.

The independent firm has concentrated monitoring of energy utilization at its main end-use point--its furnaces (it was estimated that the firm's furnaces account for seventy to seventy-five percent of the firm's total energy consumption). Detailed audits of the energy efficiency of the furnaces are conducted on a regular basis. The audits are particularly critical for they serve as the basis of measuring the effectiveness of the major element of the firm's energy conservation effort--the redesign, rebuilding, and insulation of its furnaces. As in the case of the division, the audits also provide the necessary quantitative measures to substantiate energy conservation investment proposals.

EMD3: Management Accountability

In neither of the firms was there any evidence that personnel were formally evaluated on their energy management efforts. None of those interviewed felt that they were directly evaluated on how effectively they carried out their energy related responsibilities. One member of the independent firm suggested that the necessary criteria to evaluate the effectiveness with which energy related responsibilities were discharged were as yet so nebulous and ill-defined as to be close to meaningless.

Although interviewees within the division did not consider they were formally evaluated with respect to energy management, the division as a whole was clearly seen as accountable to corporate headquarters for its energy management. This accountability to corporate headquarters is formalized through the submission of an annual plan, major capital expenditures, and specific programs for review by corporate headquarters personnel. As perceived by division personnel, a critical component of its accountability is the regular transmission of energy consumption data to corporate headquarters (e.g., total btu's consumed, nature of the energy mix, and occasionally energy efficiency of furnaces, estimated energy consumed in space heating, or required for plant maintenance, etc.). It is this data which facilitates the "bottom-line" evaluation of each division's energy management results by the corporate headquarters staff.

EMD4: Energy Efficiency Improvement
Programs/Investments

The two firms under study have made significant investments to improve their overall energy efficiency. While both firms were reluctant and/or unable to place a total dollar figure on their energy conservation investments within the last two years, they each indicated it was at least three to five million dollars.

The independent firm has undertaken a major redesign and rebuilding of all of its furnaces. The program is being implemented
over a number of years because of the substantial capital expenditures
involved and because of the undesirability of shutting down more than
one furnace at any single time. The largest furnace alone required a
capital outlay of $1-1/2 million.

Although improvement in overall energy efficiency was cited as
the major reason for embarking upon this program, a number of factors
coalesced to provide its impetus: the firm's furnaces account for
seventy to seventy-five percent of its total energy consumption; re-
structuring the furnaces to avail of energy efficiency improvement
also led to the production of a purer form of the melted product, i.e.,
glass; the redesign of the furnaces, allowed for the first time, a
high quality insulation material to be used in insulating the furnaces;
the firm has projected that the redesign of the furnaces plus the improved quality of the furnace insulation will result in a marginal
extension in the life of each furnace and such a marginal life extension could result in significant savings due to its lengthening of
the time period between which each furnace must undergo a major overhaul.

The potential for improving energy efficiency, although it was
not the sole reason, was cited as a major contributing factor by independent firm personnel in the decision to replace inefficient equipment
at a number of stages within the manufacturing process. The process
involved in the formulation and implementation of the decision to in-
vest in more (energy) efficient equipment is an explicit example of

the necessary integration of a number of distinct functional interests in energy management (in this case, production/operations management, plant engineering, plant management, accounting/finance and general management--the president). This aspect of energy management decision making will be discussed in greater detail in the next section.

The division has also made a number of investments specifically to improve energy efficiency. It has also rebuilt some of its furnaces, modified or replaced some outmoded equipment and has begun a program to insulate buildings wherever possible.

Both firms have "housekeeping" programs in operation to control heating, lighting, and ventilation. For example, the independent firm has replaced all of its incandescent lights with sodium vapor and fluorescent lights. It has also established maximum office temperature levels during the winter and maximum air-conditioning levels during summer.

Both firms had made the bulk of their investment in the early 1970s in the conversion of boilers and furnaces to utilize more than one energy source. The motivation for this investment was a series of direct intimations to the firms by their natural gas utilities over a two or three year period in the late 1960s and early 1970s that natural gas curtailments were a real possibility and/or actual slight curtailments suffered by the firms. The realization that they could not expect to receive more natural gas than that stipulated in their contract at certain times during the year spurred both firms to install a conversion facility in their boilers and furnaces.

Summary/Conclusions

A number of conclusions can be drawn from the above description
of the energy management approaches of these two energy intensive and
growth firms.

1. Both firms have delineated specific roles, responsibilities
and tasks in their efforts to institutionalize the process of energy
management. The substance and the process of integrating these roles,
responsibilities and tasks will be discussed in the final part of this
chapter.

2. Both firms considered that an energy management committee
would impede rather than facilitate the process of energy management
decision making: energy related decisions are implemented much more
effectively where there is unambiguous responsibility for the formulation and implementation of energy management strategies and programs.

3. The locus of responsibility for the formulation and implementation of energy management strategy goals falls within the engineering function in each firm. Both full-time and part-time energy
management positions are staffed by engineering department personnel.

4. Energy efficiency improvement objectives serve the purpose
of motivating management efforts in the area of energy management.
All of the interviewees suggested that the dissemination of "energy
conservation goals" created intra-firm awareness of the necessity for
energy management.

5. Both firms are in the early stages of developing what they
would consider a systematic and adequate energy data base. It is also
apparent that such a data base is not a "free good": a certain level

of resources, both human and physical (e.g., meters, computer-time, etc.) must be devoted to the generation and evaluation of energy related data. However, to the extent that energy data has been available, it has played a major role in the identification of energy conservation investment areas and in the acceptance of such proposals by top management.

6. An absence of the relevant energy data has impeded an evaluation of energy management at the individual level. Thus, both firms have found it difficult to institutionalize an accountability for energy management.

7. A substantial investment program to improve energy efficiency has been undertaken by each firm. Also, the energy implications of non-energy specific capital investments are a formal component of their capital budgeting processes.

In short, these two firms have made energy management a conscious part of their overall management process. The next part of this section will examine some firms where energy management has received relatively little attention.

SIC 3441: Non-energy Intensive, Non-growth Firms

SIC 3441, Fabricated Structural Metal, consists of "establishments primarily engaged in manufacturing iron and steel and other metals for structural purposes, such as bridges, buildings and sections for ships, boats and barges."[2]

The study sample contained two divisions and two independent firms in SIC 3441. However, given the larger number of firms in

SIC 3441 in the Pittsburgh area, it was decided to add two more independent firms for the purposes of this section. (Unfortunately, for the purpose of maintaining a paired sample between divisions and independent firms to facilitate proposition testing, it was found impossible to locate any more divisions in SIC 3441). Table VII-3 shows the sales, growth, energy intensity and employment levels of these six firms.

A number of reasons can be cited for the choice of this particular SIC for detailed analysis. (1) It afforded the largest number of firms (six) within any of the study sample's SIC classification codes which would be reasonably similar in terms of total sales, level of employment, growth and energy intensity (see Table VII-3). (2) Since 1974/75 firms in SIC 3441 have experienced depressed market conditions. Thus, the growth figures as shown in Table VII-3 are somewhat misleading; all the firms with the exception of Division B, indicated that they had experienced difficulty in maintaining their sales level over the period 1974/75 to 1976/77. The depressed market conditions are reflected in the fact that all of the firms were operating at less than capacity with one division and one independent firm operating at what they suggested was not much more than fifty percent of "normal" operating capacity. (3) All of the firms have a very low level of energy intensity; none of the firms reported total energy costs to be greater than two (2) percent of total operating costs. (4) Competition between steel fabrication firms predominately occurs through the mechanism of bidding on pre-specified work orders. In other words, the output of steel fabrication firms is almost exclusively custom-made.

TABLE VII-3

SIC 3441 FIRMS: SALES, GROWTH, ENERGY INTENSITY
AND EMPLOYMENT LEVELS

	Sales[1] (1,000,000)	Growth	Energy Intensity	Number of Employees
Division A	25	25%	2%	150
Division B	19	12%	1%	125
Firm A	15	8%	1-2%	140
Firm B	30	5%	1-2%	250
Firm C	5	25%	2%	50
Firm D	10	10%	1-2%	150

---

[1]The sales and growth figures represent the actual or estimated
sales and growth figures as reported by the interviewees.

Consequently, price competition is very keen within the industry.
Pricing is particularly important in view of the fact that the firms
interviewed, perceived geographic location (i.e., proximity to the
customer) as of minimal significance from the perspective of "competitive advantage." Thus, given the importance of price, one might
speculate that the firms in this SIC group would be engaged in intensive efforts to control costs, including their energy costs.

As can be seen from Table VII-4, which shows in summary form
an analysis of energy management in the six (6) firms studied, five
(5) of the six (6) firms (one division and the four independent firms)
have engaged in relatively little energy management. What follows will
be an appraisal of these firms' energy management efforts along four
energy management dimensions (see Table VII-4): organization for
energy management; energy data generation and analysis; management
accountability and energy efficiency improvement programs/investments.

EMD1: Organization for Energy Management

The four independent firms and Division B have not taken any
steps to make energy management an integral component of ongoing organizational management. No one individual or committee within these firms
has been assigned specific responsibility for energy management.

In two of the independent firms, the president himself, in conjunction with the plant manager and/or plant engineer, make the energy
related decisions when, as one president put it, "we have no other
choice but to make a decision." Neither did any firms show any

TABLE VII-4

ENERGY MANAGEMENT RESPONSE OF SIC 3441 FIRMS

ENERGY MANAGEMENT FUNCTIONS \ TYPE OF FIRM		DIVISIONS		INDEPENDENT FIRMS
		Division A	Division B	Four Independent Firms
Organization of Management Function	Energy Management Responsibility	Designated Responsibility		No clear designation of energy management responsibilities
	Location of Responsibility	Plant Manager Part-time		Energy management functions performed by president/plant manager/ plant engineer in very cursory manner
	Energy Management Committee	No Committee		No Committee
	Energy Conservation Efficiency Objectives	Overall Target		No real concern with energy efficiency improvement targets
Energy Data Generation and Analysis	Monitoring of Energy Utilization	Some Effort		Very little attempt to monitor Energy usage on on-going basis
	Energy Audits	Periodic		Absence of any effort to audit energy usage at main end-use points
Management Accountability	Evaluation of Energy "Managers"/ Management	No personnel evaluated in their energy management efforts.		
Energy Conservation Supply	"Housekeeping" Problems	Some attempts to control ventilation, air-conditioning, temperatures, etc., improve boiler/furnace maintenance, etc.		
	Energy Conservation "Capital Expenditures"	A few investments	One major investment	Some minor investments
	Energy "Conversion" Investments	One major investment	None	Two firms have initiated energy conversion programs

interest in establishing any kind of target or objective for their energy conservation or energy efficiency improvement efforts.

Perhaps the attitude of these five firms to managing energy is best summed up by one plant manager who stated that he didn't see any need to explicitly consider energy management (i.e., establish specific energy management responsibilities) since he believed that "the firm as presently organized could make whatever energy decisions were required." Implicit in this comment is the perception of energy as being of limited consequence for the firm's economic well-being

One division (Division A) made the plant superintendent responsible for the development and implementation of the firm's energy management endeavors. However, energy management is seen as a minor component of his job and one where "management by exception" might be described as being the norm, i.e., energy management only becomes a concern when unusual circumstances prevail, e.g., the threat of an energy supply interruption or when some proposed conservation or supply investment has to be appraised. This division also has an overall energy utilization target (btu's per ton of output) as a goal against which to measure its energy efficiency efforts. This is judged by the plant manager primarily as a motivational device; it represents a specific objective for attainment by the plant superintendent and plant foremen, the personnel who would ultimately have to implement any energy conservation/efficiency program.

EMD2:   Energy Data Base and Monitoring
        Process

Again five (5) of the six (6) firms have established few if
any procedures to monitor energy usage in a systematic manner or to
conduct audits of energy usage at main end-use points. In fact one
firm has only one natural gas meter which serves as the sole monitoring device for natural gas usage in the firm's plant, office and storage area. These firms generally see little merit in breaking down
their total energy usage consumed at different stages of the manufacturing process, or the amount of energy used for plant heating, office
heating, plant maintenance, etc., as opposed to that used strictly in
the manufacturing (fabrication) process. One independent firm's president went so far as to suggest that it would cost more in terms of
initial investment (i.e., meters, etc.) and the continued personnel
time involved in collecting, appraising and apportioning energy usage
per end-use, per unit of output, etc., than could be expected in any
consequent energy savings.

The same division, which has designated the plant superintendent responsible for energy affairs and has established an overall
energy conservation/efficiency target, is initiating a program to
facilitate daily reading of natural gas usage (i.e., the installation
of meters, the establishment of meter reading procedures, etc.). The
firm has conducted an audit of energy usage wherever the existing
metering system has allowed them to do so. (It is estimated that the
firm is dependent on natural gas for 85-90 percent of its total energy
usage.)

The suggested motivation for continuous data collection and appraisal was not energy conservation or improved energy efficiency, per se, but rather the fear of exceeding the firm's natural gas allotment. Should the firm move toward full operating capacity (it was currently operating at 55-60 percent of capacity) it would most probably exceed its natural gas allotment which was perceived as especially critical given the expectation of receiving only small increments above the current natural gas allotment.

EMD3: Management Accountability

In none of the firms is there any evidence that energy management is a factor in the evaluation of personnel. Even in the one division where energy management responsibilities are clearly assigned, how management is evaluated is not perceived as being related to how effectively energy management functions are performed.

The explanation provided by two independent firms as to why energy management is neither an explicit or implicit component of the firm's personnel evaluation and reward system is revealing. The potential for reducing the amount of energy utilized per unit of output, per direct labor hour etc., is perceived as very small. Hence, since the potential energy savings are severely limited, it is deemed a pointless exercise to charge any personnel with specific responsibility for reducing energy utilization and/or evaluating personnel as to how effective they are in controlling energy utilization.

One other independent firm and Division A intimated that energy was treated like any other controllable cost but that the discretionary area of control with regard to energy costs is considerably less than with other cost control areas (e.g., labor, raw materials). For any given level of output a certain volume of energy is required, and that energy has to be taken at the price it is sold (the latter would be particularly true for the firms in this SIC classification code since they are almost exclusively dependent on natural gas and electricity).

EMD4: Energy Efficiency Improvment
       Programs/Investments

All of the firms have made some effort to control their "house-keeping" energy costs, i.e., controlling air conditioning, ventilation and temperature, reducing unnecessary idling of equipment, improving boiler and furnace maintenance, etc. Housekeeping efforts entail little, if any, investment or other start-up costs and, thus, are relatively easy to initiate and implement.

Where any form of investment or capital expenditure is required, the efforts of these firms could be described as ranging from minimal to non-existent. In no case, does the total dollar investment to date in energy conservation activities exceed ten thousand dollars. Only one firm had attempted to install any kind of insulation; two independent firms indicated they have not undertaken any dollar outlays to improve energy efficiency.

However, one division and two independent firms have undertaken investments to provide themselves with an energy conversion capability. The intent of these efforts was to avoid dependence on any one source of energy and/or potentially interruptible supply source.

Although the extent of these investments to provide energy convertibility is not large (in no case was the already committed and/or projected expenditure to exceed $50,000), they far outweigh the commitment of resources to energy conservation/energy efficiency improvement for each firm. Only one firm (Division A) exhibited a greater degree of concern (measured by the extent of their investment) with energy efficiency/utilization than with energy supply.

Summary/Conclusion

Unlike the case of the two firms in SIC 3221, energy management has received very little attention in five (5) of the six (6) firms in this SIC category. A number of contributing factors to the absence of any concerted energy management efforts can be identified: (1) Energy costs are such a small part of the firms' total costs that firms see little merit in instituting energy cost control programs; (2) A strongly held perception that the potential to effect energy saving through available techniques/technologies is very small and, thus, not worth the effort involved; (3) Highly limited discretionary capital resources and many competing claims on available capital; (4) A tendency on the part of these firms to "manage by exception"-- only when something goes wrong does it receive adequate management attention; (5) The thin management structure (a reflection of the small size of the firms) and the lack of bouyancy in the market for these firms' products place heavy market/customer related demands on management time. The fact that one (1) of the two (2) divisions is the only firm in this SIC category which has specifically designated energy management responsibilities and established energy efficiency targets, and that the two (2) divisions have made a greater amount of investment in energy efficiency improvement than the independent firms, lends further evidence to the contention that divisions demonstrate a higher degree of strategic responsiveness in their approach to energy management than independent firms.

Given that the firms in SIC 3441 are considerably smaller in terms of annual dollar sales and are much less energy intensive than the firms in SIC 3222 and also have demonstrated by comparison with the SIC 3222 firms, relatively little effort to manage their energy resources, a major question for future research is whether there is a threshold level in terms of firm size (i.e., annual sales volume) and energy intensity, below which firms find little incentive to make any kind of concerted effort to manage their energy resources.

The next section of this chapter examines the nature and interaction of the organizational roles involved in energy management decision making as well as some of the factors which influence energy management decisions.

Energy Conservation Decision Making Processes

The purpose of this part of the chapter is to develop a descriptive model of small to medium sized firms' energy conservation decision making. Specifically, the following aspects of organizations' energy conservation decision making will be examined:

1. What is the role of different management levels or functions in energy conservation or energy efficiency improvement investment decisions?

2. What are the principal factors which appear to affect the emergence of ideas for energy conservation investments and the evaluation of ideas once they have been formulated into specific investment proposals?

The focus of this section is energy conservation investments which entail some measure of capital expenditure (e.g., the insulation of buildings, acquisition of more energy efficient equipment, redesign of furnaces or boilers, etc.) and thus require some degree of interaction between different management levels and functions (e.g., the president, plant manager, accounting/finance function, engineering function, etc.).

The division and independent firm in SIC 3221 (glass containers) whose approach to energy management was described in the previous section, will also be the primary subjects of our efforts to develop a descriptive model of firms' energy conservation decision making. When it is considered appropriate, reference will be made to other sample firms.

Major Decision-Making Roles

Figure VII-3 identifies the major roles of the four principal organization elements (i.e., the president, plant management, accounting/finance function, and engineering function), involved in the independent firm's energy conservation decision making. Although it is evident from Figure VII-3 that a "bottom-up" approach is dominant with respect to the emergence, development, evaluation and approval of energy conservation investment proposals, a "top-down" approach is also occasionally applicable.

The "bottom-up" approach is represented by the major role of the engineering function in the initiation and development of energy conservation investment proposals. In both of the firms investigated in SIC 3221, almost all of the ideas which eventually materialized as fully developed investment proposals to improve energy efficiency originated within the engineering function. (The process by which these ideas are generated and evaluated within the engineering function will be discussed more fully, shortly.)

Even in those few situations where origination of an energy conservation idea was credited to an organizational level or function other than engineering, it was the engineering function which was charged with investigating its merits or demerits as a potentially viable means for the organization to improve its energy efficiency.

Once proposals have been formally developed by the engineering function, they are usually routed to the president's office. Sometimes proposals are directed to other management functions and levels for review, evaluation, and recommendation before they are forwarded to

FIGURE VII-3

AN ORGANIZATIONAL MODEL OF THE DEVELOPMENT AND
APPRAISAL OF ENERGY CONSERVATION INVESTMENTS

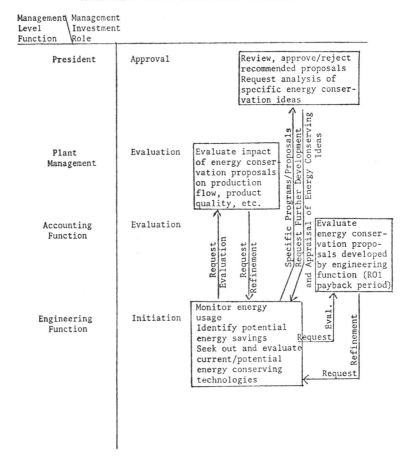

the president. If proposals go directly to the president's office, he may request their review and evaluation by plant management and/or the accounting/finance function. Of course, the president can (and apparently often does) return proposals to the engineering function for further development and appraisal.

The role of plant management and the accounting/finance function seems to be largely one of evaluating proposals which emanate from the engineering function. The role of the two management areas (i.e., plant management and accounting/finance) as sources of energy conservation ideas appears to be negligible. Neither do they retain the organizational prerogative to approve or reject energy conservation investment proposals.

The criteria applied by plant management and the accounting/finance function in the evaluation of potential energy conservation investments appear to stem from: (1) the organizational role and purpose of these functions; (2) the perceived self-interest of those performing the evaluation (which may be different from the "interest" or prescribed role of the function or management level); and (3) the perceptions of energy efficiency, potential energy savings, etc., held by personnel within these functions.

It was these latter two criteria which were pointed out by members of the engineering function in the independent firm as apparent influential factors in the way plant management and the accounting/finance functions had responded to energy conservation proposals developed by the engineering function. In other words, plant management and accounting/finance personnel, where they had been asked to respond to investment proposals, did not always do so by complete reliance on "rational" (as perceived by the engineering function) or economic criteria. In the eyes of engineering personnel they did not evaluate these investments using the same criteria as the engineering function. As the senior plant engineer put it, "they (especially plant management) look at more than the numbers involved."

The following is an illustration of the conflictual nature of the criteria applied to an actual proposed investment within a function (plant management) and between functions (plant management and the engineering function) as perceived and explicated by senior members of the engineering function within the independent firm. The firm's engineering unit is proposing to make a major overhaul of one of its furnaces which would entail completely dismantling the furnace and rebuilding it. The firm's furnaces are normally subjected to a major overhaul every four years. However, on this occasion, the engineering function is proposing to extend the period during which the furnace is "down" so that specific energy efficiency features can be incorporated into the furnace's refurbishment.

According to the engineering function's estimates, the opportunity cost of the extended period that the furnace will be "down" will be more than recouped by a combination of energy savings over the life of the furnace (i.e., the period until its next overhaul), a possible extension of the life of the furnace and improved quality of the finished product (in this case, glass).

However, plant management, while it was desirous of improved product quality, has raised a number of objections to the proposed investment:

1. It could jeopardize the firm's ability to meet its production deadlines; thus, the plant management would be conceding for a period of time some of the discretion required to meet one of its major responsibilities (i.e., meet production schedules).

2. Although the firm had some experience with investments of this kind (it had previously revamped its furnaces along similar lines though on a smaller scale), plant management remained to be convinced that this level of investment could not be better utilized to improve overall organization efficiency. It had been suggested by the plant manager that an investment of this order of magnitude to acquire more efficient production equipment would yield a higher rate of overall return to the firm.

3. The assumptions underlying the specific energy savings or improved energy efficiency levels projected by the engineering function were questioned by plant management. If the firm were not able to continue operating at close to full operating capacity, it would not have the potential to generate sufficient energy savings to realize the ROI (return on investment) projected by the engineering function.

This example helps to illustrate the conflictual nature of the criteria and perspectives which are brought to bear on the assessment of energy conservation projects by different organizational functions and roles. An examination of the president's role and his interaction with the engineering function in the development and appraisal of energy conservation projects also helps to illustrate some of the factors which influence the emergence and evaluation of energy conservation projects.

Investments which require a capital expenditure above a minimum level have to be authorized by the president. Thus the level of the president's interest in, and commitment to, the pursuit of improved energy efficiency is critical to the acceptance or rejection of a specific energy conservation investment proposal. As a consequence, the engineering function is extremely careful in how "it packages and presents proposals to the president" (and to plant management). A number of comments seem warranted with respect to the last point.

1. The recognition by members of the engineering function that how it presented proposals to management has an effect on the manner in which they are reviewed, suggests that factors other than economic criteria influence their acceptance or rejection. The senior plant engineer in the independent firm indicated that investment proposals which did not meet the accepted payback standard might still be accepted if it could be shown that they possessed some non-energy related benefits.

2. The engineering function's concern with "packaging" energy conservation projects which would most likely be compatible with the "interests" of management suggests that factors other than economic criteria alone also enter into the processes by which the engineering function itself develops and evaluates energy conservation ideas (this point will be addressed in the next part of this section).

3. The above two points suggest that the concept of "learning by experience" or "learning by doing" may be relevant from an organization decision making process perspective in the analysis of firms' efforts to improve their energy efficiency. The engineering function

learns by experience how management appraises investment projects.
This knowledge in turn becomes factored into the engineering function's
decisions on which energy conservation ideas merit close scrutiny and
development into potential investment projects.

It is evident from the above discussion that a number of organizational functions and roles interact in energy conservation decision making. What is more critical from the point of view of which
energy conservation ideas get developed into specific project proposals,
and then get approved and implemented, is the apparent divergency in
the perceptions, expectations, and criteria applied by different organizational roles. It is to the role of organizational interaction and
the impact of these divergent perspectives on the generation and evaluation of energy conservation investment ideas that we now turn.

Energy Conservation Idea
Generation and Evaluation

A major theme of the discussion so far has been the central
role of the engineering function in energy conservation decision making.
Perhaps the critical component of the role of the engineering function
in both these firms is its role in the generation and initial evaluation
of energy conservation project ideas as has been mentioned previously
(see Figure VII-3).

Figure VII-4 is an attempt to identify the main sources of energy conservation ideas and the channels by which they are captured or impress themselves upon members of the engineering function. There are
both external and internal sources of energy conservation project ideas.
Both firms mentioned that conference meetings with members of their

FIGURE VII-4

FACTORS WHICH AFFECT FIRMS' SEARCH FOR AND EVALUATION OF
ENERGY CONSERVATION AND EFFICIENCY IMPROVEMENT INVESTMENTS

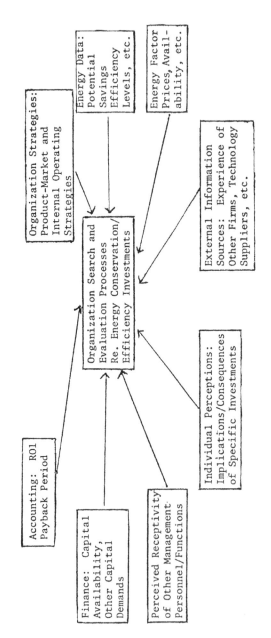

competitive firms and interactions with fellow engineers and other technical personnel was a fruitful source of energy conservation ideas. Other sources of external information which were considered useful were mostly non-personal; the professional and trade press being considered the most important. The independent firm had found manufacturers of energy conservation technologies a very valuable source of ideas on how to improve energy efficiency whereas the division suggested that such suppliers were of relatively little assistance.

The engineering function not only serves the "information gate-keeping" role with respect to external information but also performs a similar role in relation to internal energy related information. As mentioned in the previous section, it is the responsibility of the engineering function in both firms to develop whatever data on energy utilization is deemed necessary for energy management decision making. Through monitoring energy consumption patterns and the implementation of special energy audits (this is especially so in the case of the division) the engineering function is able to determine areas of potential energy savings. The division's Energy Management Coordinator has attempted to develop a crude index of potential energy savings by comparing theoretical levels of energy efficiency and actual levels of energy efficiency for some "self-contained major end-use points" (e.g., boilers, furnaces).

Identifying areas of inefficient energy utilization provides a stimulus to and a focus for firms' search patterns with respect to ways and means of improving energy efficiency. At this stage the engineering function knows what it wants to achieve (i.e., specified levels of energy efficiency at specific end-use points) but not how to achieve it. It is now that the members of the engineering staff can engage in a focused search of the external sources of information mentioned earlier for energy conserving technologies and processes.

Another source of energy conservation ideas that was reported by both firms is organizational interaction between members of the engineering function themselves and between the engineering function and other management areas. Engineering staff which do not have an energy focus in their responsibilities were identified as being occasionally the source of identification of areas of inefficient energy consumption and/or potentially applicable energy conservation technologies or processes. In both firms, the engineering function was able to point to specific instances where the president, plant manager or some other organizational member from outside the engineering function had requested an appraisal of a specific energy conservation idea, technology or process.

Since those interviewed within the engineering function in both firms indicated that not all energy conservation ideas which are considered, actually emerge as investment proposals for management appraisal, what factors can be identified which seem to have a significant influence on how energy conservation investment ideas are evaluated within the engineering function? As shown in Figure VII-4, three principal sources of influence seem to be dominant: (1) the extent of the merits or demerits of the proposed investment project as reflected in the evidence accumulated from sources external to the firm;

(2) the extent of the projected energy savings or improvement in energy efficiency; and (3) the engineering function's perception of management's receptivity to proposed energy investment projects.

Any one of these sources of influence by itself may be sufficient to lead to the rejection of a proposed investment idea while a relatively high rating on each of these three dimensions will usually be necessary for the full investigation and development of an energy conservation idea. For instance, if the engineering function learns from a professional or trade association report or member, or its acquaintances in similar firms or other external sources that a particular energy conservation technology or process has had less than favorable results, its chances of being proposed by the engineering function for implementation are very low unless the engineering function's own estimates of the potential energy savings by adopting the proposed conservation idea are very high and/or the engineering function has reason to believe that management is keenly interested in evaluating the merits of the proposed conservation idea.

Perhaps the most nebulous but nonetheless an apparently significant influence on which energy conservation ideas are pursued by the engineering function is how it perceives management's receptivity to energy conservation projects. How the engineering function perceives, and thus predicts, management receptivity to a specific energy conservation project is based on its perception and/or knowledge of a number of indicators or measures: the expected ROI or required payback period; the extent of discretionary capital funds for investment projects and how management has historically apportioned such funds; the firm's strategies and objectives as well as the goals of the other management functions; past experience of management acceptance and/or rejection of proposed energy conservation projects; and commitment of the president to the improvement of energy efficiency. Needless to say, there need not be any consistency or agreement among these perceptions with respect to any given proposed conservation project. Each one of these factors was mentioned by some member of the two firms' engineering staffs as being important in determining which projects were presented to management for approval and, also, how these projects were packaged and presented.

All of these factors--external information, projected energy savings and perceived management receptivity--are factored into the engineering function's ongoing screening or evaluation of potential energy conservation ideas. However, what the relative influence of these factors is, in decisions by members of the engineering function to accept or reject energy conservation project ideas is a question which can only be answered by further research.

As was pointed out in the discussion on decision making roles in energy management, the engineering function must work in close liaison with plant management, the accounting/finance function and especially the president, if it is to realize its responsibility, i.e., improve the firm's level of energy efficiency. The role of these other management levels and functions in the evaluation of energy conservation projects was also discussed. Thus, the factors which non-engineering personnel appraise in their evaluation of energy conservation technologies and processes must also be considered. If we consider the roles of the president, plant management, and engineering function as a combined organization search and evaluation process, a number of factors (as shown in Figure V.II-5) can be identified as having some influence on the initiation and evaluation phases of energy conservation decision making. It will be observed that many of these factors have been discussed in relation to the role of the engineering function in energy conservation idea generation and evaluation.

Summary/Conclusion

A number of conclusions can be drawn from this general discussion of energy management decision making.

1. Energy conservation decision making in medium-sized firms (i.e., annual sales between 10 and 100 million dollars) is a reasonably complex activity: a number of individuals and/or functional areas are involved and a wide range of influences affect these decisions.

2. The engineering function plays the major role in the initiation and development of energy conservation investment proposals. Almost all of the ideas which eventually materialize as energy conservation investment proposals originate within the engineering function.

3. The other major actors in the generation and evaluation of potential energy conservation investments are the president, or chief executive officer, operations/plant management and the finance/accounting function. Their role is largely the evaluation of energy conservation proposals developed by the engineering function; only rarely do they originate potential investment ideas.

4. The different perspectives brought to bear by these individuals/groups upon energy management decision making is reflected in

FIGURE VII-5

ENERGY CONSERVATION INVESTMENT IDEA GENERATION AND
EVALUATION WITHIN THE ENGINEERING FUNCTION

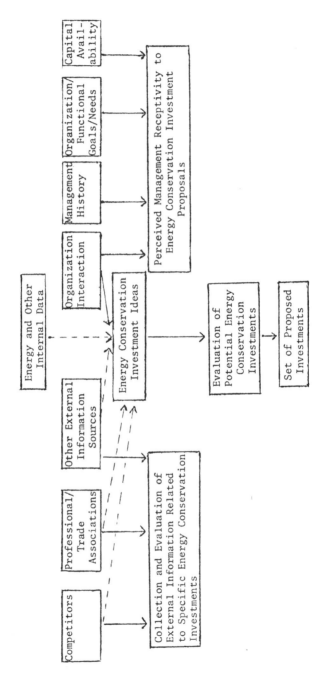

the conflictual nature of the criteria which they apply in the assessment of energy conservation investment proposals.

5. In recognition of these conflictual interests, the engineering function is careful in how it "packages" and presents proposals to management.

6. The last two points suggest that factors other than economic/financial criteria influence the acceptance or rejection of proposals. They also indicate that "learning by doing" may be relevant in the analysis of firms' efforts to improve their energy efficiency: the engineering function learns by experience how management appraises energy conservation investment projects, and this knowledge, in turn, becomes factored into the engineering function's decisions on which energy conservation investment ideas ought to be presented to management as potential investments.

7. A wide variety of both internal and external sources of potential energy conservation investment ideas are evident in both firms.

8. Three factors seem to have a significant influence on the evaluation of energy conservation investment ideas within the engineering function: (1) the favorableness of information gathered from sources external to the firm; (2) the extent of projected energy savings; and (3) the perception of management receptivity to the proposed project.

A low rating on any one of these dimensions could be sufficient to lead to the rejection of a potential energy conservation investment idea.

9. If the president, operations/plant management and the engineering function are considered as an organizational search and evaluation system for energy conservation investments, a large number of factors emerge as having some influence on the initiation and evaluation of such investments. The relative importance of these factors in relation to different energy conservation investments and in different energy management situations is a task which needs to be undertaken in future research.

In summary, this chapter has qualitatively examined energy management decision making processes in the smaller sized firms. Further support emerged for the major findings in the hypotheses/propositions testing, i.e., that divisions demonstrate a higher degree of strategic responsiveness in their approach to energy management than independent firms. A high degree of variance is evident in the extent to which firms engage in energy management: even firms within the same SIC group can adopt different energy management approaches. Energy management decision making is reasonably complex (i.e., it involves a number of management levels and functions) and a broad range of factors can influence energy related decisions.

Whereas this chapter has provided a descriptive analysis of energy management in the smaller-sized firms, in the next chapter we turn to the process of energy management decision making in large multidivisional firms.

[1]This is how SIC 3221, Glass Containers, is defined in
Standard Industrial Classifications, Office of Management and Budget,
Washington, D.C., 1972.

[2]This is how SIC 3442, Fabricated Structural Metal, is defined
in Standard Industrial Classifications, Office of Management and Budget,
Washington, D.C., 1972.

CHAPTER EIGHT

ENERGY MANAGEMENT IN LARGE MULTIDIVISIONAL FIRMS

This chapter examines energy management decision making in large multidivisional firms. The predominant focus is energy management decision making at corporate headquarters level.

The specific purpose of the chapter is to highlight the major features of the energy management approaches adopted by the study sample's eleven large corporations. For a number of reasons, the hypotheses and specific propositions underlying this study will not be tested in the case of large multidivisional firms: (1) the average annual growth rate of these firms is highly clustered (eight of the eleven firms had an annual growth rate between eleven and fourteen percent); (2) although little difficulty was experienced in determining whether these firms were energy intensive or non-energy intensive (using the criteria established in Chapter 2) two factors emerged in the course of the in-person interviews which ought to be kept in mind in any interpretation of energy intensity as an independent variable: (a) a high variance in energy intensity across divisions was true for most firms; (b) even among the firms labelled "energy intensive" a high degree of variance is evident in the degree of energy intensity (one firm estimated that energy costs as a percentage of total operating costs was 7-8 percent while another firm estimated that the same fraction was of the order of 22-23 percent); (3) with regard to the structure variable, the average size (in terms of dollar sales) of the large multidivisional firms is so large in comparison to that of the sample divisions and independent firms that it makes little sense to compare them.

This chapter is divided into two sections: the first section provides a descriptive analysis of the main features of the energy management approach of the sample's large multidivisional firms along the six (6) EMD's; and the second section details the energy management decision making system in the two firms which have developed the most comprehensive and systematic approach to energy management.

An Overview of Energy Management
In Large Multidivisional Firms

This section provides a summary of the findings on energy
management in large multidivisional firms along each of the six (6)
EMD. Its specific purpose is to highlight the critical features of
the energy management approaches adopted by these firms and, where
possible, provide some explanation for the choice of approach.

EMD1: Organization of Energy Management

All of the large multidivisional firms studied have, in varying degrees, established a specific organizational function or process
to formulate and implement energy management. Each firm has clearly
assigned energy management roles and responsibilities at corporate
headquarters. The nature of these managerial roles, tasks, and responsibilities and the process of interaction between different management
levels/groups at corporate headquarters and divisions will be discussed
in the following section.

Assignment of Energy Management Roles and Responsibilites

As is shown in Table VIII-1, all eleven firms have placed corporate responsibility for energy management in one management position.
However, the level of this position within the corporate hierarchy and
whether or not energy management is a full-time position clearly varies
from one firm to another.

TABLE VIII-1

ORGANIZATION FOR ENERGY MANAGEMENT IN LARGE
MULTIDIVISIONAL FIRMS: A SUMMARY

Elements of Organization for Energy Management \ Firms	1	2	3	4	5	6	7	8	9	10	11
Specific individual is charged with responsibility for corporate energy management	x	x	x	x	x	x	x	x	x	x	x
Individual is charged with corporate energy management responsibility reports to president	x	x									
Corporate energy management is a full-time position for individual charged with corporate energy management responsibility	x	x	x	x	x	x	x	x	x	x	x
Full-time energy management position which reports to individual with responsibility for corporate energy management	x	x	x	x	x	x	x				
Individual charged with corporate energy management responsibility has at least one other full-time (equivalent) support staff	x	x	x	x	x	x	x				
Energy management committee coordinates corporate wide energy management activity	x	x	x	x	x	x	x	x			

Two firms have established a full-time position entitled, "Director of Energy Affairs." In each case, the Director of Energy Affairs reports directly to the president. A number of support staff report directly to the Director of Energy Affairs (the energy management decision making system in these two firms will be evaluated in the next section).

In the remaining nine firms, a high ranking member of the firm (e.g., Senior Vice President of Operations, Director of Engineering, Director of Construction Technology) is charged with responsibility for development and implementation of the energy management function. Although in each of these firms the position which is held accountable for overall corporate energy management is one which directly reports to the president, it is not one which allows the incumbent to devote one hundred percent of his attention to energy management. The estimates by these individuals of the amount of their time devoted to energy management ranged from thirty to eighty percent. In each case, it was claimed that energy management was entirely compatible with their other functions.

In order to facilitate implementation of their energy management responsibilities, five of these individuals have established full-time energy management positions within their departments/functions. The role of the individuals (nominally) charged with responsibility for energy management is largely reduced to policy formulation and characterized by a large dependence on input from the full-time management position. In these firms, day-to-day corporate energy management revolves around these full-time positions (e.g., monitoring divisional energy consumption patterns, appraising energy efficiency at the plant level, determining divisions' susceptibility to energy shortages, etc.). In all five firms, each full-time energy manager also has a full-time and part-time support staff; one energy manager estimated that he had the equivalent of seven (7) full-time personnel assisting him in energy management activities.

The individual charged with energy management responsibility in one firm did not believe that a full-time energy management position was necessary. It was his contention that as a group vice president for operations he was in the best position to discharge a corporate energy management function; however, he did have "special assistants" in the engineering and accounting/finance functions. Also, it was asserted that the effective functioning of the energy management com-mittee contributed to rendering unnecessary the establishment of a full-time energy management position at corporate headquarters.

All eight of the firms discussed above have established an energy management committee (EMC) to coordinate and integrate energy management activities at corporate headquarters and between it and the divisions (see Table VIII-1). The composition of the EMC varies con-siderably among firms; however, it usually consists of the individual charged with the responsibility for corporate energy management (most often as chairperson), the full-time energy manager and/or some other full-time energy staff assistant(s), representatives from engineering, operations, R and D, accounting/finance, and, in most firms, represen-tatives from some specialized areas (e.g., construction technology, facilities planning, etc.) The role of the EMC in corporate energy management will be more fully discussed in the next section.

Thus it is evident from the above that eight of the eleven firms studied have taken a centralized approach to energy management: the firms energy management efforts are planned, controlled and monitored at corporate headquarters; divisional autonomy in energy matters is severely circumscribed (this will be even more evident when the energy management decision making system in large multidivisional firms is discussed). The reasons cited by these firms as to why they have established an energy management function and have chosen a centralized energy management approach are basically similar (although, of course, different reasons tended to be emphasized by different firms):

1. Energy has become a much more significant cost factor since the early 1970s. Many of these large multidivisional firms indicated that energy costs had risen more rapidly than either raw material costs or labor costs since the early 1970s.

2. Energy supply could no longer be taken for granted. To ensure an adequate energy supply and to distribute available energy supplies most equitably and in the best interests of the firm was not something which could be left to the discretion of the divisions.

3. The vertically integrated nature of the divisions of some firms meant that it was more critical for some divisions than for others to suffer energy shortages. Again it was contended that (re)distribution of available energy supplies in times of scarcity--a position which a number of firms had faced--could best be affected in the interests of the overall corporation by management at corporate headquarters.

4. Energy management is seen by most of these firms as of such critical importance for corporate economic well-being that it is necessary to delineate energy management responsibilities as a separate function or set of activities. Energy management is not something which can simply be added on to an existing organizational function: it cuts across many lines of authority and functional areas. As phrased by one of the interviewees "energy management, to be effective, requires its own set of independent advocates."

5. Some interviewees considered that extensive organizational economies of scale were realized through the establishment of an energy management function at corporate headquarters. Although implementation of energy management would always be a divisional task, the corporate energy management group could provide many useful inputs to the divisional efforts and also, avoid unnecessary overlapping of activities at the divisional level. For instance, monitoring the federal government's energy policies, regulations, etc., is performed by the corporate headquarters group, and divisional implications are identified and brought to the attention of appropriate divisional personnel.

However, despite the apparent force of logic in the above arguments in favor of centralized energy management, three firms are very emphatic in their intent not to centralize energy management at corporate headquarters. It is the contention of each of these firms that all phases of energy management could best be affected in a decentralized manner: the individual divisions are in a better position to manage energy and, thus, the role of corporate headquarters should be limited to that of reviewing divisional efforts through their normal planning and reporting process. A high ranking member of each firm (Corporate Treasurer, Director of Engineering and Environment, and Vice President for Operations) is charged with responsibility for corporate energy management. None of these individuals has a full-time energy management assistant; each could request assistance from specified individuals at corporate headquarters. The amount of their time devoted to energy management was estimated to be relatively small by each individual (not more than twenty-five or thirty percent).

The role of these individuals in corporate energy management would seem to be threefold:

1. reporting to the president and interested outside parties (e.g., federal agencies) the status of the firm's corporate management efforts);

2. assisting divisions with major energy management decisions (e.g., what would be the corporate implications of major energy conversion programs);

3. disseminating to the division relevant energy information, either from internal or external sources (e.g., corporate implications of new federal regulations).

All three firms do not see any merit in establishing an EMC; not enough energy management activity occurred at corporate headquarters to justify the establishment of another corporate committee.

Although each of these firms is in a predominantly energy intensive industry, energy supply and energy utilization are not perceived as sufficiently critical for corporate economic well-being that energy management should be centralized at corporate headquarters. It is suggested by all three firms that energy management as a divisional task was not much different from many of their other management concerns.

Summary

Energy management in eight firms is highly centralized with clearly defined roles and responsibilities at corporate headquarters. Formal energy management functions have emerged and are now an established feature of corporate management in a number of large multidivisional firms. However, some firms, in keeping with their general management strategies, have chosen a decentralized energy management approach: wherever possible, energy management is an activity which takes place at the divisional level.

Energy Management Targets/
Objectives

Seven of the eleven corporations have established at corporate headquarters energy management targets/objectives for the entire corporation (see Table VIII-2). The overall corporate objectives are, in most cases, stated in very general terms, for example, "[to] improve energy utilization per ton of output by ten percent over a five year period."

Almost all of the large firm interviewees mentioned the difficulties involved in developing overall corporate energy efficiency improvement objectives (e.g., different product lines, manufacturing processes, individual accounting systems, variances in energy data availability at individual plants, etc.). Although not explicitly stated by all firms which had established overall corporate objectives,

TABLE VIII-2

ESTABLISHMENT OF ENERGY MANAGEMENT OBJECTIVES/TARGETS
IN LARGE MULTIDIVISIONAL FIRMS: A SUMMARY

Critical features of Objective/Targets Setting \ Firms	Centralized approach to Energy Management								Decentralized Approach to Energy Management		
	1	2	3	4	5	6	7	8	9	10	11
General energy management objectives are established for entire corporation	x	x	x	x	x	x	x				
Energy management targets are established at division level	x	x	x	x	x	x	x	x			
Establishment of targets is a systematic part of divisional energy management	x	x	x								
Establishment of targets at divisional level is an "ad hoc" process				x	x				x	x	

it seems fair to suggest that such objectives have as their primary function the motivation of corporate efforts to improve energy efficiency; an objective or goal becomes a benchmark against which to approximately measure corporate energy management performance.

The four firms which did not establish an overall corporate objective cited some of the reasons identified above for not doing so as well as their strong conviction that objectives were best established by those who would have the responsibility of achieving them, i.e., the divisions.

All eleven firms suggested that energy management targets (i.e., specific attainable goals) were established at the divisional level. Only three firms would go so far as to suggest that such targets were developed in a systematic and continuous manner by all the divisions. For the other eight firms, the specificity of the targets and process of developing them tended to vary widely from firm to firm and even between divisions of individual firms. Four firms (including two decentralized ones) indicated that the process of establishing energy management targets and the targets themselves was largely "ad hoc": divisions did so if they felt it was necessary.

In summary, a high degree of variance is evident in the extent to which firms establish specific energy management objectives and targets. Given, that this variance does exist, a critical question for future research to examine is whether the existence of such objectives/targets leads to better energy management performance.

EMD2:   Energy Data Base and Monitoring
        Process

As is evident from Table VIII-3, there is a wide diversity in
the approach of the sample firms at corporate headquarters level to the
collection and analysis of divisional and other energy data. Six firms
(all with centralized energy management) considered that the data
assembled by their corporate energy staffs was sufficient for effective
corporate-wide energy management, i.e., monitoring and assessing divisional performance in improving energy efficiency. Five of these six
firms and one firm with a decentralized approach to energy management
have established what they believe is a relatively systematic approach
to energy data collection and analysis: (1) they conduct at least an
annual audit of divisional energy management performance; (2) some
attempt is made to establish divisional energy efficiency measures;
(3) specific individuals at corporate headquarters are charged with
responsibility for energy data collection and analysis; (4) regular
meetings have been established between corporate headquarters personnel and division management; (5) some firms require divisions to
develop a formal energy management plan (see next part of this section--
Management Accountability).

Although this study has not attempted to assess the quality
or consistency of the energy data collected at corporate headquarters
level or how effectively such data are utilized, it is clear that
approximately half the sample firms consider energy data collection
of such importance in effective corporate-wide energy management that
they have established specific processes to facilitate data collection
and its integration into corporate energy management decision making.

TABLE VIII-3

ENERGY DATA GENERATION AND ANALYSIS IN LARGE
MULTIDIVISIONAL FIRMS: A SUMMARY

Critical Features of Data Generation and Analysis	Centralized Approach to Energy Management								Decentralized Approach to Energy Management		
	1	2	3	4	5	6	8	8	9	10	11
Firms which consider they have access to sufficient data for energy management	x	x	x	x	x	x					
Continuous appraisal of divisional energy data at corporate headquarters	x	x	x	x	x				x		
Little organized effort todate to develop corporate wide energy data base						x	x	x	x	x	
Firms which indicated they were beginning to develop a more formal approach to energy data collection and analysis							x	x	x	x	

On the other hand, approximately half the sample firms have to date made little effort in the direction of establishing a systematic approach to corporate energy data collection and utilization at corporate headquarters level. A number of reasons were cited for the haphazard nature of these firms' energy information gathering efforts at corporate headquarters: (1) one firm considered that it had sufficient and appropriate data for effective corporate energy management without engaging in any formal organizational activities specifically designed to collect and analyze energy data. In comparison with the organized approach to energy data collection and analysis of the firms discussed above, the question of whether this firm actually has appropriate and sufficient data for energy management is perhaps subject to dispute; (2) two firms in particular did not see much merit in establishing a corporate energy accounting system at corporate headquarters. It was contended that such data would best be utilized at the division level; the detailed data required for effective divisional energy management was not required at corporate headquarters. In effect, these firms employ "management by exception" in their corporate energy (data) management: only when a major problem is evident at the divisional level will corporate headquarters make a substantial effort to collect and evaluate whatever energy data the division can make available; (3) related to the previous point, is the belief expressed by some firms (especially by the firms with a decentralized approach to energy management) that energy management implementation is predominantly a divisional function. Corporate headquarter's role is that of motivating, coordinating, and providing direction of divisional energy efficiency improvement programs, and disseminating information which might not otherwise be available to the divisions (e.g., the implications of federal energy policy). To achieve these purposes, it was suggested by many of the interviewees that detailed divisional energy data were not required.

It is important to note that four (4) of the five (5) firms which had shown the strongest antipathy towards energy data collection and analysis at corporate headquarters indicated they were beginning to develop a more formal approach to the question of energy information, particularly with regard to energy information sources external to the firm. Each firm had already assigned a staff assistant (or indicated that it was planning to do so) to monitor governmental policies and regulations and identify their implications for the firm. In no case, would this be a full time position.

In summary, a wide degree of difference exists among the sample firms as to the extent of energy relevant data which is required at corporate headquarters for effective corporate energy management. A partial explanation for this difference is whether firms have adopted a centralized or decentralized approach to corporate energy management.

EMD3: Management Accountability

Seven firms (six with a centralized approach to energy management and one with a decentralized approach) indicated that energy management was an element of line management's accountability in all or most divisions (see Table VIII-4). It should be noted that most large firm interviewees had difficulty in detailing how divisional

TABLE VIII-4

LINE MANAGEMENT ACCOUNTABILITY FOR ENERGY MANAGEMENT
IN LARGE MULTIDIVISIONAL FIRMS: A SUMMARY

Critical features of Management Accountability \ Firms	Centralized Approach to Energy Management								Decentralized Approach to Energy Management		
	1	2	3	4	5	6	7	8	9	10	11
Line management clearly accountable for energy management in all or most divisions	x	x	x	x	x	x			x		
Corporate Headquarters formally evaluates divisional energy consumption, efficiency trends, etc.	x	x	x	x	x	x	x	x	x		
Divisions must submit a formal plan for energy management/efficiency improvement	x	x	x	x					x	x	
Energy management considerations are an established component of divisions planning/ budgeting process	x	x			x				x	x	
Corporate headquarters is primarily concerned with divisional capital requirements for energy efficiency improvement						x	x	x			x

management was held accountable for its energy management, i.e., the process by which corporate headquarters evaluated the energy management effectiveness of divisional management.

However, it is apparent that the process by which divisional energy management accountability is operationalized varies considerably across the sample firms. With the exception of two decentralized firms, corporate headquarters monitors divisional energy consumption, trends, etc., with a view to developing appropriate energy efficiency measures. Most firms pointed out that such divisional energy efficiency measures were often very crude and were not intended to assess management's effectiveness in controlling energy costs.

Accountability is formalized in four centralized and two decentralized firms through the submission of a separate plan to headquarters which details management's approach to energy efficiency improvement. Again the level of detail and the manner in which these plans are reviewed varies considerably among these firms. The energy management plan is usually formulated by a divisional energy specialist and reviewed by the energy management group at corporate headquarters.

Most of the firms which require the divisions to submit some kind of energy management plan indicated that energy management was an integral part of most divisions' planning/budgeting processes. In other words, accountability for energy management is implicit in division's planning/budgeting scheme.

In four firms it is difficult to see what formal accountability for energy management exists, if any. These firms' primary concern with divisional energy management is the extent of the capital budget requirements for energy efficiency improvements. It is, thus, an "ad hoc" approach to evaluating (in some detail) divisional energy management efforts as distinct from their normal division performance appraisal and management evaluation processes.

In view of the different approaches to operationalizing divisional energy management accountability, a fruitful research focus would be to examine the relationship between different methods of divisional energy management performance appraisal (e.g., development of an energy management plan, energy management as another element in the division's regular planning/budgeting process, evaluation only of energy related capital expenditure as opposed to inclusion of "housekeeping" programs, etc.) and the extent of energy efficiency improvements realized by divisions or the type and extent of divisional energy efficiency improvement investment/programs.

EMD4: Energy Efficiency Improvement
        Programs/Investments

All of the firms interviewed indicated that most divisions had made capital investments to improve the energy efficiency of their manufacturing/production processes. However, the extent to which corporate headquarters personnel became involved in the formulation and assessment of such investments varied dramatically from one firm to another; some interviewees (particularly in firms with decentralized energy management) experienced some difficulty in detailing the nature and extent of divisional energy efficiency improvement investments. Thus, in some firms a much clearer picture of energy related investment behavior would have been gained had divisional executives also been interviewed.

Investments/Programs to Improve
Manufacturing/Production Process
Efficiency

Eight of the eleven firms interviewed suggested that production/
manufacturing process related energy efficiency improvements were in
most cases a consequence of production/manufacturing process changes for
other purposes (see Table VIII-5). In other words, energy efficiency
improvement, in and of itself, is not considered sufficient justifica-
tion by a majority of the sample firms for modification of production/
manufacturing processes.

Three energy intensive firms indicated they have made very substantial capital expenditures specifically to improve energy efficiency;
although it was considered an impossibility to place a dollar figure on
the total of such investments, each firm was able to identify a number
of investments which required capital outlays in excess of one million
dollars.

Three firms have made very few capital expenditures specifically to improve energy efficiency. Two of these firms are non-energy
intensive; the potential for manufacturing/production process energy
efficiency improvement related investments which would realize significant cost savings was perceived as very small.

All firms indicated that major energy related capital expenditures would normally be reviewed by corporate headquarters personnel.
In five firms (four energy intensive and one non-energy intensive)
energy related capital investments were of sufficient significance
that they were an explicit component of most divisions' annual capital

TABLE VIII-5

ENERGY EFFICIENCY IMPROVEMENT PROGRAMS/INVESTMENTS
IN LARGE MULTIDIVISIONAL FIRMS: A SUMMARY

Critical Features of EEI Programs	Centralized Approach To Energy Management								Decentralized Approach To Energy Management		
	1	2	3	4	5	6	7	8	9	10	11
Most divisions have modified production/ manufacturing processes to improve energy efficiency	x	x	x	x	x	x	x	x	x	x	x
Energy efficiency improvement is most often a consequence of production/manufacturing process changes for other purposes	x	x	x	x	x	x			x	x	
Very few capital expenditures are specifically to improve energy efficiency	x	x									x
Energy efficiency improvement is an explicit component of most divisions capital expenditures program			x	x	x		x	x			
"Housekeeping" programs receive little attention at corporate headquarters	x		x	x			x	x	x	x	x

expenditure programs. The criteria applied in assessing energy related
investments differs widely among firms (see next part of this section--
energy conservation investment criteria) as also, does the organizational
process involved in assessing these investments (see next section).

Energy "housekeeping" cost control programs either receive minimal attention at corporate headquarters (eight firms) or they are a
major component of corporate headquarter's energy related activities.
In a majority of firms, although many divisions have such programs in
operation, it was generally felt by the interviewees that it was inappro-
priate and unnecessary for corporate headquarters to be involved, largely for two reasons: (1) "housekeeping" programs were of a wide variety
and usually involved relatively little capital outlay; (2) the potential
energy savings attributable to "housekeeping" efforts was perceived
as being small (relative to that which might accrue to capital expenditures) and, in some cases, it was suggested that such savings had already been largely achieved.

In three firms "housekeeping" programs are a major thrust of
the energy management function at corporate headquarters. It is, perhaps, in these three firms that energy management is most clearly centralized at corporate headquarters. The energy management function
personnel in all three firms are involved in developing, monitoring
and assessing division energy "housekeeping" programs. For one firm,
"housekeeping" programs constitute the main component of the corporate
head office energy function activities; this firm has estimated that
heating, ventilation and lighting account for approximately thirty
percent of its total energy costs.

Further research is required to assess the impact of corporate headquarters on the investment decision process within divisions, e.g., does a centralized approach to energy management result in more capital intensive energy efficiency improvement investments by divisions?

Energy Conservation
Investment Criteria

All firms have clearly prescribed and disseminated investment criteria by which energy conservation/supply investment proposals are evaluated. In all cases, interviewees were able to specify in detail the nature of the economic criteria which energy related investments must meet.

Most firms indicated they endeavored to have common investment criteria applied by each division. The specific investment criteria applied was dependent upon the firm in question. Some firms chose after-tax criteria while others prefer before-tax criteria. In terms of "payback" period and ROI, the investment appraisal criteria ranged from two (2) years and/or forty percent before tax to six (6) years and/or fifteen percent after tax.

Economic and financial criteria (ROI, payback period) were stressed by all firms as primary: unless an investment met the firm's economic/financial standards it would not be accepted under any circumstances. Indeed, many interviewees, when questioned directly, went so far as to suggest that energy efficiency investment analysis was exclusively an economic process: unless an investment was clearly profitable it would quickly be dismissed from further consideration.

However, upon further questioning, it becomes evident that the application of standard economic/financial criteria to energy conservation/supply investment evaluation is not a straightforward exercise. Even in the most energy intensive firms, it was suggested by many interviewees that investments to improve energy efficiency must be made within the context of many considerations: for example, "Will the investment impede the flow of product," "How will it affect product quality?" "Will it significantly reduce product cost?" Thus, firms were able to identify investments which satisfied their standard economic criteria but which were not implemented for reasons similar to those just mentioned.

What may be of more significance for the level of investment in energy efficiency improvement is not the absolute level of the criteria but whether they differ from the criteria applied to other types of investment. Only two firms indicated that there was occasionally a difference: in both firms the criteria applied to energy conservation investment proposals may be more lenient than they would be for other investments. In both firms the primary reason for the occasional application of more lenient criteria was rapidly rising energy prices and, particularly, projected continuance of increasing energy prices. One of these firms also indicated that investment proposals which would help ensure a continued energy supply (e.g., investment in energy conversion) were also subjected to more lenient criteria. Both firms argued that given expected energy price increases over the next one to ten years, investments which might be assessed as non-profitable now, would be profitable in a few years time.

In consideration of the importance of energy conservation/ supply investment evaluation criteria, at least two major questions need to be clarified by further research studies: (1) what is the relative importance of the different factors (i.e., financial/economic and others) which influence the assessment of energy conservation/supply investment proposals; and (2) how does the importance accorded to the factors differ between corporate headquarters and divisions.

EMD5: Research and Development Programs

The importance accorded to energy efficiency by the sample's large multidivisional firms is evidenced in the extent to which firms have focused their R and D efforts on improving production/manufacturing process energy efficiency.

As shown in Table VIII-6, in three (energy intensive) firms (all with centralized energy management), improving production/manufacturing process energy efficiency was described as a major focus of their R and D programs. In each case it was the high cost of energy (as a proportion of total operating costs) that was seen as the major reason for R and D preoccupation with energy efficiency. Another factor which was seen as facilitating R and D orientation toward energy efficiency improvement is that each firm's R and D efforts are largely focused on improving production/manufacturing process efficiency; one firm suggested that even when its R and D program was primarily concerned with new product development, a major consideration would be production/ manufacturing process efficiency.

TABLE VIII-6

R & D PROGRAMS AND ENERGY EFFICIENCY IMPROVEMENT IN
LARGE MULTIDIVISIONAL FIRMS: A SUMMARY

Critical Features of R & D Programs	Centralized Approach To Energy Management								Decentralized Approach To Energy Management		
Firms	1	2	3	4	5	6	7	8	9	10	11
Improvement production/ manufacturing process energy efficiency is a major focus of firms' R & D programs	x	x	x								
Improving production; manufacturing process energy efficiency is a minor focus of firms' R & D programs				x	x					x	x
R & D efforts have already led to some energy improvements in production/manufacturing process energy efficiency	x	x	x	x	x					x	x
Energy efficiency improvements are a consequence of new or improved production/manufacturing processes	x	x			x						

Three more energy intensive firms and one non-energy intensive firm suggested that production/manufacturing process energy efficiency was a minor focus of their R and D programs. In each of these firms R and D was more product oriented than in the three firms which were discussed above. However, all four firms were able to indicate R and D projects where energy efficiency improvement had been a major consideration.

The output of the R and D programs in each of these seven firms has led to major improvements in production/manufacturing process energy efficiency. The recycling of raw materials has led to major energy savings in two firms; three firms cited cases where R and D teams were established specifically to investigate potential energy efficiency improvements at some major energy consuming point in the production/manufacturing process (e.g., boilers, furnaces, use of steam heat, etc.); in three firms, energy efficiency improvements were an outcome of new or improved production/manufacturing processes (one of these firms claimed that rising energy costs was perhaps the major reason why the firm began to reappraise "a production process which had remained basically the same for nearly twenty years").

Four firms believed that their R and D programs had little, if any, relationship with energy efficiency improvement: their R and D programs are predominantly product oriented.

The above suggests that some firm's R and D programs are very much concerned with energy efficiency enhancement. However, a number of questions (some of which are being grappled with by the firms, themselves) seem worthy of future research attention: (1) how can the R and D function be best coordinated with the production, engineering, plant management and other relevant functions in the interest of improving energy efficiency? What factors inhibit or induce R and D personnel to consider the energy implications of their recommendations? (Some interviewees intimated that R and D personnel seem to have very little awareness that energy efficiency is not a constant--it is affected by the nature of the manufacturing process.) How can the corporate energy management function influence corporate and/or division R and D function personnel to take a more active role in corporate energy management? (One DEA noted that although he considered the R and D function one of his most valuable sources of advice on many technical aspects of energy management, it was his opinion that the R and D function responded to his requests very reluctantly and often in not a very timely manner.)

EMD6: Development and Marketing of Energy Efficient Products and Services

The final aspect of energy management in large multidivisional firms which is investigated, is the extent to which energy related considerations have penetrated firms' product-market strategies. Unlike the other energy management components which have been discussed, product-market strategy considerations refer specifically to firm-environment interactions.

A majority of firms (seven of eleven) considered energy efficiency as of little, if any, relevance to their products/services (see Table VIII-7). Energy related factors were not accorded any consideration in decisions related to new product development, modification of

TABLE VIII-7

ENERGY EFFICIENCY AS AN ELEMENT IN LARGE MULTIDIVISIONAL
FIRMS PRODUCT/MARKET STRATEGIES: A SUMMARY

Firms Product/Market Components	Centralized Approach to Energy Management								Decentalized Approach to Energy Management		
	1	2	3	4	5	6	7	8	9	10	11
Modification of existing products/services to make them more energy efficient	x	x	x	x							
Customers' energy efficiency is seen as unrelated to firms' product/service lines					x	x	x	x	x	x	x
New products/services are being developed to improve customers energy efficiency	x	x	x	x							
Firms which have used/ are using energy efficiency as a selling point in their marketing activities	x	x	x								

existing products, identification and pursuit of new market segments, etc. The reasons cited for lack of concern with energy related factors in such decisions can be grouped in three categories:

1. Some firms did not believe their product lines could impact the energy efficiency of their customers' operations. Thus, firms see little point in incorporating energy related consideration into their product-market activities.

2. A number of interviewees suggested that even if their product lines did possess the potential to affect customers' energy efficiency levels, it would not be a matter of major concern to their customers (this was perceived as being especially so in the case of industrial customers). Two firms producing mostly capital intensive goods considered that their products were assessed by their industrial customers on two dimensions: price and efficiency/effectiveness in doing the job they were supposed to do. Thus, some firms at least see little "demand-pull" for the development of more energy efficient products and/or the marketing of existing products from an energy standpoint.

3. Some interviewees were particularly insistent that their firms were not in the "energy-business"--neither management nor their firms present and potential customers would consider these firms as related to the "energy business." In terms of how they defined their business(es) (e.g., "we are in business to produce and sell steel") it would seem that some firms preclude energy related considerations from their product-market activities.

Four firms (each with a centralized approach to energy management) have modified existing products and are developing new products to make them more energy efficient for their customers. It was intimated by these firms that these product development/modifications were initiated primarily and, in some cases exclusively, to improve customers' energy efficiency. For instance, one firm in the glass industry had "dramatically improved the thermo-efficiency" of many of its product lines. Another firm has improved the energy efficiency of many of its consumer durable products and, in some cases, it was claimed the product shape/size/style was altered to facilitate energy efficiency improvement.

None of these firms could be said to be in the energy conservation business, per se, i.e., manufacturing products specifically to improve energy efficiency or conserve energy (e.g., insulation materials, recycling equipment), yet, they considered they had enhanced their competitive competence by integrating energy related considerations into their product-market activities. These firms have, therefore, made some attempt to turn the so-called "energy-crisis" into an "economic opportunity." Thus, in comparing these four firms with the seven firms which perceived their product lines as being non-energy related, a number of research questions emerge which appear to warrant future research attention:

1. How do such factors as the nature of firms' product lines (e.g., steel, glass, food, etc.), type of end-use (e.g., industrial, consumer, service, etc.) affect firms' perceptions of the relationship between the energy environment and their product-market activities?

2. Why are some firms extremely concerned with improving their own level of energy efficiency but show little, if any, concern with the energy implications of their own products on their customers' operations?

Summary/Conclusion

The energy management approach adopted by the sample's large multidivisional firms, generally falls into two categories: a largely centralized energy management approach and a decentralized approach to energy management. In the three firms with decentralized energy management, the choice of energy management strategies and programs falls predominantly within the division's domain. In those firms with centralized energy management the major impetus and direction in energy management strategy-making resides within corporate headquarters. The following are some of the major findings with respect to each of the six (6) EMD.

1. Within each EMD a high degree of variance is evident among the sample firms. A partial explanation of the variance is the extent to which firms have centralized energy management (i.e., place responsibility for corporate energy management at corporate headquarters). The following highlights the findings along each EMD.

2. Approximately half the sample firms consider energy data generation and analysis of such importance in effective corporate wide energy management that they have already established specific processes to facilitate energy data collection (e.g., annual audit of division energy performance, specific individuals charged with responsibility for energy data collection and analyses, etc.) and its integration into corporate energy management decision making.

On the other hand, approximately half the sample firms have, as yet, made little effort to develop an energy data collection and analysis process at corporate headquarters level. The major reason indicated by these firms for not doing so is that energy management is seen as predominantly a division function.

3. Although it was indicated by seven (7) firms that energy management is an element in line management's accountability in all or most divisions, the process by which divisional energy management is operationalized varies considerably among the sample firms. In the other four firms, divisional energy management accountability only arises when capital budget allocations are required for energy efficiency improvement.

4. Energy efficiency improvement is rarely sufficient reason by itself to cause firms to modify their production/manufacturing processes. The volume of capital expenditures specifically to improve energy efficiency varies considerably from firm to firm: three energy intensive firms could identify a number of investments, each requiring an outlay in excess of one billion dollars; three other firms have made very few investments specifically to improve energy efficiency.

Housekeeping programs tend to be either a major component of corporate headquarters energy management activities or they receive minimal attention.

All firms have clearly prescribed economic/financial criteria by which energy related investments are appraised. However, satisfaction of such criteria does not guarantee that a proposed energy efficiency improvement investment will be implemented; such factors as the impact on product quality and cost and flow of work must be considered. In only two (2) firms were the standard economic/financial criteria occasionally made more lenient in the case of energy related investments--in both cases due to the expected continuance of rapidly rising energy prices.

5. In seven (7) of the sample's eleven firms, R and D output has led to major improvements in production/manufacturing process energy efficiency. The R and D program in each of these firms is at least partially concerned with improvement in production/manufacturing process efficiency. However, in the four firms where R and D is predominantly product oriented, R and D was seen as having little, if any, relationship with the improvement of production/manufacturing process energy efficiency.

6. Energy related factors were considered of little, if any, relevance to the development and marketing of products/services by a majority of the sample firms. The firms suggested that their product lines do not impact the energy efficiency level of their customers operations, and/or even if they did, their customers attach little importance to whether the products/services they purchase affect energy efficiency.

Four firms indicated that some product developments/modifications were initiated principally to improve customers' energy efficiency.

This section of the chapter has described the energy management response of the sample's large multidivisional firms along each

EMD. With this background in mind, we now focus on the process of energy management decision making.

Energy Management Decision Making in Large Multidivisional Firms

The previous section of this chapter outlined some of the major characteristics of energy management in large multidivisional firms with respect to each of the six (6) energy management dimensions. This section describes and discusses the process of energy management decision making. Specifically, this section will focus on two (2) related components of the energy management decision making process in large multidivisional firms: (1) a description of the energy management decision making system (EMDMS) which has evolved in firms with the most systematic and comprehensive approach to energy management; and (2) a description of the roles, responsibilities and functions of the principal individuals and committees (and their interaction) involved in energy management decision making.

The context within which the process of energy management decision making is described is the formulation and implementation of energy management strategies and programs. It is presented as a step toward answering the following questions: How do some firms establish an energy management policy? How are energy efficiency improvement strategies, objectives, and specific programs formulated? What are the organizational linkages between policies, strategies, objectives and programs? What procedures are employed to monitor

strategy and program implementation? It is these questions which will
be addressed in the analysis.

The energy management decision making process described in this
section is that of the two firms with the most systematic and developed
approach to energy management. However, where it is appropriate to the
discussion, energy management decision making processes in other firms
are also analyzed.

The Energy Management Decision Making System in Two Large Firms

The two firms which consititute the primary focus of this section
have attempted to establish a formal energy management decision making
system (EMDMS) to coordinate and integrate corporate energy decision
making activities. These are the only two (2) firms which have developed to date what may be called a systematic EMDMS. The key energy
management participants in the EMDMS are shown in Figure VIII-1. An
analysis of the EMDMS adopted by these two firms (it is largely similar
in both firms) facilitates a preliminary discussion of the roles, responsibilities and tasks implicit in each of the positions shown in
Figure VIII-1.

Figure VIII-2 is an attempt to capture the main EMDMS decision
points, their sequence and interactions. It also shows the output at
each stage of the process. As shown in Figure VIII-2, the EMDMS consists of the three phases; each phase will be discussed in turn.

EMDMS--Phase 1

Phase 1 establishes the overall framework for corporate energy
management. It primarily involves the Director of Energy Affairs (DEA)

FIGURE VIII-1

ENERGY MANAGEMENT ORGANIZATION STRUCTURE
IN LARGE MULTIDIVISIONAL FIRMS

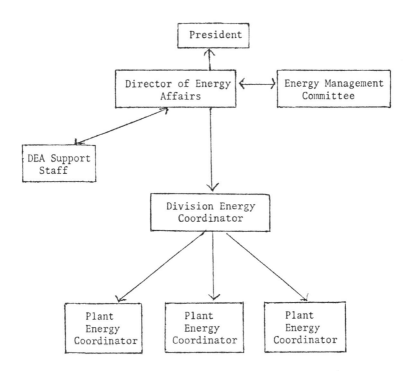

FIGURE VIII-2

ENERGY MANAGEMENT DECISION MAKING SYSTEM
IN LARGE, MULTIDIVISIONAL FIRMS

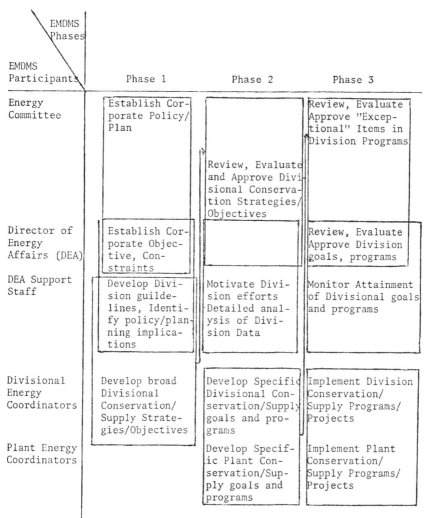

and the Energy Management Committee (EMC): thus it is largely a task performed at corporate headquarters.

The two major components of Phase 1 are: (1) to establish (or update) the corporate energy policy/planning document which entails broad energy management strategies, objectives, and constraints; and (2) to develop a broad energy management plan for each division.

The corporate energy management plan developed by the DEA and the EMC is by design, non-specific; it merely sets forth general energy management objectives, an estimate of the resources that may be available for capital expenditures, an identification and assessment of the areas where capital investment may be required, a consideration of the energy conservation and supply programs which may be required, etc. The energy management policy/plan is communicated to the DEC's (Division Energy Coordinators) and other interested division management through the medium of a "corporate energy management day": a day-long meeting attended by the DEA, the EMC, the DEA's support staff, the DECs and other interested management personnel is held at corporate headquarters to discuss the firm's energy management posture. The corporate energy policy/plan as originally developed by the DEA and the EMC constitutes the major discussion document; it can undergo substantial modification as a result of the day's deliberations.

The significance of the corporate energy policy/plan is that it provides a sense of direction for the work of the DEA's support staff and the DECs in their initial efforts to establish division energy management plans--the major output of Phase 1 and the most time-consuming part of Phase 1 activities. The divisions' broad energy management plans provide an opportunity for corporate headquarters (specifically the DEA's support staff) to review the strengths and weaknesses of the energy management approach, and also, to identify the individual energy related constraints, characteristics, and requirements of each division.

It is at this stage of the EMDMS that the DEC's, often with the assistance of their division management, try to make a special case to headquarters as to why their division requires more energy management resources, why the standard corporate investment evaluation criteria should not be applied to the division's energy conservation/supply investment proposals, etc.

The division energy management plans--the output of Phase 1-- are also intentionally general in nature. These plans represent, in outline form, the energy management objectives, strategies and overall approach which each division proposes to adopt within the appropriate EMDMS time frame. They usually include energy conservation and supply objectives, strategies to achieve these objectives, estimated energy savings, anticipated capital outlays, major internal and external constraints on energy efficiency improvement, and estimates of the extent of dependence on energy sources which might be interrupted.

EMDMS--Phase 2

The specific purpose of Phase Two of the EMDMS is to develop detailed division energy conservation and supply programs. It is a three step process:

1. First, the DEA and the EMC review, evaluate, and approve or reject the general division plans which were the output of Phase 1. The purpose of this review process is to ensure that division energy management activities are not in violation of the corporate energy policy/plan. Where inconsistencies do exist, they usually result in the DEA's office working more closely with division management and particularly with the DEC.

Discrepancies between the divisions proposed approach to energy management and the corporate policy/plan occasionally result in modifications to the corporate policy/plan. This emphasizes that the corporate policy/plan is not inflexible and that the EMDMS is not entirely a "top-down" approach to energy management.

2. The DEA and his support staff work in close conjunction with the DEC's to assist them in developing specific energy conservation and supply programs. At this stage, the principal role of the DEA's office is to spur each individual division to develop a comprehensive set of energy conservation and supply projects. Most of the large firms interviewed suggested that division energy management efforts would be less systematic were it not for these persistent inquiries and demands of the corporate headquarters management staff.

Another major role of the DEA's office is to examine all available energy related data with respect to each division, specifically the major plants of each division (e.g., the major energy sources used, energy consumption patterns, the types and results of previous energy related investments, etc.). An analysis of this type for each division

allows the DEA's office to make concrete suggestions to division management as to the type and extent of energy conservation and supply pro-
grams/projects they ought to pursue. In other words, the DEA's office
attempts to translate the proposed divisional strategies into more
specific, action-oriented programs. For instance, corporate headquarters may direct specific division plants to initiate or accelerate
their energy conservation program.

A major role of the DEA's office is the collection and dissemination of energy related information which it considers useful to
individual or all divisions, in the development and implementation
of specific energy conservation and supply programs. The source of
such information may be internal or external to the firm. Some firms
convey to DEC's, information about energy conservation or supply techniques, procedures or processes which any division may have found successful. For instance, one of these two firms distributed the detailed
results of one division's insulation program to all divisions in an
attempt to motivate those divisions to investigate the feasibility of
similar insulation programs. The DEA's office, also, often serves to
disseminate information on new energy conserving technologies to all
divisions.

3. The final step in Phase 2 is the formulation of energy
management programs by each division. This is primarily the responsibility of DEC's in conjunction with Plant Energy Coordinators (PEC's).
In most divisions other management functions such as engineering, plant
management and general management are involved in the formulation of
general programs and specific projects.

A program may contain many projects with projects varying from one plant to another. An energy conservation program to improve the energy efficiency of boilers and/or furnaces can involve many different types of investment projects ranging from a complete rebuilding of furnaces (in most cases a major capital investment project) to the installation of meters to monitor furnace/boiler energy usage.

EMDMS--Phase 3

Implementation of the energy conservation and supply programs which evolve from Phase 1 and Phase 2 is the primary focus of Phase 3. The two major segments of Phase 3 are: (1) The DEA's office reviews, evaluates and approves the divisional energy conservation and supply programs which are the output of Phase 2; and (2) Implementation of the reviewed and revised programs by the divisions.

1. A major proportion of the activities of the DEA's office is concerned with reviewing specific programs by the divisions and monitoring the implementation of such programs/projects. The DEAs interviewed (and their support staff) considered it a major part of their function to ensure that not only were division energy conservation and supply programs as comprehensive and detailed as possible, but that they were tackling the problems or opportunities which were the most effective from an energy savings perspective. The vehicle which provides the DEA's office with the best opportunity to achieve this goal is the detailed review of division energy management programs.

Major items of capital expenditure and/or programs or individual projects which the DEA's office claims are "exceptional" (e.g., a major project which the firm has not previously encountered, a program/project which the DEA's office feels is of dubious merit, etc.) are referred to the EMC for review and evaluation. In this way, the experience and viewpoints of other areas are added to that of the DEA's office.

The DEA's support staff are charged with the responsibility of monitoring the implementation of divisional programs. The monitoring process is effected through regular meetings with DECs and other relevant division management, submission of regular reports (energy consumption, data, etc.) to the DEA's office, and requests by the DEA for progress reports on major or special projects.

The concept of "organization learning" or "learning by doing" is highly relevant to this phase of the EMDMS: the DEA's support staff felt that this component of their role or responsibilities (i.e., monitoring the implementation of divisional programs) provided the most insights into "the process and the substance of energy management." For instance, in working closely with division personnel in the assessment of program success or failure, DEA support staff indicated that division personnel biases and perceptions with respect to energy management in general and specific projects in particular become evident; the nature of the covert and overt criteria applied by different division personnel becomes manifest, and, an understanding is gained of the organizational procedures involved in division energy management decision making.

2. The final phase of the EMDMS is the implementation of energy conservation and supply programs by the divisions. Energy management decision making at the divisional level, including the process of implementing energy programs, will not be discussed here, since it was covered in the previous chapter, and some comments on the role of the DEC's will be made later in this chapter.

EMDMS--Some Comments

The description of the EMDMS has highlighted the major decision points and processes in the formulation and implementation of energy management strategy. However, a number of comments on the EMDMS are warranted:

1. The evolution of the EMDMS in both firms is still in its infancy; most of those interviewed in the two firms indicated that they were (as one DEA put it) "still learning how best to do energy management."

2. The three (3) EMDMS phases and the individual steps within each phase are not as sequential as presented. Many of the activities identified occur repeatedly or are ongoing components of energy management (e.g., the EMC in its regular meetings reviews exceptional items in division programs, the DEA's office is constantly monitoring implementation of division energy management strategies and programs).

3. The EMDMS as described focuses primarily on internal energy management activities and processes, i.e., improving the firm's energy efficiency level; it does not consider external energy strategy or product-market strategies. Neither does it consider those facets of

the DEA's role which demand interfacing with the actors in the firm's environment.

4. However, the EMDMS does reflect the intent of these firms to structure and control energy management; energy efficiency improvement is considered too important to the well-being of these firms to be left to informal or haphazard decision making processes.

5. Both firms are moving toward making the EMDMS an annual process. Given the high degree of organizational learning which had to take place before energy management could reach its present state of development in these two firms, the phases and their sequence in the EMDMS did not correspond to any strict time schedule or to any of the firms' planning/budgeting cycles.

6. Some important aspects of the role of DEAs, DECs and the EMC and the interrelationships among them have not been identified in the EMDMS description: these will be discussed in the remainder of this chapter.

DEA-EMC Roles and Their Interaction

It is evident from the discussion of the EMDMS that central to the thrust of and commitment to energy management in large multi-divisional firms is the individual but related roles of the DEA's office and the EMC. Table VIII-8 shows the major energy management functions/roles of the DEA and the EMC and the interaction between them. The scope of the activities of the DEA's office and the EMC manifest the institutionalization of energy management by these firms;

TABLE VIII-8

MAJOR FEATURES OF INTERACTION
BETWEEN DEA AND EMC

Decision Type / Locus of Decision	Director of Energy Affairs (DEA)	Corporate Energy Management Committee
Corporate Energy Policy	Developed by DEA	Reviewed and evaluated by EMC to insure that it reflects corporate policy and strategies and is consistent with inputs from (e.g., legal) departments
Implementation of Corporate Energy Policy	Direct responsibility	Serves to generate support for DEA efforts
Energy Supply Evaluation	Data gathering function Evaluation of Energy Supply trends, major firm impacts	Evaluation of specific divisional impacts finance restraints, legal barriers, etc.
Energy Mix, Conversion, Fuel Allocation	Make suggestions to EMC; direct implementation of EMC decisions	Authorize alternate fuel back-up systems; recommend development of firms energy sources; allocate fuels between divisions, plants, etc.
Energy Conservation Programs	Develop program specifics; direct and monitor program implementation	Establish overall program guidelines Provide DEA requested inputs e.g., specialized engineering assistance
Assessment of Energy Related Capital Expenditures	Assessment of all capital expenditures which have energy utilization implications	Evaluation of all capital expenditures above a certain minimum figure
Federal/State/Local Legislation	Monitor regulatory developments Assess and disseminate current and potential implications	Assist DEA in identification and evaluation of regulatory impacts

it is a concrete expression of the perceived critical nature of the energy management environment on their current and future operations.

Clearly manifest in all of the eight firms interviewed which had a corporate energy management committee (EMC) is a very high degree of interaction and interdependence between the DEA (or equivalent position) and the EMC. In each firm, the DEA (or the individual with equivalent responsibilities) is the chairperson of the energy management committee.

The DEA and EMC working in close cooperation produce the major integrative mechanism for the firm's energy management efforts--the corporate energy policy document. The document is seen as serving a number of functions: (1) it facilitates integration of energy management policy and plans with the firm's product-market strategy and other resource allocation programs; (2) it provides a forum for corporate-wide discussion of the scope, orientation and implications of various energy management strategies and programs; and (3) it serves as a useful internal and external public relations exercise to generate support for the notion of actively managing the firm's energy resources.

The broad-based composition of the energy management committee serves to provide a wide range of inputs in the developmental stages of the policy document. Thus, the espoused corporate energy policy is not merely a representation of the unfounded expectations of the DEA's office. The development of explicit corporate energy policy guidelines often highlights existing and potential areas of conflict between different groups within the firm and, thus, sensitizes the

DEA to these difficulties prior to the development and implementation
of specific strategies and goals.

One other apparently major function of the EMC with respect
to corporate energy policy development and implementation which is
less explicit than many of the functions identified in Table VIII-8 is
worth noting. The EMC plays a large role in generating organizational
support for the concept of energy management, in general, and the role
and tasks of the DEA's office in particular. EMC members through formal and informal interactions within their own functional areas impress
upon management and other personnel the importance of energy management.

A major function of the DEA's role which was espoused by the
DEAs in the in-person interviews (this was also reflected in discussions with DEA support staff) is that of "selling the notion of energy
management" to other management personnel within both corporate headquarters and the divisions. The energy management function, no more
than any other functional area, cannot sustain a separate existence
from the rest of the firm's operations. As related by one of the
DEAs, it is in interaction with corporate and division general management, and the production/operations, finance/accounting, engineering
and other functional groups that success or failure of the energy
management function is determined. Thus, the energy advocacy role
of the DEA can not be underestimated; it may be particularly critical
in the early phases of the evolution of a corporate energy management
function.

Another key energy management task which is performed by the
DEA (and his support staff) is that of "environmental scanning":

i.e., monitoring governmental policies and regulations, national and local energy supply conditions, major energy conservation/supply technology developments, energy management practices, and achievements in other corporations, etc. One firm maintained a constant relationship with a number of organizations and individuals in Washington, D.C. in order to keep abreast of federal energy developments. Thus, a major role of the DEA's office is that of external energy information "gatekeeper" for the firm.

The DEA's and their support staffs also see themselves playing an energy "watchdog role": that is, the DEA's office monitors all capital expenditure programs/projects which may be likely to have energy utilization implications. These are programs/projects which are not energy specific, they arise in other management or functional areas (e.g., facilities planning, construction technology, engineering, R and D, production/operations management). Such programs/projects which may have implications for energy efficiency are forwarded by these groups to the DEA's office for analysis. In this way, energy management considerations are incorporated into the capital investment evaluation process.

DEA-DEC Interaction

Table VIII-9 shows the main areas of interaction between the DEA's offices and the DEC's; each of these areas has been discussed in the EMDMS description. However, a number of comments about the roles of the DEC's and their interaction with the DEA's office are warranted.

TABLE VIII-9

MAJOR FEATURES OF INTERACTION BETWEEN

DEAO AND DECS

Locus of Decision / Decision Type	Office of Director of Energy Affairs (DEAO)	Division Energy Coordinator
Implementation of Corporate Policy	Identify general implications of corporate energy policy for each division. Evaluate divisional constraints peculiarities, limitations, etc.	Detail divisional implications of corporate energy policy Provide divisional viewpoint on corporate energy policy: constaints peculiarities, etc.
Corporate Objectives/ Divisional goals	Establish corporate objectives Work with DEC's on developing divisional goals	Work with DEAO on developing divisional goals
Energy Conservation Program	Evaluate division programs Monitor division progress on each program element Establish agreed bench-marks to evaluate division progress Develop reporting system to facilitate monitoring and evaluation	Develop detailed division program in conjunction with plant energy coordinators Provide progress reports to DEAO on each program element
Energy Supply	Monitor corporate and divisional energy mix Identify potential energy shortages and their implications Establish program criteria for installation of alternate fuel back-up systems	Develop division energy demand projections Assess alternate energy back-up system requirements Create contingency plans for alternate systems (e.g. foreign oil embargo, industrial dispute in coal industry, etc.)
Energy Related Capital Expenditures	Solicit and evaluate major capital expenditures in divisions conservation and supply programs	Detail conservation and supply program capital expenditures Itemize energy implications of non-energy specific capital expenditures

1. All of the sample firms have established positions entitled "Division Energy Coordinator" for at least some of the divisions. Whether the positions are generally full-time or part-time varies from firm to firm; DECs are full-time positions in the two firms whose EMDMS was described.

2. The role of the DECs in the formulation and implementation of energy management strategies and programs is a pivotal one: in effect, they play the energy "advocacy" and "gatekeeper" roles at the division level that has already been described in the case of the DEA at the corporate headquarters level.

3. Almost all DECs have a strong engineering background with a preponderance of DECs coming from the plant engineering function.

4. A problem which part-time DECs must grapple with is that they "serve two masters." They report to the DEA but the latter does not have line authority over them: they also report to their functional area heads (e.g., head of engineering). Thus, conflicts in the demands placed upon DECs inevitably exist.

Summary/Conclusion

This section has described the energy management decision making system (EMDMS) in two large multidivisional firms, and has highlighted some of the main features of the roles of the principal individuals and committees involved in the formulation and implementation of energy management strategies and programs. A formal EMDMS with clearly prescribed roles and responsibilities as well as organizational mechanisms for interaction among them is emerging in at least some large multidivisional firms. Management of energy resources is perceived as of such importance for the economic welfare of the enterprise that some firms now are in the process of establishing what may be described as an energy management function.

The EMDMS established in the two large multidivisional firms with the most developed approach to energy management is basically a three phased process:

1. In Phase 1, the corporate energy policy/plan is developed in broad outline by the DEA in conjunction with the EMC. One of the significant aspects of the corporate energy policy/plan is that it provides the framework within which the DEA's support staff and the DECs develop tentative division energy management plans--the major output of Phase 1.

2. Phase 2 results in the formulation of specific division energy management programs. The DEC's often draw on the resources of the DEA's office in the development of these programs. The DEA's office also often takes the initiative to motivate division efforts to establish comprehensive energy management programs. A major role of the DEA's office is evident in Phase 2: the collection and dissemination of information which divisions may find useful in their energy management efforts.

3. Phase 3 represents the implementation of division energy management programs and the monitoring of their success or failure by the DEA's office. The DEA's office and the EMC must review and approve all division energy management programs--the output of Phase 2--before they are implemented by the divisions.

The momentum and direction of the energy management function is provided by the Director of Energy Affairs (DEA) and his full-time support staff. The DEA's office coordinates all corporate energy management activities; a high degree of interaction with the EMC, the DECs and other division line management is very apparent in the role of the DEA's office.

The EMC provides a diversity of perspectives in the evaluation of energy management strategies; it also serves to generate corporate-wide support for the notion of energy management, and in particular the role and tasks of the DEA's office.

The role of the DEC's office is critical in energy management strategy formulation and implementation: it is they who must ensure that energy management is a formal part of division management activities. The DEA's office is dependent upon them to implement corporate energy management programs and to provide guidance for the development of appropriate directions for corporate energy management strategy.

In summary, large multidivisional firms are responding to the complex and turbulent energy environment. Firms have begun to establish organizational mechanisms to manage their energy resources. Some of the sample's large multidivisional firms have institutionalized an energy management decision making process: whether these firms have realized superior energy efficiency improvements over firms which have adopted a less systematic approach can only be answered by future research.

CHAPTER NINE

CONCLUSIONS

The findings of this study point to several conclusions. The intent of this chapter is to indicate some of the important conclusions that can be derived from the study's results. This chapter is organized as follows: first, the limitations of the study are noted; second, the major energy management related conclusions with respect to large multi-divisional firms and smaller sized firms are indicated; third, some managerial implications for the successful introduction and implementation of energy management in industrial organizations are discussed; fourth, the implications of the study for governmental agencies interested in motivating industrial energy efficiency are set forth; fifth, some issues with respect to the current status and future research directions in the academic fields of business strategy/policy and organizational innovation are raised; and, finally, some areas worthy of future research in the context of energy management are identified.

Study Limitations

Any interpretation of the results of this study must be couched in a number of caveats. The restricted geographic base of the study sample and its unrepresentativeness of the mix of U.S. industry (see Appendix C) imply that we must sacrifice a certain degree of general-izability of results. The preponderance of firms in the Primary Metals industry in the study sample (especially with respect to large multi-divisional firms) suggests a major degree of caution in generalizing from these results.

The small sample of small organizational units permitted only tentative statistical analysis of the hypotheses and propositions of this research. Also, the definitions of two of the three independent variables (i.e., growth and energy intensity) utilized in the hypotheses testing were chosen to facilitate consistency in interpretation; alternate definitions of growth and energy intensity which might be employed could lead to different results.

The explication of energy management decision making processes is cross-sectional in nature, i.e., a snapshot of energy management decision making at one point in time is captured and interviewees are asked to delineate the evolution of events which has led to present circumstances. A longitudinal study of energy related decision processes would provide richer insights into the organizational or behavioral influences at play in energy management.

However, given the exploratory nature of this research, it is hoped that the results of the hypotheses testing and the intensive investigation of energy management decision making in selected firms will provide the guidance necessary for further research utilizing broader data bases. Viewed in this light, this study may be seen as one of the necessary steps toward conceptual and empirical development in an area (i.e., energy management) which has received relatively little systematic attention.

Energy Management Related Conclusions

Since a detailed summary of the research findings is presented at the end of each section in the previous two chapters, only the highlights of the conclusions which can be drawn from this research are noted here. Conclusions are presented separately with regard to the smaller sized firms and the larger multidivisional firms.

Smaller Sized Firms

This study hypothesized that growth firms, energy intensive firms and divisions would demonstrate a greater degree of strategic responsiveness in their approaches to energy management than non-growth firms, non-energy intensive firms and independent firms respectively. Only in relation to growth firms did this study fail to generate any evidence to support these hypotheses. The research findings most strongly supported the hypothesis that divisions would be more involved in energy management than independent firms. It may be that these findings are a reflection of the unrepresentative nature of the study sample: small (i.e., annual sales of $10-100 million) independent firms in other regions which are less dependent on an industrial base characterized by mature (e.g., Primary Metals) industries might have demonstrated a higher degree of energy management innovativeness.

It is evident that energy management is a task which is taken seriously by many of the study sample's smaller sized firms. Some firms have institutionalized energy management along each of the six (6) EMD's investigated in this study. (See Chapter 2 for a definition and discussion of the Energy Management Dimensions.) Organizational

commitment to the notion of energy management is manifest in the establishment of full-time and/or part-time energy management positions,
and specific energy management objectives/targets (EMD1); the development of energy efficiency measures and energy auditing processes (EMD2);
a concern with establishing energy management as a component of line
management's accountabilities (EMD3); the implementation of extensive
energy efficiency improvement programs and investments (EMD4); the
orientation of R and D programs to the improvement of production/
manufacturing process energy efficiency (EMD5); and the integration
of energy efficiency considerations into product/market strategies
(EMD6).

The relative emphasis placed upon the EMD's (as well as the
components of individual EMD) can vary considerably among firms which
have largely the same characteristics (i.e., growth, energy intensity,
product lines, manufacturing technologies, etc.). For instance, with
regard to the two firms in SIC 3221 (the energy management approaches
of these firms was described in Chapter 7), the independent firm chose
not to appoint a full-time energy manager but had invested more financial resources in energy efficiency improvement than the division.
This is particularly interesting in view of the fact that the division
interviewees suggested the division was not constrained in its investment behavior by capital limitations.

A number of firms with very low levels of energy intensity
have done relatively little to institutionalize energy management.
Although many other factors were also identified as inhibiting attention to energy management (e.g., lack of capital resources, a tendency

to manage by exception, etc.), there may be a threshold level of energy intensity below which firms consider they have relatively little incentive (in terms of potential energy savings) to devote time and effort to the management of energy resources. The partial support found in the statistical analysis for Hypothesis 2 (i.e., that energy intensive firms would show a greater degree of strategic responsiveness in their approach to energy management than non-energy intensive firms) also supports this contention. If a threshold level of energy intensity does exist, below which firms perceive little incentive to improve energy efficiency, governmental programs aimed at initiating energy conservation efforts in these firms will most likely meet with little success.

A critical feature of energy management in all the firms which are attempting to develop and institutionalize energy management is the major role of the engineering function. Even in those firms which have done relatively little in terms of systematic energy management, the role of the engineering function (i.e., plant/industrial/electrical engineering staff) is central to whatever tasks are considered and/or implemented. Engineering function staff are usually charged with the initial investigation and development of energy efficiency improvement investment proposals; indeed, most energy conservation ideas emanate from firms' engineering functions. When full-time and/or part-time energy management positions are established they are usually located within the engineering function. It is the engineering function which implements firms' energy conservation/supply investments and it also monitors the success or failure (in terms of energy savings) of the firm's energy conservation strategies and programs. Thus, the improvement of energy efficiency is perceived as predominantly an engineering task by most of the sample firms.

However, centralizing energy management in the engineering department has its disadvantages as well as its advantages. While the engineering function may assume the role of energy advocacy and gate-keeping within the firm, it must work through line management (i.e., plant/operations management) in order to implement the firm's energy management strategies. A number of instances of production/operations management's reluctance to support engineering department proposals to improve energy efficiency because of their potential impact on production flow, product quality, etc., were evident in this research. The engineering function in many firms is charged with responsibility for energy management but the success of its efforts is highly dependent on the cooperation of other departments/functions. Thus, external agents (e.g., Department of Energy) must focus their efforts to influence the direction of energy management activity to other areas within the firm as well as to the engineering function.

One of the significant impediments to the implementation of energy management programs as described by full-time and part-time personnel is their "dual responsibility": they report to their superiors within their functional area and they report (with regard to their energy management responsibility) to some management member(s) outside their functional area (e.g., the president or vice president for operations). The nature of the organizational dilemmas faced by the occupant of these positions of dual responsibility has been amply

illustrated in the literature on "project management" or "matrix management" (Cleland and King, 1974). The result is that conflicting demands
are placed upon those with assigned responsibilities for energy management. From the point of view of those filling these positions, none
of the organizations interviewed have developed a satisfactory solution
to this problem.

Although the thrust of energy management may reside within the
engineering function, it is clear that a critical prerequisite to the
establishment of an energy management function, and thus, to the success of energy management related programs, is the commitment of a
firm's president or chief executive officer to the notion that energy
resources must be managed. Many interviewees were at pains to point
out that unless the firm's president was willing to commit organizational resources to the formulation and implementation of energy management strategies, the efforts of production/operations management
and the engineering function would result in little more than the implementation of "housekeeping" details.

A conclusion of major import is that a very diverse set of
factors can potentially influence the emergence and evaluation of
energy conservation investment ideas/proposals (see last section of
Chapter 7). The manner in which energy conservation ideas find their
way into organizations, are nurtured, evaluated and finally emerge as
fully fledged investment proposals is neither a "simple" process (i.e.,
a process which is easy to understand, describe and evaluate) nor a
"rational" process (i.e., a process in which the same set of organizational procedures are followed or the same set of organizational

factors are dominant in each case). Neither is the evaluation of
investment alternatives (i.e., energy conservation ideas that have
been developed into specific investment proposals) a process which
utilizes financial/economic criteria exclusively. While the latter
may often be employed as the initial criterion, other factors (e.g.,
unavailability of capital, deleterious impact on production schedules,
managerial perceptions of energy savings and energy price movements,
etc.) can inhibit or facilitate the adoption of energy conserving
technologies.

Large Multidivisional Firms

All of the large multidivisional firms investigated in this
study have responded to the complex and uncertain energy environment
along the lines suggested by the "social response process" model found
in Ackerman (1973), Ackerman and Bauer (1975) and Murray (1976). The
"social response process" model as delineated by these authors describes the manner in which firms institutionalize their response to
socio-political issues by way of decision making procedures, resource
allocation, etc. However, major differences are evident in the
approaches adopted by these firms to institutionalize the energy
management process.

In eight of the eleven firms, energy management is clearly
centralized at corporate headquarters. The organizational framework
which has evolved in relation to corporate energy management has resulted in major limitations on division discretion in energy management decision making. For example, policy/planning initiatives and
the evaluation of major investment proposals are corporate headquarter's

functions. This is particularly so in those firms which have established a full-time corporate energy management office under a "Director
of Energy Affairs" and have an EMC (energy management committee) which
takes its role seriously. In these firms, clearly identified energy
management related tasks and assigned accountabilities are evident at
both corporate headquarters and division level.

Three firms have consciously chosen to decentralize energy
management: to the extent possible, the formalization and implementation of energy management strategies are division functions. Relatively little corporate-wide energy management coordination and direction
takes place at corporate headquarters. Although two of these three
firms are highly energy intensive, it was the contention of all the
interviewees in these firms that energy management is most appropriate-
ly a division activity: corporate headquarters was variously described
as not having the skills, knowledge or detailed familiarity with division problems and operating procedures to effect corporate-wide energy
management.

In a few of the large multidivisional firms with centralized
energy management, a very formalized and structured EMDMS (energy management decision making system) is evolving to formulate and implement
corporate energy management strategies and programs. The EMDMS constitutes a substantial investment of management time and resources at both
the corporate and division levels; it is the embodiment of large firms'
commitment to the management of their energy resources. A high degree
of organizational learning or "learning by doing" is evident in the
evolution of the EMDMS as described by individual interviewees since

firms first began to move toward formalized energy management decision making in the wake of the 1973 Arab oil embargo. In effect, the EMDMS serves to institutionalize and retain the insights gained by these organizations in their energy management efforts.

Management Policy Implications

A number of recommendations with regard to the formalization and implementation of energy management can be made to business managements which intend to initiate energy management or intensify their present energy management activities. These recommendations pertain to the institutionalization of energy management, i.e., the initiation and integration of energy management procedures into the decision making fabric of the organization.

The development of an energy management capability is not something which happens quickly; in many of the firms studied (and especially so in the case of large multidivisional firms) organizational learning with regard to management of the firm's energy resources is still taking place after three or more years commitment to the notion of energy management. Organizations, therefore, need to be patient in establishing an energy management capability. Initial energy savings may be exacted with relatively little investment of resources (e.g., housekeeping programs), but major improvements in energy efficiency can require a large degree of organizational set-up and learning time.

A major key to successful energy management is the existence of clearly assigned energy management responsibilities. The establishment of an Energy Affairs Office, or in smaller organizations, a full-time or part-time energy management position, creates within an organization a point of energy management advocacy; the "watch-dog" role inherent in these positions is particularly critical in the early phases of a firm's efforts to get on the energy management "learning curve." The establishment of such positions also manifests to the entire organization top management's commitment to and interest in management of the firm's energy resources.

Closely related to the last point is the necessity to determine and promulgate energy efficiency improvement objectives. Objectives not only provide a yardstick against which energy conservation efforts can be measured, but their very existence can generate management interest and motivate efforts which some firms have suggested would otherwise be difficult to do. Even when a firm decides that an overall energy efficiency objective is unrealistic, the same purposes can be realized by establishing specific goals in the case of energy efficiency improvement projects which are clearly divisible (e.g., insulating a furnace, recycling waste heat, controlling ventilation, etc.).

A prerequisite to the success of energy management objectives as a motivational device is the development of energy efficiency measures. Energy data generation and analysis is predicated on the ability to establish energy efficiency measures; such measures provide management with the means to evaluate energy management success in general or specific projects.

The examination of the diverse factors which influence the emergence and evaluation of energy conservation investment proposals suggests that a task force or committee may be essential to the search

for and assessment of energy efficiency improvement projects. Where
these tasks fall mainly within the domain of a single department or
individual, departmental or individual interests may prevail over
organizational interests. It may be particularly critical to have
plant/operations management involved in these task forces not only to
provide more balanced appraisal of energy conservation investments but
also to provide an organizational forum whereby the impact of these
proposed investments on management groups other than the engineering
function can be identified and considered.

Federal Policy Implications

In the introduction to this study, mention was made of the
large volume of governmental resources expended in the hope of influ-
encing industrial energy management decision making. Given the findings of this study, a number of implications for federal policy makers
merit noting.

First, the decision processes involved in energy management,
even in medium sized firms (i.e., annual average sales of $10-100 mil-
lion) are reasonably complex. A number of the firm's personnel bring
to bear their own individual perspectives, interests and motivations
on major energy management issues. A number of intervention points
may, therefore, have to be considered by a federal agency; the Department of Energy may be well advised to take these differential intervention points into account in the design of the content and the identification of the targets of its communication strategies. For instance, the engineering function may require very detailed technical

and operating data to evaluate a new energy conserving technology, while the existence of the technology and an outline of its superiority over technology in use may need to be communicated to a firm's president, or chief executive officer, plant management and other personnel to ensure firm-wide awareness and serious consideration of the technology. The technical data required by the engineering group may be of little assistance to a chief executive officer (he will probably depend on the engineering function for an evaluation of this kind of data in any case), but an awareness that the technologies exist may lead a chief executive officer to direct the engineering function to conduct an in-depth appraisal of them.

A primary focus or target of federal agencies' programs and contact ought to be the location of energy advocacy and information within the firm, i.e., full-time or part-time energy management positions in smaller sized firms and the DEA's (Director of Energy Affairs) office and DEC's (Division Energy Coordinator) in large multidivisional firms. A search for such intervention points in individual firms should improve the efficiency and effectiveness of federal information dissemination strategies. Also, these particular intervention points might be the most efficient and effective means of providing feedback to the Department of Energy on the benefits and demerits of its current and potential programs.

Department of Energy programs may also want to take into account the extent to which firms are already on "the learning curve" with respect to energy management. If divisions are more actively engaged in energy management than independent firms (at least in some industries) more intensive efforts may be required to initiate consideration of energy conserving behavior and techniques in the latter types of firms. Similar efforts may also be required, if as already suggested, there is a threshold level, in terms of firm size (i.e., annual dollar sales) and/or energy intensity, below which firms engage in little, if any, energy management.

The findings of this study also suggest some implications for the content of federal programs. Concentration on the economic benefits of new energy conserving technologies alone may not be sufficient to induce their adoption if the organizational and behavioral influences which impact the evaluation of such technologies are not addressed (the scope and nature of these influences was discussed in the last two sections of Chapter 7). An understanding of the latter set of factors can help explain actions which may be regarded by the Department of Energy as counter-intuitive but which may play a large role in firms' refusal to adopt energy conserving behaviors and practices.

Finally, much of the above has direct implication for the communication media employed in federal programs. Given (a) the complexity of the energy management decision making process, (b) the desirability of communicating different kinds of information to different individuals/groups within organizations, and (c) the need to recognize the variety of economic and non-economic factors which influence the assessment of energy conservation activities, personal forms of contact may be significantly more important in impacting firms' behavior than non-personal communication modes. This may be especially true where the energy conserving technique or behavior is new to the market and/or to the firm, since firms may prefer to learn from the experiences of other organizations in adopting the technology or behavior. Personal forms of contact ranging from demonstrations to working directly with individual firms may provide a much greater opportunity to overcome points of resistance to the adoption of energy conserving practices than any other form of generalized non-personal communication.

Implications for Theory and Research in Business Strategy/Policy and Innovation

This study has examined the integration of concepts from the academic fields of business strategy/policy and organizational/technological innovation in the context of energy management. A number of implications for further research in each of these areas can be identified from the findings of this study.

Business Strategy/Policy

Strategy formulation is most frequently depicted in the business strategy/policy literature as a "rational" process: i.e., a set of logical and sequential steps with clearly defined choice criteria at each stage (Steiner and Miner, 1977; Hofer and Schendel, 1978). A growing body of literature is emphasizing that the "rational" side of strategy is embedded in political/behavioral/organizational processes (Richards, 1978; McMillan, 1978). The findings of this study suggest that the "rational" and behavioral elements are both involved in strategy formulation but that their relative impact may vary depending on the stage of the strategy formulation process.

The initial evaluation of specific projects largely reflects the rational approach to strategy formulation: a set of potential projects are identified but in order to be accepted for further consideration there must be unambiguous evidence that a particular project will meet the firm's standard economic/financial criteria (i.e., ROI, payback period, etc.). However, this does not necessarily mean that all, or indeed, any of these projects will be approved for implementation. Two different types of behavioral/organizational factors which can adversely impact the adoption of energy efficiency improvement projects were evidenced in this research (see last two sections of Chapter 7). One, any key individual(s) in the decision making process who is (are) ill-disposed toward investments to improve energy efficiency (e.g., because of a perception that energy prices will not continue to rise as sharply as they have in the past) may act as a major organizational impediment to the approval of projects which otherwise satisfy the firm's choice criteria. Two, relative departmental power and influence may also serve to impede (or facilitate) the implementation of investment proposals which are deemed acceptable to the firm's financial/economic criteria. A number of cases were identified in this study where line (plant) management resisted investments to improve energy efficiency which emanated from the engineering function, due to their potential impact on production scheduling, cost control and product quality. These results support the findings of Bower (1970), Berg, (1965), Murray (1976) and Ackerman (1973) that both economic and non-economic factors are involved in the process of strategy formulation and implementation.

However, before any set of investment alternatives (i.e., strategic choices) can be evaluated, investment ideas must first emerge within the organization and be developed into fully fledged investment proposals. This phase of the strategy formulation process has received very scant attention in the business strategy/policy literature (Mintzberg, 1977). The findings of this study suggest that organizational and behavioral influences can significantly impact which potential investment ideas are formulated into investment proposals. Thus, any theory of strategy formulation must explicitly incorporate rational and behavioral elements: either, alone, is insufficient to explain the outcomes of the strategy formulation process.

Although the business policy/strategy literature has recognized that the strategy formulation process can be very different among types of organizations (Mintzberg, et al., 1976), Hickson et al. (1978) in a review of the literature on strategic management decision making suggest that there is little recognition or empirical evidence to support the proposition that the strategy formulation process can differ within a given organization depending upon the issue, area of concern or decision in question. In some of the large multidivisional firms examined in this study, a reasonably discrete strategy formulation process for energy management decisions is emerging within these organizations: energy management decisions are analyzed, formulated and approved by different individuals than the more conventional product-market strategy decisions. Although the energy management decision making process may be reasonably similar to that occasionally found in the literature with respect to product-market strategy decision making (Lorange and

Vancil, 1975; Hofer and Schendel, 1978), the choice criteria at major decision points can be very different (e.g., internal operating efficiency considerations are clearly of major concern in energy management decisions as well as firm-environment considerations). Many insights into the strategy formulation process (both its rational and behavioral/political elements) could be gained were it investigated across a range of areas (e.g., divestments, acquisitions, new product introductions, energy management, financial management, etc.) within individual firms and among firms.

The findings of this study suggest that there may be significant differences in strategy formulation not only with respect to issue areas across firms but also with respect to major decisions within an issue area (e.g., energy management) in individual firms. For instance, energy supply decisions (e.g., building new storage capacity, conversion to alternate fuels) and conservation decisions can differ with respect to the frequency with which these decisions occur, the initial impetus for each decision (e.g., supply interruption versus knowledge of new energy conserving technology), the extent to which information gathering (both external and internal to the firm) and evaluation is required, the number of management personnel involved in the decisions and the diversity of their interests, the number of alternative courses of action identified with respect to each decision, and, the length of time involved in decision making (e.g., after a supply interruption some supply decisions have been made very quickly, whereas some conservation decisions may be prolonged for months, if not, years). Many other items could also be added to this list of differences between energy supply and energy conservation decisions. Thus, our concept of strategy making may need to be more narrowly focused at the level of individual decisions: generic descriptions of strategy formulation as are usually found in the business strategy/policy literature (particularly those which emphasize its "rational" elements) may be too general to explain (i.e., predict) the process of strategy making or its outcomes at the level of individual decisions.

A number of studies have explored the relationship between organizational structure and corporate strategy (Chandler, 1962; Fouraker and Stopford, 1968; Channon, 1973; Rumelt, 1974; Wrigley, 1970). These studies have attempted to determine the relationship between corporate economic performance in terms of firms' product line relationship and degree of diversification and/or divisionalization. However, the findings to date have been less than conclusive (Steiner and Miner, 1977). An alternate route to examine the structure/strategy relationship may be to focus on the structure of decision making processes. Although a divisionalized structure was common to all of the large firms in this study, the energy management decision making structure varied considerably from highly centralized to largely decentralized. Similarly differences were also evident in the energy management decision making processes in the divisions and independent firms studied. In other words, in order to explain the energy efficiency performance of firms, we may have to look to factors other than (or as well as) their organizational structure. Thus, the performance of firms in terms of improved energy efficiency and the choice of means (strategy) to improve energy efficiency may be a function of the structure and process of energy management decision making employed by firms and not their organizational structure, per se.

The choice of goals and strategy formulation are often represented as separate elements in strategy making (Hofer and Schendel, 1978): the most appropriate strategies are chosen to achieve predetermined goals. As described in this study, energy management objectives and strategies are often decided upon in a series of iterative stages; it is difficult to decifer whether objectives are established prior to any explicit consideration of strategies. What is clear is that objectives and goals do undergo change as specific energy management strategies are considered (e.g., the emergence of a new energy conserving technology can alter a firm's prior estimates of potential energy efficiency improvements). Further research is required to examine the relationship between goal formation and strategy formulation; it may be that the strategy/policy literature's prescription to establish objectives prior to strategy development is something which is unrealistic in practice.

Organizational/Technological Innovation

The event or result and the process approaches to studying innovation (which were described in Chapter 3) are both insufficient alone to explain the innovation behavior of organizations. While the event or result approach provides correlations between the characteristics of firms and/or innovations and firms' decisions to adopt or reject innovations, it provides little of the insights of the process approach (i.e., the identification of the stages or phases in an

innovation decision ordered along the temporal dimensions of their
anticipated sequence) into how innovation decisions are made. As
demonstrated in this study, the two approaches can be interwoven to
test a priori hypotheses and generate hypotheses for future research.
Consequently, it may be profitable in terms of refining our understanding of innovative behavior in organizations to reexamine innovation studies which have depended primarily on one of these approaches:
i.e., a reconceptualization of the concepts, variables and findings
of previous research with a view to the integration and synthesis of
what we already know about the process of organizational innovation.
Hunter and Rubenstein (1978), Warner, (1974) and Rowe and Boise (1974),
although in different contexts, have also called for a reappraisal of
past research in the study of organizational innovation.

Part of the required synthesis may be the necessity to study
the relationship between organizational and technological innovations.
Previous research has focused almost exclusively on one or other of
these innovation categories.[1] The findings of this study indicate
that a prerequisite to the adoption of technological innovations (i.e.,
energy conserving technologies) may be one or more organizational innovations, e.g., a "policy" innovation (e.g., the decision of the firm
to improve its energy efficiency), a "people" innovation (e.g., the
establishment of an energy advocacy position such as an EMC and/or
a full-time or part-time energy management position) or "organization
structure innovations" (e.g., the integration of energy management
into line management's accountabilities). Although technological
innovations can, of course, take place in the absence of these types

of organizational innovations, the latter serve to facilitate the former.

The adoption of any given technological innovation is therefore likely to be the consequence of a series of events or activities within a firm. Cross-sectional studies which categorize firms into "adopters" and "non-adopters" of technological innovations at any given point in time, and focus exclusively on financial/economic characteristics of the firm and the innovation in question,[2] will most probably fail to capture the complexity of the organizational decision making influences which can facilitate or inhibit the decision to adopt a given innovation. One such example which was evident in this study is the role and expectations of plant/operations management and the accounting/ finance department which can influence the emergence, evaluation and approval of investment proposals. Thus, longitudinal studies are required to assess the impact of these organizational influences on innovative behavior over time, and to provide further insights into why firms manifest innovative behavior in some contexts and not in others.

Related to the last point is the observation that in the technological innovation literature, the sources of innovation (or investment) ideas have received considerable attention (Myers and Marquis, 1969; Utterback, 1975), but the influences which impact the early evaluation of such ideas (i.e., before they are developed into initial proposals) have been the subject of much less systematic research. Individual and organizational perceptions and beliefs can vitally affect organizational propensities to innovate (e.g., modify its strategies) but the nature of the impact is something about which we know very little (Zaltman, Duncan and Holbek, 1973). Both cross-sectional and longitudinal studies are required to fully explore the relationships between individual and organizational perceptions and beliefs and innovative behavior.

The concept of strategy itself may provide a useful integrative mechanism and theoretical umbrella within which to examine innovative behavior. Strategy may be relevant to explanations of innovative behavior irrespective of whether the event or result or the process approach to studying innovation is utilized. For instance, the R and D strategy and the product-market strategy of firms might be used to predict whether firms would adopt specific organizational or technological innovations. Similarly, investigations of firms' strategy formulation process(es) (e.g., who is involved in the process, the kind of evaluation criteria employed, etc.) may provide indicators of the organizational barriers and inducements to innovative behavior. Although, the notion of strategy is obviously more difficult to operationalize than many of the explanatory variables which have been utilized in previous innovation studies, the possibility that it may be a more powerful explanatory construct with a wide range of potential applications (i.e., different types of strategies) requires that it be the subject of future empirical research.

Even though this study was not specifically intended to examine the relevance or impact of organizational learning on energy management, the relationship between the two was evident in many phases of the study. The experience which an organization gains in dealing with particular phenomena and events (e.g., the management of energy

resources) can differentiate one organization from another in terms of
how they approach specific problems (e.g., some firms have developed
more systematic energy management decision-processes than others). A
thorough delineation of the relationship between organizational learning and strategy formulation and implementation and the adoption of
organizational and technological innovations would represent a distinct conceptual contribution to the extant theories in both these
fields.

One final reflection on the nature of this study is worth
noting: it has major implications for theoretical and empirical progress in strategy/policy and innovation studies. Research in these
fields needs to adopt methodologies that are sensitive to the underlying processes which explain the findings obtained through quantitative
measurements. In this study, the statistical tests of the propositions
told us very little about the organizational processes involved in
energy management. Campbell (1977) has underscored this point when
he suggests

> . . . in the successful laboratory sciences, quanti-
> fication both builds upon and is cross validated by,
> the scientists pervasive qualitative knowledge. . . .
> If we are to be truly scientific, we must reestablish
> this qualitative grounding of the quantitative in
> action research. (emphasis added)

Therefore, it is proposed that research strategies in business
strategy/policy and organizational/technological innovation should
focus not only on hypotheses testing, but also on hypotheses generation
through efforts to gain process (qualitative) understanding of underlying phenomena. Such a posture also has the added benefit (as occurred

in this study) of sensitizing the researcher to the complexity of the processes and phenomena under study and thus, preventing the derivation and promulgation of conclusions which may be that only in name.

Future Research in Energy Management

A number of directions for future research in energy management can be posited as a result of the findings of this study. Many research questions with respect to individual EMD have already been identified as part of the data analysis in Chapters 7 and 8. This section will highlight some of the more significant research directions which might be taken by future studies in energy management.

A much larger sample of firms is required before the hypotheses which received some statistical support in this study can be accepted (i.e., that divisions and energy intensive firms will demonstrate a higher degree of strategic responsiveness in their approaches to energy management than independent firms and non-energy intensive firms). Larger sample sets will permit the application of multivariate statistical techniques to determine the degree of interaction among structure (i.e., divisions, independent firms) energy intensity and other firm characteristics (e.g., profitability, industry type, geographic location, energy mix, etc.) as determinants of the energy management approach employed by firms. Different definitions of energy intensity, growth and firm size are advisable, since any one definition of these firm characteristics will not capture the variance which is implicit in these concepts.

From previous comments about the desirability of examining both the rational and behavioral/political aspects of strategy formulation in energy management, such research should include internal (i.e., behavioral/organizational) characteristics of firms (e.g., existence of full-time energy management positions, specific energy management efficiency improvement objectives, etc.) as well as the more commonly utilized structural firm characteristics (e.g., industry type, profitability, sales level, etc.) in any effort to determine firms' propensity to adopt energy conserving technologies.

Different organizational approaches to energy management need to be correlated with energy management performance, i.e., improvements in energy efficiency. This study has not attempted to relate energy management strategic responsiveness to energy efficiency improvements due to the problems inherent in measuring energy efficiency improvement, the inconsistencies in such data from one firm to another, and the inability and/or unwillingness of some firms to reveal such data. However, it is clear that the criterion of enhanced energy performance must be incorporated into future research in energy management; otherwise, such organizational phenomena as EMC's and energy management objectives can merely be a facade to shelter inactivity or "non-decision making" (Bachrach and Baratz, 1962, 1970; Lukes, 1974).

The investigation of the impact of different organizational approaches to energy management on energy conservation performance may be particularly interesting in the case of large multidivisional firms. Divisional energy conservation performance might be compared between firms with centralized and decentralized approaches to energy management. Similarly, energy management decision making processes and the nature of the organizational influences impacting such decisions might be compared. It may be that in firms with decentralized energy management, energy conservation performance is comparable to that in firms which use a centralized approach to energy management, but the organizational forces impelling such performance are likely to be quite different.

A number of economic and non-economic factors are identified in this study as having some impact on the emergence, evaluation and approval of energy conservation investment proposals. Further research to examine the role of these factors in strategy formulation and the adoption of innovations has been previously suggested. A similar research strategy should also be implemented in the context of energy management which would not only improve our understanding of the interactions among the mix of factors which facilitate or impede improvements in energy efficiency but also provide insights into appropriate federal policies to influence industrial energy management behavior.

An area worthy of further research attention is an investigation of the differences which appear to exist in the approaches adopted by some firms to energy supply and energy conservation decisions. If there are significant differences among (a) the factors which provide the impetus for these decisions; (b) the organizational importance attached to these decision areas, and (c) the evaluation criteria applied to supply and conservation investments, these differences must be taken into account by federal policies which seek to influence energy supply and energy conservation decision making as well as by decision making theories which seek to explain and predict managerial behavior with respect to such decisions.

Many part-time and full-time energy management personnel find themselves as elements in a matrix form of organization, i.e., they report to two different individuals. We need to investigate the consequences of these dual responsibilities for firms' efforts to improve their energy efficiency.

By the same token, the perceptions and attitudes of other management personnel toward the concept of energy management and the role of energy management personnel need to be systematically investigated. The president, line management, the accounting/finance function and other management members can potentially make the task of energy management personnel extremely onerous.

Finally, it should be noted that the exploratory nature of this research has been such that more questions have been raised than were answered. As enumerated by Kerlinger (1973) exploratory studies have three purposes:

> to discover significant variables in the field situa-
> tion, to discover relations among variables, and to
> lay the groundwork for later, more systematic and
> rigorous testing of hypotheses.

It is hoped that the emphasis in this study on identifying important variables and the interrelationships among them in the context of energy management and on raising research questions for future empirical investigation, will have laid some of the groundwork for "more systematic and rigorous testing of hypotheses."

FOOTNOTES

[1]An examination of the studies reported in Chapter 5 under the headings, "The Innovation Adoption Process," and "The Economics of Technical Change" reveals that few studies have explicitly focused on the organizational changes which may be required to facilitate the adoption of technological innovations. This is particularly true of the studies discussed under the heading, "The Economics of Technical Change."

[2]This is predominantly the approach employed by many economists to the adoption of technological innovations which we have referred to throughout this study as the event or result approach to the examination of innovative behavior. For a description of these types of studies, see the studies reported under the heading, "The Economics of Technical Change" in Chapter 5.

APPENDIX A

CORPORATE HEADQUARTERS QUESTIONNAIRE

Q1. Is any individual charged with overall responsibility for energy
management (energy consumption and supply)?

( ) Yes   ( ) No   ( ) Not Sure

If yes,

(a) What is this individual's organization title?

_____

(b) Is energy management a full-time job for this person?

( ) Yes   ( ) No   ( ) Not Sure

(c) To whom does he/she report?

_____

(d) Could you briefly describe this individual's tasks/functions
responsibility in energy related matters?

_____

_____

_____

_____

(e) Comments

_____

_____

_____

_____

_____

_____

Q2a. Does the firm have an energy management committee or energy coordinating committee?

( ) Yes   ( ) No   ( ) Not Sure

b. Are different individuals charged with responsibility for energy conservation and energy supply?

Different Individuals ( ) Yes   ( ) No   ( ) Not Sure

Different Committee   ( ) Yes   ( ) No   ( ) Not Sure

c. Has the firm established specific targets or objectives _vis-a-vis_ energy conservation?

( ) Yes   ( ) No   ( ) Not Sure

If yes, could you briefly describe these targets/objectives.

_____

_____

_____

_____

_____

d. Comments

_____

_____

_____

_____

_____

_____

_____

_____

_____

_____

Q3a. Does the firm have access to sufficient and appropriate data to measure its energy efficiency (e.g., energy consumed per unit of output, per man-hour, etc.)?

( ) Yes   ( ) No   ( ) Not Sure

b. If yes, does the firm use this data to develop measures of its energy efficiency?

( ) Yes   ( ) No   ( ) Not Sure

c. Comments

_____

_____

_____

_____

_____

_____

_____

_____

_____

_____

_____

_____

_____

_____

_____

_____

_____

_____

Q4a. Has the firm conducted energy audits of its main operating units or divisions?

( ) Yes   ( ) No   ( ) Not Sure

b. If yes, how often are these energy audits conducted?

( ) Is an ongoing process

( ) Annually

( ) Periodically

( ) Other

c. Comments

_____

_____

_____

_____

_____

_____

_____

_____

_____

_____

_____

_____

_____

_____

_____

Q5a. Within the last three years has the firm adopted corporate-wide programs to:

	In All Divisions	In Most Divisions	In a Few Divisions	Not in Any Divisions
(a) add insultation to buildings, plants, etc.	( )	( )	( )	( )
(b) control energy wastage (e.g., lower thermostat, less frequent use of air conditioning, more efficient usage of air conditioning, etc.)	( )	( )	( )	( )
(c) reduce unnecessary idling of equipment	( )	( )	( )	( )
(d) improvement of boilers, furnaces, etc.	( )	( )	( )	( )

(e) (1) _____

_____

(2) _____

_____

(3) _____

_____

(4) _____

_____

Q6a. How many of the firm's divisions have made production or process changes specifically to improve energy efficiency/energy conservation?

( ) All Divisions   ( ) Most Divisions   ( ) Few Divisions

( ) No Divisions

b. Could you briefly describe the most significant of these productions/process changes and the amount of the investment involved in each.

_____

_____

_____

_____

_____

_____

_____

_____

c. Comments

_____

_____

_____

_____

_____

_____

_____

_____

_____

Q7a. Is energy management/energy efficiency a part of division management's formal (written) accountability?

In all Divisions	In Most Divisions	In Some Divisions	Not in any Divisions
( )	( )	( )	( )

b. If energy management/energy efficiency is a part of division management's formal (written) accountability, please indicate how this is so.

_____

_____

_____

c. Is division management required to submit a plan to improve division energy efficiency?

( ) Yes   ( ) No   ( ) Not Sure

d. Comments

_____

_____

_____

_____

_____

_____

_____

_____

_____

_____

_____

_____

Q8a. Does the firm have an R & D group?

( ) Yes   ( ) No

b. If yes, to what extent is the firm's R & D efforts devoted to developing more energy efficient/energy conserving technologies for the firm's own use in its manufacturing/ production processes?

( ) Very much   ( ) Slightly   ( ) Not at all   ( ) Not Sure

c. Has the firm's R & D efforts led to the development of more energy efficient/energy conserving technologies which the firm has already adopted (or is in the process of adopting)?

( ) Yes   ( ) No

d. If yes, could you please describe some of these energy conserving technologies.

_____

_____

_____

_____

_____

_____

_____

_____

_____

_____

_____

_____

Q9A. Has the firm made any alterations or changes in any of its existing products or services (e.g., redesign products/services), in order to make them more energy conserving for its customers?

( ) Yes   ( ) No   ( ) Not Sure

If yes, could you briefly describe the nature of these changes?

_____

_____

_____

_____

B. (a) Are new products, services, etc., being developed by the firm with a view to conserving energy for the firm's customers?

( ) Yes   ( ) No   ( ) Not Sure   ( ) Not Applicable

(b) If yes, how will the firm's customers benefit? (Please explain briefly.)

Product, Services, etc.   How Customers Will Benefit

_____   _____

_____   _____

_____   _____

C. Has your firm attempted to use energy efficiency as a selling point for any of its products and/or services in its marketing activities?

( ) Yes   ( ) No   ( ) Not Sure

If yes, what was/were the firm's reasons for adopting this strategy?

_____

_____

_____

_____

APPENDIX B

QUESTIONNAIRE FOR DIVISIONS AND INDEPENDENT FIRMS

Q1. Is any individual charged with overall responsibility for energy management, (energy consumption and supply)?

( ) Yes   ( ) No   ( ) Not Sure

If yes,

(a) What is this individual's organization title?

_____

(b) Is energy management a full-time job for this person?

( ) Yes   ( ) No   ( ) Not Sure

(c) To whom does he/she report?

_____

(d) Could you briefly describe this individual's tasks/functions/ responsibility in energy related matters?

_____

_____

_____

(e) Comments

_____

_____

_____

_____

_____

Q2a. Does the firm have an energy management committee or energy coordinating committee?

( ) Yes　　　( ) No　　　( ) Not Sure

b. Are different individuals charged with responsibility for energy conservation and energy supply?

Different Individuals　( ) Yes　　( ) No　　( ) Not Sure

Different Committee　　( ) Yes　　( ) No　　( ) Not Sure

c. Has the firm established specific targets or objectives vis-a-vis energy conservation?

( ) Yes　　　( ) No　　　( ) Not Sure

If yes, could you briefly describe these targets/objectives.

_____

_____

_____

_____

_____

d. Comments

_____

_____

_____

_____

_____

_____

_____

Q3a. Does the firm have access to sufficient and appropriate data to measure its energy efficiency (e.g., energy consumed per unit of output, per man-hour, etc.)?

( ) Yes   ( ) No   ( ) Not Sure

b. If yes, does the firm use this data to develop measures of its energy efficiency?

( ) Yes   ( ) No   ( ) Not Sure

c. Comments

_____

_____

_____

_____

_____

_____

_____

_____

_____

_____

_____

_____

Q4a. Has the firm conducted energy audits of its main operating units
(production departments/units, boilers, furnaces, etc.)?

( ) Yes   ( ) No   ( ) Not Sure

b. If yes, how often are these energy audits conducted?

( ) Is an ongoing process

( ) Annually

( ) Periodically

( ) Other

c. Comments

_____

_____

_____

_____

_____

_____

_____

_____

_____

_____

_____

_____

_____

Q5a. Within the last three years has the firm been able to:

    (a) add insulation to its buildings, ( ) Yes ( ) No ( ) Not Sure
        plant, etc.

    (b) lower thermostat during winter   ( ) Yes ( ) No ( ) Not Sure

    (c) use air conditioning less
        frequently during summer   ( ) Yes ( ) No ( ) Not Sure

    (d) control energy wastage (more
        efficient usage of lighting
        system, ventilating, etc.)   ( ) Yes ( ) No ( ) Not Sure

    (e) reduce unnecessary idling of
        equipment   ( ) Yes ( ) No ( ) Not Sure

    (f) improve maintenance of boilers,
        furnaces, etc.   ( ) yes ( ) No ( ) Not Sure

b. What has been the total dollar investment in the above efforts
   to be more energy efficient in the last three years?

_____

_____

_____

_____

c. Comments

_____

_____

_____

_____

_____

_____

Q6a. Has the firm made any production or process changes specifically to improve energy efficiency/energy conservation?

( ) Yes　　　　( ) No　　　　( ) Not Sure

b. If yes, could you briefly describe the most significant of these production/process changes and the amount of the investment involved in each.

_____
_____
_____
_____
_____
_____
_____

c. Comments

_____
_____
_____
_____
_____
_____
_____
_____
_____
_____

Q7a. Is energy management/energy efficiency a part of line management's formal (written) accountability?

( ) Very much so   ( ) Slightly   ( ) Not at all

  b. If energy management/energy efficiency is a part of line
      management's formal accountability, could you please indicate
      in what respects this is so?

      _____

      _____

      _____

      _____

      _____

      _____

  c. Is management of the main operating units required to submit
      a plan to improve their energy efficiency?

      ( ) Yes   ( ) No   ( ) Not Sure

  d. Comments

      _____

      _____

      _____

      _____

      _____

      _____

      _____

      _____

Q8a. Does the firm have an R & D group?

( ) Yes   ( ) No

b. If yes, to what extent is the firm's R & D efforts devoted to developing more energy efficient/energy conserving technologies for the firm's own use in its manufacturing/ production processes?

( ) Very much ( ) Slightly ( ) Not at all ( ) Not Sure

c. Has the firm's R & D efforts led to the development of more energy efficient/energy conserving technologies which the firm has already adopted (or is in the process of adopting)?

( ) Yes   ( ) No

d. If yes, could you please describe some of these energy conserving technologies.

_____

_____

_____

_____

_____

_____

_____

_____

_____

_____

_____

_____

Q9A. Has the firm made any alterations or changes in any of its existing products or services (e.g., redesign products/services), in
order to make them more energy conserving for its customers?

( ) Yes   ( ) No   ( ) Not Sure

If yes, could you briefly describe the nature of these changes?

_____

_____

_____

_____

B.   (a) Are new products, services, etc., being developed by the
firm with a view to conserving energy for the firm's
customers?

( ) Yes   ( ) No   ( ) Not Sure   ( ) Not Applicable

(b) If yes, how will the firm's customers benefit? (Please
explain briefly.)

Product, Services, etc.   How Customers Will Benefit

_____   _____

_____   _____

_____   _____

C.   Has your firm attempted to use energy efficiency as a selling
point for any of its products and/or services in its marketing
activities?

( ) Yes   ( ) No   ( ) Not Sure

If yes, what was/were the firm's reasons for adopting this
strategy?

_____

_____

_____

_____

APPENDIX C

The 1972 Census of Manufacturing indicates that the Pittsburgh SMSA is the 12th largest when all SMSAs are ranked by value added by manufacturing industrial. However, the "mature" nature of the industrial base of the Pittsburgh area (i.e., older industries such as Primary Metals) is reflected in the drop in ranking from 10th in 1967 (it was also ranked 10th in 1963).

The preponderance of the Primary Metals Industries in the Pittsburgh SMSA is readily seen when we note that the two digit SIC classification code, SIC 33, Primary Metals, accounts for 46 percent of total manufacturing employment. Similar percentages for other Northern SMSAs are: Buffalo, 28 percent; Cleveland, 20 percent; Baltimore, 14 percent; Columbus, 8 percent; Philadelphia, 5 percent; and Akron, 4 percent.

Toward the opposite end of the industrial spectrum is Chemical and Allied Products (SIC 28), which is a substantially newer and more "growth" oriented industry than Primary Metals; the Pittsburgh SMSA has a lower percentage of its workforce in this industry (four percent than any of the above mentioned areas).

Specifically, with respect to smaller businesses, the Pittsburgh area also manifests peculiar characteristics. If we consider the SBA (Small Business Administration) regions, the Pittsburgh region has considerably fewer such businesses (1,277 per 100,000 population) than the at large national average of 1,616 per 100,000 population. The

Pittsburgh figure can be compared to the figures for the other SBA

regions: Boston, 1,396; Cincinnati, 1,435; Cleveland, 1,452;

Chicago, 1,489; St. Louis, 1,555; Houston, 1,645; Seattle, 1,795;

and Miami, 1,962.

BIBLIOGRAPHY

BOOKS

Ackerman, Robert W. Managing Corporate Responsibility. Boston, Harvard University Press, 1975.

Ackoff, Russell L. A Concept of Corporate Strategy. New York: Wiley, 1970.

Ackoff, Russell L. Redesigning the Future: A Systems Approach to Societal Problems. New York: John Wiley and Sons, 1974.

Allison, Graham T. Essence of Decision: Explaining the Cuban Missile Crisis. Boston: Little, Brown, 1971.

Andrews, Kenneth R. The Concept of Corporate Strategy. Homewood, Illinois: Dow Jones-Irwin, Inc., 1971.

Ansoff, H. Igor. Corporate Strategy. New York: McGraw-Hill, 1965.

Ansoff, H. Igor; Declarck, R. P.; and Hayes, R. L. From Strategic Planning to Strategic Management. New York: John Wiley and Sons, 1976.

Bachrach, P. and Baratz, M. S. Power and Poverty: Theory and Practice. London: Oxford University Press, 1970.

Baumol, William J. Economic Theory and Operations Analysis. Englewood Cliffs, N.J.: Prentice-Hall, 1977.

Bell, Daniel. The Coming of Post-Industrial Society. New York: Basic Books, Inc., 1973.

Bloomstrom, R. H. and Davis, K. Business and Society: Environment and Responsibility 3rd ed., New York: McGraw Hill, 1975.

Bower, J. L. Managing the Resource Allocation Process: A Study of Corporate Planning and Investment. Boston: Harvard Business School, Division of Research, 1970.

Burns, Tom and Stalker, G. M. The Management of Innovation. London: Tavistock Publications, 1961.

Cannon, J. Thomas. Business Strategy and Policy. New York: Harcourt, Brace and World, 1968.

Carter, C. F. and Williams, B. R. Industry and Technical Progress: Factors Governing the Speed of Application of Science. London: Oxford University Press, 1957.

Chamberlain, Neil W. The Limits of Corporate Responsibility. New York: Basic Books, Inc., 1973.

Chandler, Alfred D. Strategy and Structure. Cambridge, Mass.: MIT Press, 1962.

Channon, Derek F. The Strategy and Structure of British Enterprise. Boston: Graduate School of Business Administration, Harvard University, 1973.

Christensen, C. Roland; Andrews, Kenneth R.; and Bower, Joseph L. Business Policy: Text and Cases. Homewood, Ill.: Irwin, 1973.

Churchman, C. West. The Systems Approach. New York: Dell Publishing Co., 1968.

Cleland, David I. and King, William R. Systems Analysis and Project Management. 2nd ed., New York: McGraw-Hill, Inc., 1975.

Commoner, Barry. The Poverty of Power: Energy and the Economic Crisis. New York: Alfred A. Knopf, 1976.

Cyert, R. M. and March, J. G. A Behavioral Theory of the Firm. Englewood Cliffs, N.J.: Prentice-Hall, 1963.

Doctors, S. The Role of Federal Agencies in Technology Transfer. Cambridge, Mass.: MIT Press, 1969.

Drucker, Peter. The Age of Discontinuity. New York: Harper and Row, 1969.

Eckaus, Richard S. Basic Economics. Boston: Little, Brown and Company, 1972.

Ferkiss, Victor. Technological Man: The Myth and the Reality. New York: Braziller, 1969.

Freeman, David M. Technology and Society: Issues in Assessment Conflict and Choice. Chicago: Rand McNally College Publishing Company, 1974a.

Freeman, S. David. Energy: The New Era. New York: Vintage Books, 1974b.

Fromm, Eric. The Revolution of Hope: Toward a Humanized Technology. New York: Harper and Row, 1970.

Galbraith, Jay. Designing Complex Organizations. Reading, Mass.: Addison, Wesley, 1973.

Glueck, William. Business Policy, Strategy Formulation and Management Action. New York: McGraw Hill, 1976.

Gross, Neal; Giacquinta, Joseph B.; and Berstein, Marilyn. Implementing Organizational Innovations: A Sociological Analysis of Planned Educational Change. New York: Basic Books, 1971.

Hofer, Charles W. and Schedel, Dan. Strategy Formulation: Analytical Concepts. New York: West Publishing Company, 1978.

Jewkes, J.; Sawers, D.; and Stillerman, R. The Sources of Invention. New York: W. W. Norton, 1969.

Kast, Fremont E. and Rosenzweig, James E. Organization and Management: A Systems Approach, 2nd ed. New York: McGraw-Hill, 1974.

Katz, Robert L. Management of the Total Enterprise. Englewood Cliffs, N.J.: Prentice-Hall, Inc., 1970.

King, William R. and Cleland, David I. Strategic Planning and Policy. New York: Nostrand Reinhold Publishing Company, 1978.

Langrish, J.; Gibbons, M.; Evans, G.; and Jerome, F. R. Wealth From Knowledge. New York: MacMillan, 1972.

Lawrence, J. W. and Lorsch, P. R. Organization and Environment: Managing Differentiation and Integration. Boston: Division of Research, Harvard Business School, 1967.

Lodge, George A. The New American Ideology. New York: Knopf, 1975.

Luck, David J. and Prell, Arthur E. Market Strategy. New York: Appleton-Century-Crofts, 1968.

Lukes, S. Power: A Radical View. London: Macmillan, 1974.

MacMillan, Ian C. Strategy Formulation: Political Concepts. New York: West Publishing Company, 1978.

McAvoy, Paul W. and Pindyek, William. Price Controls and the Natural Gas Shortage. Washington, D.C.: American Enterprise Institute for Public Policy Research, 1975.

McNichols, Thomas J. Policy Making and Executive Action: Cases on Business Policy. New York: McGraw-Hill, 1972.

Mancke, Richard B. The Failure of U.S. Energy Policy. New York: Columbia University Press, 1974.

Mansfield, Edwin. Industrial Research and Technological Innovation. New York: W. W. Norton and Company, Inc., 1968.

Mansfield, Edwin; Rapoport, John; Schnee, Jerome; Wagner, Samuel; and Hamburger, Michael. Research and Innovation in the Modern Corporation. New York: W. W. Norton, 1972.

March, J. G. and Olsen, J. P. Ambiguity and Choice in Organization. Norway: Universitetsforlaget, 1976.

March, J. G. and Simon, H. A. Organizations. New York: Wiley, 1958.

Myers, S. and Marquis, D. G. Factors in the Transfer of Technology. Cambridge, Mass.: MIT Press, 1969.

Nabseth, L. and Ray, A. V., eds. The Diffusion of New Industry Processes: An International Study, London: Cambridge University Press, 1974.

Nelson, R.; Peek, Merton, J.; and Kalachek, Edward, D. Technology, Economic Growth and Public Policy. Washington, D.C.: The Brookings Institute, 1967.

Newman, William H. and Logan, James P. Strategy, Policy and Central Management. Cincinnati: South-Western Publishing Company, 1972.

Paine, Frank T. and Naumes, William. Organizational Strategy and Policy. Philadelphia: W. B. Sanders and Company, 1975.

Pavitt, K. and Wald, S. Conditions for Success in Technological Innovation. Paris: Organization for Economic Cooperation and Development, 1971.

Pettigrew, Andrew. The Politics of Organizational Decision-Making. London: Tavistock, 1973.

Richards, Max D. Organizational Goal Structures. New York: West Publishing Company, 1978.

Robertson, B.; Achilladelis, B.; and Jervis, P. Success and Failure in Industrial Innovation: Report on Project Sappho. London: Center for the Study of Industrial Innovation, 1972.

Rogers, E. Diffusion of Innovations. New York: The Free Press, 1962.

Rogers, Everett M. and Shoemaker, F. Floyd. Communication of Innovations: A Cross Cultural Approach. New York: The Free Press, 1971.

Rumelt, R. Strategy, Structure and Economic Performance. Cambridge, Mass.: Harvard University Press, 1974.

Schmookler, Jacob. Invention and Economic Growth. Cambridge, Mass.: Harvard University Press, 1966.

Schon, Donald A. Technology and Change. New York: Delacorte Press, 1967.

Schumacher, E. F. Small is Beautiful, Economics as if People Mattered. New York: Harper and Row, 1975.

Schurr, Sam H., ed. Energy, Economic Growth and Environment. Baltimore: The John Hopkins University Press, 1972.

Selznick, Philip. Leadership in Administration. New York: Harper and Row Publishers, Inc., 1957.

Simon, H. A. Administrative Action. New York: The Free Press, 1947.

Steiner, George A. Top Management Planning. New York: MacMillan, 1969.

Steiner, George A. Business and Society. New York: Random House, 1977.

Steiner, George A. and Miner, John B. Management Policy and Strategy. New York: MacMillan Publishing Company, Inc., 1977.

Thompson, James D. Organizations in Action. New York: McGraw-Hill, 1967.

Tilton, John E. International Diffusion of Technology: The Case of Semiconductors. Washington, D.C.: The Brookings Institute, 1971.

Toffer, Alvin. Future Shock. New York: Random House, 1970.

Uyterhoeven, Hugo R.; Ackerman, R. W.; and Rosenblum, T. W. Strategy and Organization: Test and Cases in General Management, 2nd ed. Homewood, Ill.: Irwin, 1977.

Zaltman, Gerald; Duncan, Robert; and Holbek, Jonny. Innovations and Organizations. New York: Wiley, 1973.

ARTICLES

Ackerman, Robert. "How Companies Respond to Social Demands." Harvard Business Review 73 (July-August 1973).

Ackerman, Robert W. "Influence of Integration and Diversity on the Investment Process." Administration Science Quarterly 15, No. 3 (September 1970); 341-351.

Aiken, Michael and Alford, Robert R. "Community Structure and Innovation: The Case of Public Housing." The American Political Science Review 64 (September 1970): 843-864.

Alchian A. "Reliability of Progress Curves in Airframe Production." Econometrics 31 (October 1963): 679-693.

Allen, T. J. "Information Needs and Uses." In Annual Review of Information, Science and Technology, pp. 3-31. Edited by C. A. Cuandra, Encyclopedia Britannica, Chicago, 1969.

Allen, T. J. and Cohen, S. I. "Information Flow in an R & D Laboratory." Technology Review 70, No. 3 (October-November 1967).

Ansoff, H. Igor; Avner, Jay; Brandenburg, Richard G.; Fortner, Fred E.; and Radosevich, Raymond. "Does Planning Pay? The Effect on Success of Acquisitions in American Firms." Long Range Planning 3, No. 2 (December 1970): 2-7.

Arrow, K. "The Economic Implications of Learning By Doing." Review of Economic Studies 29 (June 1962): 155-173.

Baker, Norman R.; Siegman, Jack; and Rubenstein, Albert H. "The Effects of Perceived Needs on the Generation of Ideas or Industrial Research and Development Projects." I. E. E. E. Transactions for Engineering Management EM-14, No. 4 (December 1967).

Becker, Selwyn, W. and Whisler, Thomas L. "The Innovative Organization: A Selective View of Current Theory and Research." The Journal of Business 40 (October 1967): 462-465.

Beckman, M. J. and Sato, R. "Aggregate Production Functions and Types of Technical Progress: A Statistical Analysis." American Economic Review 59 (March 1969): 88-101.

Berg, C. A. "Process Innovation and Changes in Industrial Energy Use." Science 10 No. 199 (February 10, 1978): 608-614.

Berg, N. A. "Strategic Planning in Conglomerate Companies." Harvard Business Review 43 (May/June 1965): 79-92.

Blackman, Jr., A. Wade. "The Market Dynamics of Technological Substitutions." Technological Forecasting and Social Change 6 (1974): 41-63.

Bungaard-Nielsen, M. and Fiehn, Peter. "The Diffusion of New Technology in the U. S. Petroleum Refining Industry." Technological Forecasting and Social Change 6 (1974).

Butler, R. J.; Hickson, D. J.; Wilson, D. C.; and Axelsson, R. "Organization Power, Politicking and Paralysis." Organization and Administrative Sciences (Winter 1977/78) to appear.

Carter, E. E. "The Behavioral Theory of the Firm and Top Level Corporate Decisions." Administrative Science Quarterly 16, No. 4 (1971): 413-428.

Child, John. "Organizational Structure, Environment and Performance--The Role of Strategic Choice." Sociology 6, No. 1 (January 1972): 2-22.

Cooper, A. C. "R & D is More Efficient in Small Companies." Harvard Business Review 42, No. 3 (May/June 1964): 75-83.

Cooper, A. C. and Schendel, D. E. "Strategy Determination in Manufacturing Firms: Concepts and Research Findings." Proceedings of the American Marketing Association, Fall Conference (August-September 1971).

Darmstadter, Joel. "Energy Consumption: Trends and Patterns." In Schurr, Sam H., Energy, Economic Growth and Environment. Baltimore: The John Hopkins University Press, 1972.

Darmstadter, Joel and Landsberg, Hans H. "The Economic Background." In The Oil Crisis: In Perspective. Daedalus Fall (1975): 15-38.

Dill, William R. "Environment as an Influence on Managerial Autonomy." Administrative Science Quarterly 2, No. 4 (1958): 409-443.

Duncan, Robert B. "Characteristics of Organizational Environments and Perceived Environmental Uncertainty." Administrative Science Quarterly 17, No. 2 (June 1972): 313-327.

Eastlack, Joseph P. and McDonald, Philip R. "CEO's Role in Corporate Growth." Harvard Business Review 48, No. 3 (May-June 1970): 88-98.

Emergy, R. E. and Trist, E. "The Causal Texture of Organizational Environments." Human Relations 18: 21-31.

Enos, J. L. "Invention and Innovation in the Petroleum Industry" in The Rate and Direction of Innovative Activity: Economic and Social Factors. Edited by R. R. Nelson, Princeton, N.J.: Princeton University Press, 1962.

Evan, William and Black, G. "Innovation in Business Organizations: Some Factors of Staff Proposals." Journal of Business 40 (1967): 519-530.

Fouraker, Lawrence E. and Stopford, J. M. "Organizational Structure and Multi-national Strategy." Administrative Science Quarterly 13, No. 1 (June, 1968): 47-64.

Frankenoff, W. P. and Granger, C. H. "Strategic Management: A New Managerial Concept for an Era of Rapid Change." Journal of Long Range Planning (April 1971): 7-12.

Freeman, S. David. "Towards a Policy of Energy Conservation." Bulletin of Atomic Scientists 27 (October 1971): 8-12.

Gerstner, Louis V. "Can Strategic Planning Pay Off." Business Horizons 15, No. 6 (December 1972): 5-16.

Gray, V. "Innovation in the States: A Diffusion Study." American Political Science Review 67 (December 1973): 1174-1185.

Griliches, Zui. "Hybrid Corn: An Exploration in the Economics of Technological Change." Econometrics 25 (October 1957): 501-522.

Guth, W. "Toward a Social System Theory of Strategic Planning." Proceedings of the Midwest Meetings of the Academy of Management, Chicago, Academy of Management, April 1973.

Hamburg, D. "Invention in the Industrial Research Laboratory." Journal of Political Economy 71 (April 1963): 71-95.

Herold, David M. "Long Range Planning and Organizational Performance: A Cross Validation Study." Academy of Management Journal 15, No. 1 (March 1972): 91-104.

Hickson, D. J.; Butler, R. J.; Axelsson, R.; and Wilson, D. "Decisive Coalitions," in King, B. T.; Streufert, S.; and Fiedler, F. E., eds., Organizational Effectiveness, 1978.

Hirsch, Werner Z. "Manufacturing Progress Functions." Review of Economics and Statistics 34 (May 1952).

Hirsch, Werner Z. "Firm Progress Ratios." Econometrics 24 (April, 1956).

Hofer, Charles W. "Towards a Contingency Theory of Business Strategy." Academy of Management Journal 18 (December 1975): 784-816.

Hogan, W. P. "Technical Progress and Production Functions." Review of Economics and Statistics 40 (November 1958): 407-11.

Irwin, Patrick H. "Towards Better Strategic Management." Long Range Planning (December 1976).

Karger, D. W. "Integrated Formal Long Range Planning and How to Do It." Long Range Planning 6, No. 4 (December 1973).

Kendrick, J. W. and Sato, R. "Factors, Prices, Productivity and Growth." American Economic Review 52 (December 1963): 974-1003.

Knight, K. "A Descriptive Model of the Intra-firm Innovation Process." Journal of Business 40 (October 1967): 478-496.

Lindblom, Charles E. "The Science of Muddling Through." Public Admin-
    istration Review 19 (1959): 79-88.

Lipson, Harry A. "Do Corporate Executives Plan for Social Responsibil-
    ity." Business and Society Review 12 (Winter 1974-5): 80-82.

Litschert, R. J. "Some Characteristics of Long Range Planning: An
    Industry Study." Academy of Management Journal 14, No. 1 (March
    1971): 33-43.

Mansfield, Edwin. "Technical Change and the Rate of Innovation."
    Econometrics 29 (October 1961): 741-766.

Mansfield, Edwin. "The Speed of Response of Firms to New Techniques."
    Quarterly Journal of Economics 77 (May 1963): 290-311.

Mansfield, Edwin. "Size of Firm, Market Structure and Innovation."
    Journal of Political Economy 71 (December 1963): 556-576.

Mansfield, Edwin. "The Economics of Industrial Innovation: Major
    Questions, State of the Art and Needed Research." In Technolog-
    ical Innovation: A Critical Review of Current Knowledge. Edited
    by Kelly, Patrick and Kranzberg, Melvin, Atlanta, Ga.: Advanced
    Technology and Sciences Study Group, Georgia Tech., January 1975.

Mansfield, Edwin and Rapoport, F. "Adoption of Technological Innova-
    tions by Organizations." Management Science 21 (August 1975):
    1380-1386.

Miernyk, William H. "Rising Energy Prices and Regional Economic Devel-
    opment." Growth and Change 8, No. 3 (July 1977): 1-7.

Mintzberg, Henry. "Policy as a Field of Management Theory." Academy
    of Management Review 2, No. 1 (January 1977): 88-101.

Mintzberg, Henry; Raisinghani, Duru; and Thoret, Andre. "The Structure
    of 'Unstructured' Decision Processes." Administrative Science
    Quarterly 21, No. 2 (June 1976): 246-275.

Mohr, Lawrence B. "Determinants of Innovation in Organizations."
    American Political Science Review 63 (March 1969): 111-126.

Murray, Edwin A. "The Social Response Process in Commercial Banks:
    An Empirical Investigation." Academy of Management Review 1,
    No. 3 (July 1976): 5-15.

Neghandi, Anant R. and Reimann, Bernard C. "Task Environment, Decen-
    tralization and Organizational Effectiveness." Human Relations
    26, No. 2 (1973): 203-214.

Nelson, R. "Aggregate Production Functions and Medium Range Growth Projections." American Economic Review 54 (September 1964): 575-606.

Newgren, Kenneth. "Social Forecasting: An Overview of Current Business Practices." In Carroll, Archie B. Managing Corporate Social Responsibility. Boston: Little, Brown and Company, 1977.

Palmedo, Philip F. "Approaches to Regional Energy Analysis." Growth and Change 7, No. 4 (October 1976): 25-32.

Penrose, Edith. "The Development of Crisis." In The Oil Crisis: In Perspective Daedalus Fall (1975): 39-58.

Perrow, Charles. "A Framework for Comparative Analysis of Organizations." American Sociological Review 32 (1967): 194-208.

Roberts, Edward. "Entrepreneurship and Technology." In Factors in the Transfer of Technology, Edited by Marquis, Donald and Gruber, William, Cambridge, Ma.: MIT Press, 1969.

Rowe, Lloyd A. and Boise, William B. "Organizational Innovation: Current Research and Evolving Concepts." Public Administration Review 34 (May-June 1974): 284-293.

Sapolsky, Harvey M. "Organizational Structure and Innovation." The Journal of Business 40, No. 4 (October 1967): 497-510.

Sawyer, George C. "Social Issues and Social Change: Impact on Strategic Decisions." MSU Business Topics 21, No. 3 (Summer 1973): 15-20.

Schendel, D. E. and Hatton, K. T. "Business Policy or Strategic Management: A Broader View for an Emerging Discipline. Proceedings of the Academy of Management, 1972.

Schmookler, Jacob. "The Changing Efficiency of the American Economy, 1869-1938." Review of Economics and Statistics 34 (August 1952): 214-31.

Sherperd, Herbert A. "Innovation Resisting and Innovation Producing Organizations." Journal of Business 40, No. 4 (October 1967): 470-476.

Solow, R. M. "Technical Change and the Aggregate Production Function." Review of Economics and Statistics 39 (August 1957): 312-20.

Thompson, Victor A. "Bureaucracy and Innovation." Administrative Science Quarterly 10, No. 1 (June 1965): 1-20.

Thune, Stanley S. and House, Robert J. "Where Long Range Planning Pays Off." Business Horizons 13, No. 4 (August 1970): 81-87.

Utterback, James M. "The Process of Technological Innovation Within the Firm." Academy of Management Journal 18, No. 2 (March 1971): 75-88.

Vancil, Richard F. "Strategy Formulation in Complex Organizations." Sloan Management Review 17, No. 2 (Winter 1976).

Vancil, Richard F. and Lorange, Peter. "Strategic Planning in Diversified Companies." Harvard Business Review 53 (January-February 1975): 81-91.

Walker, Jack L. "The Diffusion of Innovation Among American States." American Political Science Review 63 (September 1969): 880-899.

Warner, Kenneth E. "The Need for Some Innovative Concepts of Innovation: An Examination of Research on the Diffusion of Innovations." Policy Sciences 5 (1974): 433-451.

Wilson, Ian H. "Socio-Political Forecasting: A New Dimension to Strategy Planning." Michigan Business Review (July 1974).

Wilson, James Q. "Innovation in Organizations: Notes Toward a Theory." In Approaches to Organization Design, edited by Thompson, James D. Pittsburgh: University of Pittsburgh Press, 1967.

Wrapp, H. E. "Organization for Long Range Planning." Harvard Business Review 35 (January-February 1957): 37-47.

PUBLIC DOCUMENTS

U. S. Department of Commerce. Project Reports of Voluntary Industrial Energy Conservation. 1974-77.

U. S. Department of Energy. Fact Book: Organization and Functions. 1977.

U. S. Department of Energy. Annual Report to Congress, 1977, Vol. 111, Statistics and Trends of Energy Supply, Demand and Prices. Energy Information Administration. Washington, D.C.: May, 1978.

U. S. Energy Research and Development Administration. Energy Coal Conversion and Utilization. 1975 Technical Report. Washington, D.C.: 1976.

U. S. Energy Research and Development Administration. A National Plan for Energy Research and Development: Creating Energy Choices for the Future. Vol. 1, The Plan, Washington, D.C.: 1976.

U. S. Energy Research and Development Administration. Managing the Social and Economic Impacts of Energy Developments, Washington, D.C.: July, 1976.

U. S. Executive Office of the President. The National Energy Plan. Washington, D.C.: The White House, April 29, 1977.

U. S. Federal Energy Administration. Project Independence: A Summary. Washington, D.C.: November 1974.

U. S. Federal Energy Administration. "Energy Conservation in the Manufacturing Sector." In Project Independence Blueprint, Final Task-force Report. Washington, D.C.: November 1974.

U. S. Federal Energy Administration. General Public Attitudes and Behavior Regarding Energy Saving. Highlight Report, Vol. IX. Washington, D.C.: April 1975.

U. S. Federal Energy Administration. 1977 National Energy Outlook. Draft. Washington, D.C.: January 15, 1977.

U. S. Office of Technology Assessment. Analysis of the Proposed National Energy Plan. Washington, D.C.: June 1977.

Reifman, Alfred; Canaday, Henry; Franssen, Herman; Gushee, David; and Mark, Clyde. U. S. Energy Policy--Major Issues and Options. Congressional Research Service, Library of Congress. Washington, D.C.: March 3, 1976.

CONGRESSIONAL HEARINGS

U. S. Congress, House of Representatives. Subcommittee on Energy and Power of the Committee on Interstate and Foreign Commerce. Energy Choices Facing the Nation and Their Long Range Implications: Mobilizing for Social Goals. Hearings. 94th Congress Second Session. Washington, D.C.: U. S. Government Printing Office, 1976.

Myer, Dale D. Presentation to the Subcommittee on Advanced Energy Technologies and Energy Conservation Research, Development and Demonstration of the Committee of Science and Technology during Hearings on 1979 Department of Energy Authorization. January 30, 1978.

Press, Frank. Presentation to Subcommittee on Advanced Energy Tech-
    nologies and Energy Conservation Research, Development and Demon-
    stration, during Hearings on Earth Resources and Drilling Tech-
    nology. June 7, 1978.

REPORTS

Carnegie Mellon Institute of Research. Regional Energy Policy Alter-
    natives: A Study of the Allegheny County Region. Final Report,
    Phase 2. Pittsburgh: October 10, 1977.

Daedalus. The Oil Crisis in Perspective. Vernon, Raymond, ed.
    Fall, 1975.

Energy Policy Project of the Ford Foundation. A Time to Choose:
    America's Energy Future. Cambridge, Mass.: Ballinger Publishing
    Co., 1974.

Gross, Neal; Lazeridis, Lazaros; and Widmer, Thomas. "Potential Fuel
    Effectiveness in Industry." A Report for the Energy Policy
    Project of the Ford Foundation. Cambridge, Mass.: Ballinger
    Publishing Company, 1974.

Tannenbaum, M. Report of the Ad Hoc Committee on Principles of
    Research-Engineering Interaction. Report No. MAB 222-M.
    National Academy of Sciences--National Research Council,
    Material Advisory Board. Washington, D.C.: 1966.

PAPERS

Bourgeois, L. Jay, III. "Strategy and Environment: A Conceptual
    Integration," Unpublished paper, Graduate School of Business,
    University of Pittsburgh, 1978.

Brooks, Harvey. "The Energy Problem." Paper delivered at the Bicen-
    tennial Symposium, Oak Ridge National Laboratories, Oak Ridge,
    Tennessee, October 5, 1976

Campbell, D. T. "Qualitative Knowing in Action Research." Kurt Lewin
    Award Address, Society for the Psychological Study of Social
    Issues, Meeting with the American Psychological Association,
    1974.

Grant, John H. "Corporate Strategy: A Synthesizing Concept for
    General Management." Unpublished paper, Graduate School of
    Business, University of Pittsburgh, 1975.

Hickson, David J.; Astley, W. Graham; Axelsson, Runo; Butler, Richard J.; and Wilson, David C. "Strategic Decision-Making in Organizations: Concepts of Process and Content." Unpublished paper, University of Bradford Management Centre, England, 1978.

Richardson, Elliot L. and Zarb, Frank G. "Perspective on Energy Policy," Energy Resources Council, Washington, D.C.: December 16, 1976.

Ringbakk, K. S. "Organized Corporate Planning Systems: An Empirical Study of Planning Practices and Experiences in American Big Business." University of Wisconsin, Unpublished doctoral dissertation, 1968.

Wrigley, Leonard. "Divisional Autonomy and Diversification," Harvard University, Unpublished doctoral dissertation, 1970.

Wygal, Don. "An exploratory Study of Performance and Process in an Industrial Safety Program." University of Pittsburgh. Unpublished doctoral dissertation, 1977.

For Product Safety Concerns and Information please contact our EU
representative GPSR@taylorandfrancis.com Taylor & Francis Verlag GmbH,
Kaufingerstraße 24, 80331 München, Germany

Printed and bound by CPI Group (UK) Ltd, Croydon, CR0 4YY

08/05/2025

01864401-0002